Exotic Visions in Marketing Theory and Practice

Exotic Visions in Marketing Theory and Practice

ALF H. WALLE

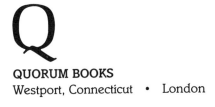

QUORUM BOOKS
Westport, Connecticut • London

658.8
W19e

Library of Congress Cataloging-in-Publication Data

Walle, Alf H.
    Exotic visions in marketing theory and practice / Alf H. Walle.
      p. cm.
    Includes bibliographical references and index.
    ISBN 1–56720–394–9 (alk. paper)
    1. Marketing research. 2. Marketing—Social aspects. I. Title.
HF5415.2.W283   2002
658.8—dc21   2001018033

British Library Cataloguing in Publication Data is available.

JK
Copyright © 2002 by Alf H. Walle

All rights reserved. No portion of this book may be
reproduced, by any process or technique, without
the express written consent of the publisher.

Library of Congress Catalog Card Number: 2001018033
ISBN: 1–56720–394–9

First published in 2002

Quorum Books, 88 Post Road West, Westport, CT 06881
An imprint of Greenwood Publishing Group, Inc.
www.quorumbooks.com

Printed in the United States of America

The paper used in this book complies with the
Permanent Paper Standard issued by the National
Information Standards Organization (Z39.48–1984).

10 9 8 7 6 5 4 3 2 1

To my father, Alf H. Walle, Sr.,
to my mother, Adeline B. Walle,
and to my brother, Richard V. Walle

University Libraries
Carnegie Mellon University
Pittsburgh, PA 15213-3890

Contents

Preface

In recent years, marketing and consumer researchers have made un-precedented strides toward the embrace of a wide range of research strategies that stem from the social sciences and the humanities. The cross-disciplinary initiatives within marketing/consumer research are helping our profession to gain intellectual maturity and to function as an equal partner within the greater intellectual world. Marketing/consumer research can no longer be accurately portrayed as sitting on the intellectual sidelines, borrowing much and contributing little in return.

In recent years, I have come to view my mission as a marketing/consumer researcher in particular, and as an intellectual in general, to be one of those contributing to this process of mutually beneficial cross-disciplinary merging. That was certainly the purpose of my recent book, *The Cowboy Hero and Its Audience: Popular Culture as Market Derived Art* (2000a). There, an icon of popular culture (the cowboy hero) was interpreted using an eclectic array of concepts that was equally influenced by the methods of marketing and the analytic techniques of literary criticism, American studies, and popular culture theory. That monograph, furthermore, was self-consciously written in a manner designed to be useful to both humanists and marketing/consumer researchers. The whole intent of the exercise was to demonstrate how marketing and consumer theory have a vital contribution to make to the broader intellectual community as well as performing "journeyman duty" within the more confined arena of business scholarship.

This embrace of cross-disciplinary methods was further emphasized in my book *Rethinking Marketing* (2000b), an eclectic demonstration of how widely varying qualitative methods from the humanities can be

usefully integrated into the mainstream of marketing/consumer research. That book begins with a cluster of chapters that, while being
"humanistic" in tone and method, are not directly linked to any particular school of humanistic analysis. Having demonstrated the value of
the "humanistic" style of analysis, a wide array of specific humanistic
techniques were applied to the questions facing marketing/consumer
research. That book ended with a plea to further expand the paradigms
that we use in our work through cross-disciplinary borrowing.

Here, I have taken my own advice and I seek to further expand the
role of social theory within marketing/consumer research. It is my belief
that much cross-disciplinary research does not provide an adequate tracing of ideas back to their original roots. I do not blame published scholars
for this situation because, on many occasions, literature reviews must be
culled to a bare minimum due to restrictions of space. This syndrome
especially impacts journal articles. Thus, on many occasions, ideas are
ripped from their intellectual context in counterproductive ways. In the
monograph format used here, it becomes possible to provide a greater
linking of ideas with their precedents. I have used the luxury of available
space to provide overviews of Immanuel Kant, Friedrich Hegel, and Karl
Marx, three intellectual titans who have profoundly stimulated the modern intellectual tradition. It is my belief that by tracing many of the ideas
we hold today back to their origins, it becomes easier for us to envision
the key concepts underlying our work and why they are important.

Having provided this introductory material, the book moves on to the
analysis of structural methods which I have divided into "mental structural" approaches, which deal with the nature of the human mind, and
"social structural" approaches, which center upon the structures of society. These discussions carefully sidestep the rhetoric of "structuralism
vs. poststructuralism" and deal with a wide variety of structural methods as valid and useful analytic methods that have much to contribute
to marketing/consumer research.

My discussions of structural analysis are followed (in Part III) by "Individualistic and Poststructural Perspectives." Here, I point to the great
strides currently being made by poststructural analysis and useful alternatives to it. My approach is not dogmatic or partisan; it merely points
to a variety of tools and how they can be embraced in useful and efficient
ways. Thus, while poststructural analysis is a premier method in many
circumstances, conflict theory (which evolved out of structural analysis)
deals with many of the same issues, and it may be superior to poststructural analysis in a number of circumstances.

Today, marketing/consumer researchers are increasingly embracing a
wide variety of exotic methods. Doing so extends the range of available
analytic techniques and broadens the relevance of our work beyond the
business world. We, as a discipline, are on the cusp of profound intel-

lectual breakthroughs; reaching this goal, however, will require a more robust orientation. It is hoped that this book will provide some illustrative suggestions regarding how to proceed in that direction.

REFERENCES

Walle, Alf H. (2000a). *The Cowboy Hero and Its Audience: Popular Culture as Market Derived Art*. Bowling Green, OH: The Popular Press.
Walle, Alf H. (2000b). *Rethinking Marketing*. Westport, CT: Quorum Books.

Acknowledgments

This book is a product of its time. In recent years, the humanities and qualitative social sciences and marketing/consumer research have converged in important ways. This trend creates an environment where the ideas presented here could come to publication. It is appropriate to thank and acknowledge all who have contributed to this more open and respectful intellectual atmosphere.

In recent years, the humanities and qualitative social sciences have become a rich source of inspiritation for forward-thinking marketing/ consumer researchers. The process by which these "non-scientific" methods have become established has been slow and painful. These researchers, furthermore, put their careers in harm's way by pursuing research that was "outside the dominant paradigm." Thus, I first acknowledge all those in marketing/consumer research who have helped bring about a greater acceptance of the qualitative analytic techniques that our profession now takes for granted. A great many individuals have contributed to this process. While some individuals deserve specific recognition, I hesitate to single them out because, in the process, I might unfairly slight others. Thus, I will simply point, with praise, to this general research stream, those who have advanced its agenda, and their accomplishments.

Having provided this recognition to qualitative marketing/consumer researchers, it becomes necessary to applaud the various donor disciplines that have influenced my thinking. This book is largely written in the belief that the current (and legitimate) vogue of applying poststructural analysis to marketing/consumer research has unfortunately masked the vast contributions that structural methods can and should make to our discipline. As a result, I have spent the majority of my time in an attempt to correct this unhealthy imbalance.

In doing so, I initially returned to the roots of the modern Western intellectual tradition with chapters on Immanuel Kant, Friedrich Hegel, and Karl Marx. It would be hard to imagine today's intellectual community without the contributions of these seminal figures. They and their ideas have become so much a part of the collective vision of the modern world, however, that we sometimes "can't see the forest for the trees." Since these pioneers could easily be ignored, it is fitting and proper to focus upon these "mighty oaks" and to acknowledge that many of us are intellectual "acorns" that spring directly from them.

Having done so, a majority of my attention is spent on various structural methods. After general overviews on mental and social structuralism, individual chapters discuss specific applications of social structural thought. While the leaders and innovators of these research strategies are praised in specific chapters, I would like to specifically single out Ruth Benedict, Margaret Mead, Edward T. Hall, Fredrik Barth, Erving Goffman, Henry Nash Smith, and Richard Slotkin. This is a purely subjective acknowledgment that centers upon who I am and who I have become, due to their help. Thus, I do not present these individuals as superior to the many other illustrious contributors to the social structural paradigm; I merely acknowledge that I work within their tradition.

On a purely personal note, I would like to thank Leslie Fiedler. I came to humanistic scholarship from the social sciences (anthropology). Fiedler provided a means by which I was able to expand my skills by overlaying literary criticism/folklore upon my preexisting social structural thinking. His leadership and friendship are much appreciated.

Exotic Visions in Marketing Theory and Practice

CHAPTER 1

Introduction: Beyond Science

In the last 15 years, marketing/consumer researchers have made great strides toward embracing a broader array of analytic tools and techniques. These exotic visions are alternatives to the scientific method, and they are rapidly gaining prestige within our profession. Even though "standard" scientific techniques may continue to dominate, the growth of alternative research tactics has been impressive and their embrace has far-reaching implications. Although it would be premature to state that these exotic methods have gained parity with their more established scientific counterparts, they are gaining respect, even if it is sometimes given grudgingly.

While those who embrace these exotic visions do not repudiate the achievements of science, they do reject the complete domination of scientific and quantitative methods that has prevailed for so long. In order to remedy that situation, these researchers have actively incorporated a vast toolkit that stems from (among other intellectual traditions) the liberal arts, the humanities, and the social sciences. These advances are revolutionizing marketing/consumer research by opening up and legitimizing strategies of research that were long ignored and/or stigmatized; our profession is more robust and more responsive as a result of the positive and progressive example set by these researchers.

While the achievements of science have been many, the type of rigor that is demanded by the scientific method often creates an intellectual straightjacket that unduly inhibits research. Typically, scientific analysis is not pursued unless it can be conducted according to the rules dictated by its methodology. Although insisting that research must be rigorous is a legitimate course of action, refusing to investigate important topics merely because a specific and circumscribed type of rigor cannot be achieved is not a bona fide or defendable tactic. Over time, forward-thinking marketing/consumer researchers have come to the conclusion that science is a tool and not a shackle; as a result of this recognition, exotic visions that encompass alternative, but equally legitimate, codes of rigor have been embraced. The end result of this increased flexibility is the current vogue of "qualitative techniques" within marketing/consumer research. This book is written as a part of and as an apology for that tradition.

Today, the stranglehold of the scientific method has significantly weakened; as a viable alternative, qualitative marketing/consumer researchers have introduced a variety of exotic visions that stem from diverse intellectual traditions. Far from suffering from fuzzy-minded thinking, the donor disciplines that are inspiring our field possess their own codes of rigor that, while different, are every bit as rigid as those embraced by the scientific method. The strategy of the qualitative research stream within marketing/consumer research has been to borrow from these disciplines, as required, and thereby provide the profession with a wider array of analytic tools.

Expanding the field in this way is sorely needed. Human beings and their environments are profoundly complex; as a result, on many occasions human behavior cannot be adequately modeled or analyzed using scientific and/or quantitative procedures. Unfortunately, in many quarters the term "scientific" has become synonymous with "rigorous"; where this is the case, any method that falls short of the canons of science has been discredited accordingly. This tendency to equate science with a monolithic envisioning of rigor is, of course, inappropriate because scientific investigation is merely one legitimate strategy of analysis; others exist.

We are currently in the dawn of a profound movement that is gravitating toward the embrace of a broader and more substantial toolkit within marketing/consumer research. Thus far, however, qualitative marketing/consumer researchers have been rather eclectic in their choice of techniques; specific methods that have seemed to be particularly appropriate are applied to the task at hand, with relatively little attention being paid to their broader intellectual pedigree and its implications. These researchers then go on to justify their use of specific exotic methods using "the proof is in the pudding" rationales; techniques that "work" are lauded accordingly. There is nothing inherently wrong with this eclectic modus operandi; such tactics are especially useful in the early days when a recipient discipline casts a wide net and seeks to sample a broad range of ideas and methods.

A potential long-term problem with this kind of eclectic borrowing, however, is that the intellectual traditions from which ideas derive and the synergistic power that unites them can easily be ignored. Eclectic borrowing that incorporates especially useful ideas from outside disciplines, useful and legitimate though it often is, takes place in isolation and tends to be ad hoc in nature. As a result, the full implications inherent in borrowing new concepts may not be adequately considered. As marketing/consumer research becomes more intertwined with these exotic visions, however, examining the full ramifications and implications of borrowed ideas becomes increasingly essential. Marketing/consumer research is now at the point where this sort of intellectual soul searching must take place. I hope that my thoughts will serve a useful role as qualitative researchers in marketing/consumer research pursue this important dialogue and as our use of qualitative methods reaches maturity.

In this Introduction, the stage is set for what will follow. First, I provide a discussion of the origins of the scientific method, as it has come down to us; in doing so, I trace the scientific intellectual tradition back to the age of the Enlightenment. Having provided this historic backdrop, a brief overview of alternative qualitative methods is presented with reference to the romantic movement. Hardly an intellectual footnote, romantic thought provides the intellectual foundation that underlies the exotic methods that are currently being embraced by qualitative marketing/consumer researchers. By providing this preliminary material, later chapters are placed within a broader intellectual context and one that is meaningful to our profession.

THE ENLIGHTENMENT AND ITS SHADOW

The age of the Enlightenment was one of the great intellectual movements of Western civilization. As we shall see, the Enlightenment continues to cast a long shadow and its example has bolstered a respect for the scientific method within both scholarly and practitioner research. The stage for the emergence of the Enlightenment was an intellectual climate that could no longer be confined by dogma and by an unquestioning belief in the intellectual and religious authorities that had long dominated Western thought.

The leaders of the Enlightenment, rejecting tradition, celebrated the power of human reason. During this era, the intellectual world stood in awe of the achievements of intellectual giants such as Isaac Newton (1643–1727) who, with the aid of human reason, had discovered the principles of gravitation and the profound (and universal) impact that it exerts. Newton brought the scientific revolution of the 17th century to a culmination and, in the process, he helped to forge the general principles of analysis that have dominated scientific research ever since. Newton, paralleling modern science, used careful methods of observation and analysis, insisted that researchers must be impartial and uninvolved, and generalized empirical data into hypotheses, theories, and laws.

It is impossible to overestimate the achievements of Newton and the British scientific method that he helped to establish. The emerging scientific method enjoyed impressive successes in explaining the natural world; over time, furthermore, parallel techniques were applied to an ever-widening intellectual arena. If the principles of gravity could be distilled using the scientific method, why not the laws that underlie human behavior and social life? By examining people in scientific ways, researchers became confident that they could transcend the dogma and sloppy thinking that had inhibited understanding for thousands of years. Inspired by Newton, but largely following the lead of John Locke, the 18th-century leaders of the Enlightenment believed that knowledge derives purely from experience and from observations that are interpreted through the use of impartial and objective human reason. Thus, the Enlightenment placed a high value upon empirical observation and emphasized drawing conclusions that used reason to generalize from the observed facts.

As with other impassioned and one-sided intellectual movements, the dominance of the Enlightenment as a coherent and unified entity eventually collapsed. Nonetheless, its emphasis upon the scientific method has largely survived. Although innumerable advances in ad hoc techniques have been made since Newton's time, the basic skeleton of the scientific method that he advocated has survived largely unaltered.

These scientific methods, of course, were born of the "hard" or "physical" sciences, and they continue to dominate in that sphere. Increasingly, however, the techniques of science became linked to the analysis of human beings and social life. Observations were made, statistical correlations were verified, and predictions of future human behavior were projected. The orientation of Auguste Comte and those who forged general social theory in his image clearly reflect this tradition. Although researchers acknowledged that people and society are profoundly complex, the essence of the scientific method was still viewed as an appropriate analytic instrument and one that could be applied to questions involving people, not merely to an analysis of the physical world.

The dominance of scientific and quantitative methods within marketing/consumer research can be viewed as a specific example of this general tendency. Inspired by the Enlightenment, they seek to apply formal methods to the study of human behavior. By employing scientific methods and applying them to the particular questions under investigation, marketing/consumer researchers sought to create a rigorous foundation for their discipline and one that was based solely upon empirical observation and reason. Without doubt, many impressive results have been derived from this endeavor.

Eventually, however, certain limitations inherent in applying the scientific method to the analysis of people and social life emerged. Human beings and society are profoundly complex; the sheer complexity of this subject matter, coupled with an inability to "control" all relevant variables when conducting research, loom as profound limitations. On some occasions, scientific researchers attempt to control the relevant variables (such as in a laboratory situation), but in doing so the research can easily become overly simplistic and, therefore, compromised. The alternative option is to relax scientific standards by attempting to deal with the complexities of the world and, in the process, abandon some of the scientific controls that are so vital to the scientific method. Without doubt, the legitimacy of both options must be evaluated and weighed on a case-by-case basis.

Those who maintain a commitment to the scientific method choose to live with the problems that are inherent in their methodology (even if various "corrections" or adjustments are implemented). These researchers, for example, may employ scientific research designs even if in doing so they might oversimplify reality in questionable and counterproductive ways. Some scientifically oriented researchers, on the other hand, may choose not to pursue whatever questions cannot be examined according to scientific principles. Each of these decisions, although defendable, constitutes a significant tradeoff, and both need to be evaluated accordingly.

Many contemporary investigators, however, have become increasingly impatient with the limitations that are ingrained in a strict adherence to the methodological guidelines demanded by science. These researchers insist that the lost options inherent in only pursuing "respectable" scientific investigation are often so great that alternatives to scientific must be available. These are the scholars who are currently advocating the use of qualitative methods within marketing/consumer research. And, as will be demonstrated below, these progressive researchers tend to (overtly or covertly) advocate methodological choices that are reflective of the romantic movement that emerged in the late 18th / early 19th century. In order to demonstrate this affinity, a brief overview of romanticism is useful.

THE ROMANTIC MOVEMENT

While the techniques of science and their embrace by the Enlightenment led to great intellectual strides, the method's emphasis upon rational thought and empirical reality simultaneously created blind spots and oversimplifications. While these limitations were tolerated by the leaders of the Enlightenment, others found them to be totally unacceptable. The pendulum shift back from the rational and scientific vision of the Enlightenment to more intuitive means of understanding is generally called the romantic movement.

Perhaps a good place to begin our tour of romanticism is with a brief consideration of Jean-Jacques Rousseau and his rejection of rational thought and civilization. Rousseau, of course, is best remembered for his celebration of what has come to be called the "noble savage." According to his "Discourse on the Origin of Inequality among Mankind," Rousseau insisted that science and society have ultimately corrupted mankind because modern life forces people away from nature and the authentic state of existence that inevitably takes place in a naturalistic setting. According to Rousseau, people are most comfortable and fulfilled when they exist in a primitive state; as a result, he views the simple life of the folk as inherently superior to that of their civilized cousins. This premise, of course, militates against the value of science and its accomplishments and it rejects the Enlightenment's celebration of progress and civilization; not surprisingly, the French philosopher Voltaire, a major spokesperson for the Enlightenment, attacked Rousseau and they became bitter enemies. Nonetheless, Rousseau provided a convincing rationale that suggested that inherent weaknesses existed within the philosophy of the Enlightenment. And, as time went on, the Enlightenment lost power while Rousseau and the romantic vision he inspired gained strength; romanticism ultimately emerged as a major social/intellectual movement and as the spirit of the age.

A strong catalyst that led to the embrace of the romantic vision was Napoleon's admirable efforts to introduce much-needed legal reforms into the countries that he conquered. The so-called "Napoleonic Code" can best be viewed as a product of the late Enlightenment. As will be recalled, the leaders of the Enlightenment believed that it is possible, through reason, to create a better world; the Napoleonic Code was a series of legal standards that had been created through reason and, therefore, Napoleon (a friend of the Enlightenment) assumed that they could be implemented everywhere in a positive and productive manner.

Reality, however, was very different from the Enlightenment's belief that rational thought was inherently superior and that, given a chance, it would invariably prevail. Even though the standards of the Napoleonic Code were enlightened, a great outcry against them arose because local populations insisted that the legal framework controlling people's lives should derive from them and their traditions and not merely be forged by rationalistic outsiders and dictated from above. These strong passions led to the formulation of the *volksgeist* theory of the law, which emphasized that the law is an overarching social structure that needs to be attuned to the feelings of the local community and that the law should not merely be a well-crafted rational code devoid of social and cultural content.

Throughout the nineteenth century, romantic nationalism continued to deal with the emotional and irrational aspects of specific peoples that stemmed from their national and ethnic heritage. This epoch of cultural striving and self-identity, of course, has never ended. Students of consumer response, for example, often recognize that people typically act according to their ethnic and cultural heritage and that their behavior must be viewed accordingly.

Not only is mankind emotional and irrational; researchers often need to analyze the behavior of people and society in ways that transcend scientific thinking. Thus, while romantic intellectuals tended to acknowledge that science is able to effectively and efficiently study the physical world in purely practical ways (even though science cannot account for phenomena such as the beauty of nature and the awe that it inspires in people), they also insisted that human beings and human emotions are so complex that alternatives to the scientific method of analysis are often required when they are investigated.

The implications of these romantic perspectives have profound consequences for marketing/consumer research. Science, the romantics affirm, is incapable of fully investigating human behavior and social life. As a result of this inability, alternatives are badly needed, and the romantic emphasis upon a broader framework of analysis provides these alternatives. Thus, the power of science is undercut by limitations that can be mitigated by the romantic vision.

The era of the Enlightenment and the reactions against it point to divergent methods of conducting research. The Enlightenment champions science and rational thought as the pinnacle of human achievement. The modern scientific method, as it has evolved, is a broadening and an expanding of this tradition. Romantic thought, in contrast, points to the limitations of science and it offers analytic alternatives. These romantic options are clearly associated with the qualitative disciplines, such as the humanities and liberal arts, traditions that are currently influencing marketing/consumer research.

Today, marketing/consumer reserchers are questioning the complete dominance of science; as this process progresses, the fruits of romantic thought are increasingly being integrated into the analytic toolkit of marketing/consumer research.

THE TASK AT HAND

This book provides one interpretation of how the vision of the romantic era is exerting a positive impact upon contemporary marketing/consumer research. As such, it celebrates and introduces an array of qualitative methods that can be usefully incorporated into our profession. This book agrees with the romantic theorists in affirming that human beings and social life are so complex that they often need to be understood using analytic styles that transcend science. Various chapters connect methodological options to the needs of today's marketing/consumer researchers.

The chapters in Part I deal with profoundly important, but often ignored, intellectual superstructures upon which modern social thought has been constructed. Because knowledge is cumulative, researchers often rely upon contemporary abstractings of the achievements of earlier thinkers. Although doing so is legitimate, this tactic of analysis can also result in key elements (that covertly underlie our thinking) to be skirted. To avoid this unfortunate potential, I provide fresh interpretations of Immanuel Kant, Friedrich Hegel, and Karl Marx; by doing so, the influence exerted by these thinkers and their impact upon our world is overtly acknowledged.

Writing while the Enlightenment was the dominant force in the West, Kant, although not totally rejecting science, pointed to other ways of knowing and understanding. Kant believed that those who advocated the scientific method did not adequately factor the power and the uniqueness of the human mind into their models. Human thought, Kant affirmed, is more than merely a processing of empirical evidence since the human mind (an instrument of analysis) operates according to its own rules and possesses its own techniques by which information is organized and synthesized. After Kant presented his vision (commonly known as the "Kantian turn" in philosophy), there was an increased focus upon people and how they think; as a result, formal methods (such as those of science) have often come to be viewed as artificial and limiting, even when it is acknowledged that they are often productive and useful.

Friedrich Hegel, building upon Kant, largely focused upon the overarching culture, society, or nation. Using the term *"volksgeist"* to refer to what we call "national character," Hegel explained behavior in terms of social identities and structures. Hegel habitually used an organic metaphor to depict society; cultures are portrayed as synergistic entities that work in systematic/structured ways for the benefit of all. This metaphor ultimately became an inherent part of social theory and (although losing some prestige since the 1960s) the organic model has exerted a profound impact upon social thought and upon marketing/consumer research that deals with and builds upon social theory. By understanding Hegel's perspectives on their own terms, a unifying force in social thought is traced back to its intellectual roots.

Karl Marx, while influenced by Hegel, tempered Hegel's emphasis upon the organic model and Hegel's underlying premise that social structures work for the greater benefit of all members of society. Thus, Marx emphasized conflict between various parts of a social system, and he was interested in social dynamics, not merely with exploring how a society operates in a homeostatic sort of way. For many years, of course, Marx was viewed as a partisan and provocative propagandist; when this perception prevailed, it was hard to objectively envision his contributions to general social theory. Today, however, with the decline of the socialist bloc, it is, at long last, possible to accept that Marx is a profoundly important social theorist, and one who was long unduly ignored or stereotyped due to the political tensions of an earlier era; I (along with many other intellectuals in diverse disciplines) seek to transcend the simplistic dismissal of Karl Marx and Marxist analysis that long prevailed, and I seek to raise them to the proper and prestigious position that they deserve.

Moving from these preliminary discussions, Part II presents a cluster of chapters that focuses upon various permutations of the structural method. Initially, a dichotomy between what I call "mental structuralism" and "social structuralism" is spotlighted. Mental structuralism refers to models that concentrate upon the inherent structure of the human mind; like Immanuel Kant, mental structuralists direct their attention toward the inherent and universal ways in which people think. In the contemporary intellectual milieu, mental structuralism is often equated with the perspectives of Claude Levi-Strauss; in reality, however, other mental structural models (such as those of Sigmund Freud and Carl Gustav Jung) exist, and they have exerted a strong and multifaceted influence.

Social structuralism, in contrast to mental structuralism, is a powerful and pervasive paradigm that largely stems from the work of Friedrich Hegel and his *volksgeist* model. After an initial chapter that examines the general traditions of social structural thought, three structural models are presented. They are not offered as an exhaustive listing of options, but merely as an indication of the flexibility possessed by the structural model. The particular methods discussed include the culture at a distance method that stems from social anthropology, the myth and symbol method that applies structural principles to literary criticism and American studies, and Erving Goffman's dramaturgical method that links social structures to the conscious and purposeful behavior of specific social actors. The goal of these discussions is to present specific social structural tools that have a distinct and overt contribution to make to marketing/consumer research.

While social structural models deal with the larger society, increasingly there has been a tendency to focus upon the dilemmas of individual people and circumscribed groups who must ultimately make decisions in a complex and (some would argue) absurd world; these issues, of course, are akin to Kant's focus upon the individual. First arising in the 19th century as rejections of Hegel's emphasis upon society and his ignoring of the individual, these individualistic perspectives came of age after World War II with the vogue of existential thought. In dealing with these social and intellectual movements, a discussion of the existential tradition is provided, as well as an updating of the individualistic perspective via poststructuralism. Although these movements are significant and have exerted a strong influence upon marketing/consumer research, they are not considered in more depth in this book because they have already been widely analyzed in our literature. Nonetheless, I acknowledge that these models are clearly able to transcend structural models that place an overemphasis upon harmony and homeostasis; for that reason, they have made a significant contribution to marketing/consumer research.

The achievements of those who have applied poststructural models to marketing/consumer research, unfortunately, have drawn attention away from a variety of social structural models that are also able to deal with conflict, strife, and the specific needs of individuals and circumscribed groups. One such research stream is modern "conflict theory," which is an outgrowth and refinement of social structural theory. A concluding chapter suggests that this research stream can often be used in many situations where poststructural analysis has traditionally served. Furthermore, because conflict theory has direct linkages to classic structural theory, in many cases it can usefully emerge as the method of choice for marketing/consumer reserchers who choose to work within a social structural intellectual tradition.

A FINAL STATEMENT

In recent years, marketing/consumer reserchers have come to embrace a variety of exotic visions in order to transcend the limitations inherent in the scientific method. This book is written as a part of that research stream. As these alternatives to science become increasingly entrenched within our field, perceiving this work as part of a coherent intellectual tradition becomes increasingly necessary.

Understandably, there has been a tendency for qualitative scholars to embrace whatever methods appeared to be fruitful and to justify their use accordingly. As these methods become more deeply a part of our profession, however, a more overarching vision of qualitative methods and their intellectual pedigree is required. It is my hope that this book will, in some small way, help marketing/consumer reserchers to come to grips with the challenges they face and the opportunities that lie before them.

Kant, Hegel, and Marx:
Three Often-Ignored Pioneers

Scholars, at times, are not adequately aware of the history and full implications of the ideas that they embrace and rework. As a result, their perspectives may fail to acknowledge the far-reaching implications of the theories and concepts that they champion (or confront), the power of these ideas, and the intellectual baggage that is carried with them. To mitigate these potentials, Part I of this book presents, in a fairly elementary manner, an overview of the intellectual building blocks that have given rise to contemporary thought. I assume that most readers are familiar, to a greater or lesser degree, with the ideas that are presented here; after all, they form an important part of the bedrock of the Western intellectual tradition.

Nonetheless, it is one thing to be aware of one's intellectual heritage, on the one hand, and to forcefully focus upon it when grappling with specific problems, on the other. Intellectual borrowing, by its very nature, strategically seeks to save time and effort through the legitimate process of adapting and borrowing from the work of others. And we, as borrowers, tend to gravitate toward models and refinements that have been carefully tailored to our needs; in this manner, researchers can save time and the quality of their efforts can often be improved. The dark side of doing so, however, is that the full potential of earlier thinking can become ignored or diluted when scholars go straight to revisionists and do not confront the actual thinking upon which their ideas are ultimately based.

Thus, in the process of lifting ideas from beyond their original context, later thinkers may begin to overlook important implications inherent in the thinking they refine or rebut. Although I am sure that the reader has not fallen victim to this potential, I must admit that, on occasion, I have. Thus, I hope that the reader will bear with me as I work through the basic foundations upon which this book is based.

In order to do so, the first cluster of chapters in this book deals with basic chains of thought that have exerted a profound impact upon the modern world. Three intellectual giants (Immanuel Kant, Friedrich Hegel, and Karl Marx) are analyzed on their own terms. The shadow cast by their work is profound and it extends much further than might be supposed at first glance. As a result, it is first important to present my views of these scholarly forefathers and to nest their thought within the evolving intellectual world to which we fall heir.

As interpreted here, Immanuel Kant is a largely unprecedented scholar who firmly demonstrated the limitations inherent in the scientific method. The field of marketing/consumer research is currently in a phase of expanding beyond the scientific method. Ultimately we, as a discipline, are moving in this direction because we feel that the human mind has powers of observation that, in various circumstances, transcend the abilities of mere empirical observation and/or statistical analysis. Ultimately, developing a means of getting beyond mere empiricism was the major achievement of Kant and, therefore, it is important to consider what he struggled to accomplish; that is my attempt in Chapter 2.

Friedrich Hegel, discussed in Chapter 3, is a pivotal intellectual force because he took the ideas of Kant and mated them with the then-emerging disciplines of biology and economics. In addition, since Hegel emphasized that individual countries/cultures/nations have their own unique ethos, he popularized concepts that have come to be called "national character." Hegel's use of the organic metaphor in analyzing cultures, furthermore, is the forerunner of what has come to be known as the theory of "social structuralism" that has had a profound impact upon both the social sciences and the models employed by literary and cultural critics.

Not only have many scholars carefully refined and adapted Hegel's perspectives, others have actively reacted against him and his example. Karl Marx and his emphasis upon conflict, not cooperation, is an early example of this tendency. (Because of his profound importance, Marx is the third member of the trio of intellectual ancestors to be considered here; his influence is discussed in Chapter 4.) While Hegel focused upon the harmony of the social system, Marx concentrated upon conflict. In addition, Marx (somewhat building upon Hegel's interest in economics) dealt with social evolution in terms of economic influences.

Besides Marx, the existential movement and its offshoots (deconstructionism, postmodernism, and so on) also provide alternatives to Hegelian analysis. These perspectives emphasize the plight of the individual, not the functioning of the larger collective society and, therefore, they are self-conscious alternatives to Hegel's emphasis upon the culture at large.

Having presented these thumbnail sketches of Kant, Hegel, and Marx, Chapter 5 discusses the broader intellectual traditions that helped set the stage for the chapters to follow. It is hoped that by getting back to the basic intellectual building blocks presented by Kant, Hegel, and Marx, an adequate foundation for embracing an array of qualitative techniques that stem from their work is provided.

The goal of this book is to better crystalize the role of qualitative techniques within contemporary marketing/consumer research; the first step in doing so is to encourage a proper appreciation of our intellectual ancestors.

CHAPTER 2

Kant and the Tempering of Science: A Metaphor for Marketing

In the late 18th century, when Immanuel Kant transformed the intellectual world with his *Critique of Pure Reason (1781)*, the age of the Enlightenment (which raised rational thought to the pinnacle of human achievement and potential) reigned supreme, and the methods of science dominated the intellectual world. Between that time and today, many advances in the analytic techniques of scientific research have been made; nonetheless, today's scientifically oriented analysts would feel largely at home if magically thrust back into the era of the Enlightenment. The scientific orientations so prevalent today were clearly in vogue 250 years ago.

While not overturning or repudiating science, Kant clearly expanded upon it. He did so by championing humanistic thought and by reinforcing the notion that not all knowledge can be quantified in scientific ways. In doing so, Kant set the philosophy of knowledge upon a new path (usually called the "Kantian turn" in philosophy). The qualitative models and methods that are profoundly impacting contemporary marketing scholarship and consumer research are clearly indebted to Kant and his vision. In the final analysis, Kant's achievement can be used as a convenient metaphor when evaluating the rise of qualitative methods within marketing thought.

THE RISE OF SCIENCE

Here, I will initially discuss the rise of the scientific method in the 17th and 18th centuries in order to place Kant and his contribution within a proper perspective. Doing so establishes a foundation for evaluating

Kant and for appraising how his thinking impacts and meshes with qualitative marketing/consumer research.

Although it would be possible to begin our analysis at an earlier era (such as that of Francis Bacon and Isaac Newton, or even the ancient Greeks), the work of John Locke will be our point of departure. Locke emphasizes that human knowledge stems from the empirical data that is provided by the senses (i.e., stems from actual experience). In choosing this focus, Locke was consciously reacting against the philosophy of René Descartes and his deductive methods of analysis that started with reason (and the assertion that "I think, therefore I am") and went on to extend reason outward in order to understand the larger world. Locke reversed this order by beginning with experience and then extrapolating an understanding of the world from empirical observation. Locke's basic premise and slogan is "tabula rasa": the notion that, at birth, the mind of a person resembles a blank slate that contains nothing until experience writes on it. Thus, knowledge is based purely upon experience, not upon anything that is innate within the mind itself.

Thinkers such as Descartes, who came before Locke, often claimed that people possess innate knowledge as a gift from or an artifact of the rational God who made them. Such perspectives, of course, are the opposite of Locke's theory that knowledge is based solely on experience, and he repudiated these speculations in his *Essay Concerning Human Understanding* (1690), a profound undercutting of the theory of innate knowledge. Locke's empiricism emphasizes the importance of actual experience as the basis of all knowledge and it discounts intuitive speculation and deductive analysis. Starting with the foundation laid down by Francis Bacon early in the 17th century, Locke placed the empirical method on a firm intellectual foundation and he encouraged further developments that led to the flowering of what has come to be known as British empiricism and the modern scientific method.

The rise of British empiricism was directly linked to the fact that since the techniques of scientific inquiry were emerging as dominant, they required an underlying philosophy that was capable of channeling scientific reasoning in systematic and rigorous ways. Locke and the British empiricists who followed him were very successful and influential; we can easily view the modern scientific method we use today as an extension of Locke's philosophy. The underlying chain of thought of this intellectual tradition goes something like this:

1. All knowledge is based on experience.
2. Nonetheless, we must channel experience in productive ways.
3. In specific, we must eliminate the biases of the observer from the process of observation.

4. We must also make sure that what we observe is truly representative of reality.

5. By doing so, empirical observation can be placed within a rigorous context.

This is the modern scientific method in a nutshell, and it has led to sophisticated strategies of sample selection, statistical analysis, criteria for objective observation, and so on.

From Locke's time until the era of Kant, the British empiricists (such as George Berkeley and David Hume) increasingly refined the tools of analysis that were needed to facilitate the development of an empirically based scientific method. Although many methodological advances have been made since the time of these writers, the British empiricists of the 18th century created a foundation for scientific thought and procedure that has remained unshaken to this day.

Although empiricism, as a philosophical movement, is primarily identified with Britain, its ideas were quickly embraced by members of the Enlightenment who primarily came from France. Ultimately, the Enlightenment can best be viewed as a progressive movement of international scope that affirmed that rational human thought possesses the potential to remake the world in utopian ways.

This was the intellectual monolith that Kant faced in the late 18th century. The methods and spirit of science had come to dominate to such a degree that the power of the human mind, as an essential and inevitable tool of analysis, was generally ignored.

THE "KANTIAN TURN"

It was Immanuel Kant who reaffirmed an interest in the human mind as an important component that must be considered when exploring how people understand the world. The empiricists emphasized the role of observation to such a degree that the function of human thought, as a process that is distinct from observation, was discounted and overlooked. Kant, however, suggested that certain kinds of knowledge (or at least certain ways by which the mind interprets observations) are not dependent on empiricism alone; instead they are based on inherent abilities that exist within the human mind. Dealing with the inherent powers of the human mind (without focusing solely upon empirical observation) is generally called the "Kantian turn" in philosophy.

In essence, Kant, in his *Critique of Pure Reason* (1781), forcefully challenges Locke's notion that the human mind is merely a passive "tabula rasa" or empty slate upon which empirical observation writes its messages as the mind itself remains passive. Instead, Kant suggests that the human mind possesses certain innate methods of analyzing reality that are inherent and, therefore, human thought and knowledge are not solely based on empirical evidence or observation. In specific, Kant lists 12 categories or concepts of human thought that he lumps under the headings of "Quantity," "Quality," "Relation," and "Modality." At issue here is not the specific categories that Kant enumerated, but his theory that the human mind possesses inherent abilities that transcend mere observation and experience.

Kant, while not undercutting or challenging the empirical roots of knowledge, nonetheless argues that another key factor must be considered; that factor is the nature of the human mind. Thus, Kant asserts that the analytic nature of the human mind (the 12 categories of thought he describes) exists before empirical experience and, therefore, it cannot be viewed as stemming from what specific individuals had perceived. In view of this fact, Kant viewed these categories of thought as independent of experience. Dealing with the human species and the analytic strengths and abilities it possesses, Kant suggests that these mental powers exist in all normal people.

The key point that Kant drives home is that the human mind is able to create knowledge out of observed data because the mind has the innate ability to organize empirical reality in meaningful ways. It is the human mind that takes the evidence supplied by empirical observation and weaves it into a tapestry from which knowledge can be derived. This profound observation (self-evident as it might seem, once stated) brought about one of the great transformations in the history of human self-reflection, scholarship, and philosophy.

These Kantian perspectives have exerted a profound effect upon our view of knowledge and human thought. Two powerful paradigms of thought that can be traced back to Kant involve the works of Friedrich Hegel and Karl Marx. Since they are dealt with in Chapters 3 and 4, however, our discussions of them and their influence are postponed until later. Here, we will briefly analyze the impact of Kant upon the romantic era and how romanticism provides a viable alternative to the scientific method.

KANT AND THE ROMANTIC ERA

Throughout the 18th-century era of the Enlightenment, the intellectual world embraced the notion that scientific knowledge is able to create a heaven on earth; the potential of science was seen as being boundless and as serving mankind in generally positive ways. Although clearly a dominant paradigm, the sentiments of the Enlightenment were not universally embraced by all thinkers. Although most scholars conceded the notion that science could explain various mechanical phenomena (such as the law of gravity and the motions of the planets around the sun), this ability was viewed as being rather insignificant by many intellectuals (especially in Germany). And scientific reasoning, critics of the Enlightenment suggested, was surely not the only way of knowing and perceiving the world, and certainly not the most profound.

During the high tide of the Enlightenment, however, it was difficult to overtly challenge the dominant premises and paradigms that this powerful movement embraced. Kant, however, provided the wedge by which the unbridled dominance of science could be challenged. This is true because Kant pointed to knowledge (and ways of knowing) that existed independently of science and empirical observation. Once the implications of Kant's theories became recognized, intellectuals began to be self-reflective and sought to understand human nature on its own terms and in intuitive ways that transcended science.

A major movement that embraced this basic position is known as romanticism. Emphasizing the human spirit, romanticism focuses upon human feelings and it deals with them in ways that typically go beyond rational thought and scientific observation. A key aspect of this movement is to focus upon "simple folk" who had not been transformed by the habits and cares of the modern world and who continue to live close to the earth in an age-old manner. Thus, poets like William Wordsworth celebrated the noble yeoman and the joys of rustic life. An underlying premise of the romantic movement is the belief that people have needs, feelings, and emotions that transcend rationality and the modern civilized world. A definitive statement of the emerging romantic movement, for example, is the preface to the second edition of *Lyrical Ballads* (1800) by William Wordsworth and Samuel Taylor Coleridge, where the importance of human feelings and the human imagination is clearly emphasized and celebrated. In romantic poetry and prose, imagination came to be elevated over reason and emotions were viewed as being superior to logic, while intuition was acclaimed as outshining scientific knowledge.

To a large extent, this perspective can be envisioned as an embellishment of the work of Jean-Jacques Rousseau. Today, Rousseau is primarily remembered for his theory of the "noble savage" and his belief that science, art, and social institutions corrupt and pervert mankind instead of leading to meaningful progress. Rousseau went on to suggest that the natural, or primitive state of existence is inherently superior to civilized life. These sentiments are in direct conflict with those of the then-dominant Enlightenment; nonetheless, Rousseau won a following and today he is more widely recognized than Voltaire.

By the early 19th century, Rousseau's ideas (bolstered and amplified by Kant's vision) were providing a forceful challenge to the dominance of science; this trend was taking place just as the excesses of the industrial revolution (themselves artifacts of science) were becoming increasingly apparent, obvious, and hurtful. The basic orientation of the romantics was centered around and celebrated the individual. English poets, such as Lord Byron and Percy Bysshe Shelley, typified the romantic hero both in their poetry and in their personal lives; they repudiated social and political oppression, and they defended the struggles for liberty that were taking place during their era. These efforts are mirrored by the works of Russian poet Aleksandr Pushkin, whose celebration of liberty (1820) resulted in his exile. In a typical romantic style, Pushkin's work was inspired by the folklore of the common people. Rural people who had not been "corrupted" by civilization were held up as role models and as inspirations.

The dissatisfaction of romantic intellectuals with the ethos of civilized society often resulted in a harsh critique of urban society that is clearly Rousseauean in nature. In "La Maison du Berger" [The Shepherd's Hut] (1844), by French poet Alfred Victor de Vigny, for example, a humble cottage is depicted as more noble and stately than a palace. This sentiment, of course, parallels those of Rousseau, who had written that people were born free but that civilization put them in chains; de Vigny and other romantics clearly echo these sentiments. Central to these themes is a concern with primitive mankind, an awe of untamed nature, a preoccupation with the unspoiled scenery of rural hinterlands, and (what was perceived to be) the innocent life of rustic folk.

What is important to us here is that with the help of Kant, the romantics rejected aspects of modern life that were celebrated and embraced by the Enlightenment; they also sought to overcome the domination of the scientific method. As an alternative, they celebrated innate and intuitive human thought and they depicted science as limited and inhibiting, even though it was acknowledged to be useful in some ways. The Kantian turn in philosophy had a major role in these transformations.

AN ALTERNATIVE TO SCIENCE

As will be argued, the pattern identified above (which saw the initial dominance of the Enlightenment/scientific vision coupled with the pendulum shift represented by the romantic vision) is clearly analogous to the evolution of modern marketing scholarship and research methodologies that are increasingly inspired by the qualitative humanistic tradition. First, however, it is important to center upon how romantic thought came to embrace its own unique methodology and its own rationale for conducting research and analysis.

Any number of 19th-century intellectual movements can be analyzed in order to demonstrate this pattern. Here, I will briefly discuss three illustrative examples: (1) the rise of folklore, (2) the development of psychoanalysis, and (3) the emergence of anthropological fieldwork techniques. Each will be briefly addressed; these isolated discussions will then be synthesized in a general statement.

Folklore

In the 19th century, stemming in part from the romantics' celebration of the rustic life, a group of scholars came to focus upon remnant enclaves of folk society that were viewed as vestiges of the past. These rustic people were studied in order to preserve and understand their cultural traditions that, it was believed, were in the process of being swallowed up and destroyed by the industrial age.

The term "folklore" refers to the traditions of any homogeneous group of rural people (although contemporary folklorists view all people as "folk" who embrace folklore traditions). These folk customs are typically preserved and passed from one generation to the next without the aid of the written word. The term folklore was coined in 1846 by William John Thoms (1803–1885), an English scholar. In Thoms' era, there existed a profound concern, triggered by the sensibilities of the romantic era, that the traditions and heritage of the rustic past would soon be lost, and that the only way in which this legacy could be preserved was for scholars to go to the field and record surviving examples of folklore before the folk died off and/or before they were "contaminated" by the modern world.

On the one hand, drawing upon romantic principles, these hinterland people were perceived as possessing the clues that were needed to appreciate what is truly important and meaningful in life. Thus, the generic noble savage was often studied and emulated. Aborigines and American Indians, for example, were envisioned as existing close to nature and, thereby, these people were able to live the life of the "noble savage," serving as role models for those of us who are products of and trapped within the modern civilized world.

Folklore theory no longer assumes that folk traditions will inevitably die out; increasingly, they are viewed as possessing vitality and power. In line with such beliefs, marketing/consumer researchers have long noted that much consumer response stems from examples initially provided by hinterland people, ethnic groups and circumscribed populations. Rock and Roll music, for example, started out as the musical expression of rural, lower-class Blacks and Whites of the American South. Blue jeans were once the garb of the working class. Many fashionable foods were originated by ethnic groups. Given this situation, folklore, as it has evolved, provides orientations and strategies of analysis that transcend the earlier focus upon the imminent extinction of the folk and, thereby, are of value to marketing/consumer researchers.

While the concept of the noble savage possesses a seductive appeal, many other people embraced folklore in ways that were closer to home. The romantic era saw the rise of "romantic nationalism" in which members of specific societies and nations sought to systematically regain and reassert their unique and distinctive cultural heritage. The strategy for doing so was to study rural people who had not been "adulterated" and homogenized by the modern civilized world; these intellectuals sought to extrapolate an atrophied or neglected national culture from such vestigial evidence. On occasion, the study of folklore led to "high art" being inspired by its example. The classical music of the Norwegian composer Edvard Grieg and the Czech Bedrick Smetana (1824–1884) are instances of this tendency, and the pre-Raphaelite movement in both art and literature reflects these sentiments. These are important examples of consumer culture and they have many modern counterparts (such as the vogue of "primitive" or "naive" artists such as Grandma Moses) whose products are successfully marketed to an upscale and sophisticated clientele.

The embrace of the generic noble savage and the rise of romantic nationalism as a major social movement can be viewed as self-conscious alternatives to the scientific vision of the Enlightenment. Science and rational thought are rejected in favor of intuition, emotion, and life close to nature and/or one's cultural roots, and these tendencies have exerted profound impacts upon how it is perceived and analyzed.

Psychoanalysis

In the era of the Enlightenment, the rational aspects of mankind were emphasized. This tendency was so pronounced that it needed to be tempered and channeled in appropriate ways. Throughout the romantic era, the intuitive and emotional aspects of mankind were celebrated in contrast to the Enlightenment's focus upon rationality and science. Initially, however, mankind continued to be viewed in primarily rational terms. As time went on, however, the emotional and irrational nature of mankind came to be acknowledged as a prevalent part of life. The work of Sigmund Freud was instrumental in beginning the process of correcting the Enlightenment's overemphasis upon rationality through an acknowledgment of mankind's emotional and irrational nature.

Freud clearly recognized the importance of unconscious and irrational psychological processes, and he emphasized that these phenomena are very different from conscious and rational thought. The rules and methods of logic that are so important in conscious thought, for example, do not apply to the inner workings of the unconscious mind; and many of the mainsprings that impact and channel human motivation and behavior are irrational and/or they exist below the level of conscious thought.

A basic assumption of Freudian theory is that human behavior is greatly influenced by unconscious, instinctual, and non-rational impulses. Through Freud's work (and the contributions of those who have built upon Freud's model), a better understanding of the role of the unconscious and of irrational drives and motives has resulted. A moment's reflection will demonstrate how psychoanalysis can be viewed as an outgrowth of romantic thought that focused on human thought and how it, in turn, was indebted to the Kantian inward focus.

This kind of "depth psychological" model has long been embraced by marketing/consumer research. Even the most superficial review of our profession will reveal a significant interest in consumer decision-making processes that lie below the level of consciousness; marketing strategists have been especially interested in these covert influences because, since people are not aware of how these internal influences work, they cannot easily guard against them. Romantic thought emphasized the emotional and the irrational, and it depicted both as vital components of human existence. This is the exact position embraced by Freud. And, like romanticism, psychoanalysis centered upon phenomena that rationalists tended to ignore. By transcending the rationality of the Enlightenment, more robust and appropriate models of mankind and human behavior resulted. Their value to an understanding human behavior is universally recognized.

Anthropological Methods

The classic fieldwork methods of anthropology can be viewed as the antithesis of "scientific" research and analysis. While formal scientists strive to distance themselves from the phenomena being investigated, anthropological fieldworkers take pride in their intimate association with the subjects they study. The basic strategy is for the researcher to interact within an alien culture in intimate ways in order to gain an intuitive grasp of how it operates and how its members perceive the world and respond to it.

The strategy is to gain an intuitive grasp of the society under investigation and then use this knowledge in order to construct (or reconstruct) a vision of how the culture operates. As with psychoanalysis, classic anthropological fieldwork techniques assume that much of human life is powered by non-rational and unconscious mainsprings. Anthropological fieldworkers, furthermore, affirm that understanding a society is best accomplished in a manner that transcends purely rational thought. Thus, the impact of the romantic movement is clearly present. Thus, while disciplines such as economics may embrace rational perspectives, anthropology typically centers upon more emotional and irrational considerations. And, as with psychoanalysis, it is clearly linked to the inward look that Kant emphasized. The contemporary naturalistic research approach of marketing/consumer research that has risen to prominence is clearly inspired by this tradition.

Each of these research streams can be seen to bear the imprint of the romantic era that, in turn, had been profoundly influenced by the Kantian turn in philosophy. All of these approaches to mankind transcend rational thought and each strategically does so in order to better understand humanity by evaluating people and their products on their own terms. Although Kant did not totally reject empiricism and science, he did celebrate and focus upon the nature of the human mind. This achievement led to a new emphasis upon aspects of life that transcend the purely rational character of mankind and the scientific method as an inherently superior technique of analysis. This trend, in turn, led to a number of alternative models and methods that, while not totally rejecting science and the empirical method, did transcend and augment them in useful and provocative ways. This situation mirrors contemporary transformations in marketing/consumer research.

PARALLELS IN MARKETING/CONSUMER RESEARCH

Largely paralleling these developments (in a covert and circumscribed sort of way), marketing/consumer researchers are embracing a broader, qualitative toolkit stemming from the humanities and the qualitative social sciences. A first wave of this transformation can be discussed using the rise of the focus group method as a specific example. As the reader is aware, focus groups consist of a convenience sample of 6 to 12 people who are placed in a room; with the aid of a facilitator, these informants are encouraged to brainstorm about a specific topic of interest to the client (a marketing manager, advertising agency, and so on). Using this method, the facilitator is able to quickly gather information regarding the topic being investigated through the use of methods that bypass the complicated procedures associated with the scientific method.

Initially, the focus group method was viewed as a "quick and dirty" means of gaining information, and the method (though useful) was viewed as tainted and compromised. Eventually, however, practitioners began to recognize that the focus group method was able to generate valuable insights that would be impossible to gain using formal, scientific methodologies. This is true because of the synergistic nature of the groups that are brought together in a focus group setting. Often the members of the focus group, brainstorming with little input from the facilitator, are able to crystalize issues in ways that science cannot achieve. Realizing this potential, researchers came to view the focus group as a viable method to be embraced on its own terms and not merely as a debased or compromised alternative to scientific analysis.

Thus, the focus group method has emerged as a "respectable" method and one that is evaluated on its own terms.

This initial phase of practitioner-inspired advances has been followed by a second wave in which marketing scholars have gone to other disciplines (such as the humanities and qualitative social sciences), borrowed relevant concepts and methods from them, and adapted these tools and techniques to the needs of marketing/consumer research. Invariably, this work embraces the methods of the humanities and the qualitative social sciences in ways that are hinged around the Kantian turn toward an inward look at the mental life of mankind.

In contemporary marketing/consumer research, for example, techniques inspired by literary criticism are making a strong and impressive impact upon the evolution of the research methods in the field. To a large degree, the methodologies embraced by these researchers involve techniques and perspectives that largely derive from methods of deconstructionism; in Kantian fashion, these methods seek to understand the inner workings of the human mind, not merely the larger external world.

While poststructural literary theory provides a major inspiration, the qualitative social sciences have also exerted an influence. Thus, scholars such as Russell Belk, John Sherry, and Melanie Wallendorf have adapted the techniques of the ethnographic method to the needs of marketing/consumer research that, as discussed above, owe a profound debt to Kant. Although much of this work stems from Hegel, his work is deeply influenced by Kant. Some humanistic research in marketing/consumer research that stems from literary criticism, furthermore, is also indebted to Hegel's social structural methods, such as my monograph on the marketing of the cowboy story from 1820 to 1970 (Walle 2000); wherever the focus is upon culture as a distinct and synergistic mental structure, the impact of Hegel exerts a powerful impact.

Today, modern marketing/consumer researchers are transcending (while not rejecting) the classic scientific method. This work tends to be covertly based upon the underpinnings provided by Kant. During the era when the scientific method reigned supreme, the impact of Kant was slight; today, with a more flexible array of tools available to marketing/consumer researchers, Kant's impact is growing and the value of his vision is being recognized.

REFERENCES

de Vigny, Alfred. (1844). "La Maison du Berger" [The Shepherd's Hut]. In James Doolittle, *Alfred de Vigny*. New York: Twayne, 1967, p. 96.

Kant, Immanuel. (1781). *Critique of Pure Reason*, trans. Werner S. Plurar. Reprint, Indianapolis, IN: Hackett, 1996.

Locke, John. (1690). *Essay Concerning Human Understanding*. Reprint, New York: Dover, 1959.

Rousseau, Jean-Jacques. (1755). *Discourse on the Origin of Inequality among Mankind*, trans. Maurice Cranston. Reprint, Harmondsworth, UK: Penguin, 1984.

Thoms, William. (1946). "Folklore." *Athenaeum* (August 22).

Walle, Alf H. (2000). *The Cowboy Hero and Its Audience: Popular Culture as Market Derived Art*. Bowling Green, OH: The Popular Press.

Wordsworth, William and Coleridge, Samuel. (1800). Preface to the second edition of *Lyrical Ballads*. London: Biggs and Cottle.

CHAPTER 3

Friedrich Hegel: Social Structure as Overarching Monolith

Friedrich Hegel lived and wrote in the era immediately following the achievements of Immanuel Kant. As a result, Hegel was profoundly influenced by the Kantian turn in philosophy. As we saw in Chapter 2, Kant focused upon the operation and influence of the human mind and the impact of the human thought process upon the creation of knowledge. Hegel, building upon Kant, created a model of society that was largely based upon romantic principles.

Hegel lived during the early flowering of German romanticism that was largely concerned with the will of the individual, not merely rational thought. Thus, strong-willed and heroic individuals such as Napoleon were celebrated and revered (even by their enemies) because they personified the inextinguishable will of mankind; the heroic spirit was admired as a monumental force that exists above and beyond rational thought. Thus, when Beethoven, in a fit of rage, withdrew the dedication of his Third Symphony to Napoleon, he renamed it the Heroic Symphony; in the early 19th century, Napoleon and the universal heroic spirit were interchangeable.

Besides glorifying the heroic spirit, the romantics viewed nature in spiritual terms—with the same feeling with which people may view a pristine redwood forest today. Typically, the romantics came to equate nature with "God" or at least with a sacred universal force that possesses a profound spiritual dimension.

Hegel embraced these perspectives and forged them into his own paradigm of nature, history, society, and culture. Hegel, of course, did much more than this; here, we will center upon these achievements because (1) they strongly influenced what has come to be known as the classic "structural" method of the social sciences, (2) they profoundly influenced the social/economic determinism of Karl Marx, and (3) many of the more "individualistic" philosophies of our era are an overt reaction against Hegel and his vision. These influences will be discussed in later chapters. First, it is necessary to look at Hegel himself.

HEGEL AND THE FLOW OF HISTORY

Hegel views history as the work of the all-powerful spirit of the universe driving toward perfection. In doing so, Hegel combines the notion of the will of the heroic individual striving for fulfilment with the idea that nature is divine and spiritual. In addition, Hegel views the world and its products (such as cultures and intellectual traditions) as akin to living organisms. Perhaps the best way to grasp Hegel's vision is to briefly examine the acclaimed preface of his *The Phenomenology of Spirit* (1977). Hegel begins (in a book written for his fellow philosophers) by observing that the history of philosophy overtly appears to be one of bitter debates between rivals, with one school of thought actively seeking to debunk its opponents and antagonists.

Hegel goes on to remind the reader that each clique of philosophical thought elevates its position to the pinnacle of "truth," forcefully denounces alternative positions, and depicts its own pronouncements as unwavering laws. But, Hegel continues, truth is not a rigid and static thing. Ultimately, new schools of thought inevitably arise and, in turn, a system of thought that is victorious at one point in history is inevitably rebutted in the next.

Hegel offers an alternative to the position that schools of thought are rivals that ultimately discredit each other; instead of viewing different schools of philosophic thought as adversaries, they can also be viewed as cooperating and collaborating even if, in the heat of battle, the individuals who exist at a particular moment may not recognize this truth. Ultimately, philosophy and knowledge are perpetually growing and refining themselves; each emerging school of thought, therefore, can be viewed as one more stride toward a greater and more robust intellectual maturity. Thus, schools of thought can best be viewed as rungs on an intellectual ladder that climbs toward perfection, not as rival systems in mortal combat with one another.

It is important to note here that Hegel affirms that knowledge must not be viewed merely in absolute terms, but with reference to its history and the environmental milieu in which it arises and exists. This kind of analysis is closely intertwined with Hegel's vision of the flow of history. So viewed, typical examples of philosophy and human thought cannot be legitimately judged as being "right" or "wrong"; instead, they must be evaluated in terms of the circumstances in which they exist.

Hegel came to depict human achievements and progress in a similar way. Cultures and nations, he argues, are always struggling toward perfection. Being an idealist under the influence of Kant, Hegel depicts the universe (or, perhaps, the creator of the universe) as a great spirit or mind that is perpetually seeking to perfect itself and bring its ideas to life. And Hegel depicts nations and cultures as circumscribed subcomponents of the larger nature (with their own unique traditions and spirits) that are, likewise, striving to realize their essences. Thus, viewing the world from an historical and spiritual perspective, Hegel envisioned a gradual and progressive unfolding of potentials, not merely hostility and competition.

In order to demonstrate this vision, Hegel uses his acclaimed metaphor from biology in the preface of *The Phenomenology of Spirit*:

The bud disappears in the bursting forth of the blossom, and one might say that the former is refuted by the latter; similarly, when the fruit comes, the blossom is shown up in its turn as a false manifestation of the plant, and the fruit now emerges as the truth of it instead. (1977: 2)

Hegel does two separate things here. On a superficial level, he affirms that human knowledge exists within an ongoing historical process of refinement and that the appropriate way to interpret intellectual history is to look for transformations over time. More subtle is the fact that Hegel embraces the notion that social and intellectual institutions can best be viewed with reference to an organic model.

HEGEL AND THE ORGANIC METAPHOR

This organic model (that Hegel initially employed in metaphoric ways) rose to paramount and overarching significance in Hegel's work. Hegel lived in an era when great strides were being made in biology; not only was he the product of an era that was profoundly influenced by Kant, he also existed in the era of Jean Baptiste Lamarck (1744–1829), the French naturalist who coined the word "biology" and who articulated the essence of biological evolution 50 years before Charles Darwin published his *On the Origin of Species* (1859) by speculating that species evolve over a period of many generations. In his *Philosophie Zoologique* (1809), for example, Lamarck proposed the theory that animals acquire different characteristics in response to their environment. Thus, Lamarck's work can be viewed as an important avant garde of evolutionary theory (even though the specific biological mechanisms he proposed have been discredited).

Embracing and reacting to the theoretic notions of biology as they

were emerging in the early 19th century, Hegel was struck by the fact
that living creatures tend to be complex entities that are composed of
different, albeit cooperating components and that, by working together,
these parts gain a synergism that they do not possess individually. Biology provided innumerable examples of the interdependent segments
(of an organism) working together in a systematic way for the common
good and controlled in some kind of hierarchical fashion.

Ultimately, Hegel applied the organic model to his analysis of specific
cultures. According to this metaphor, cultures are like living creatures.
Thus, parallel to a living thing, a culture is arranged in some kind of
hierarchical order. This basic model or metaphor has survived into our
era. Thus, business thinkers often depict businesses and organizations as
organisms in which the actions of the various parts of the culture are
controlled by specialists (management, strategic planners, and so on)
who concentrate upon strategy and tactics. Cultures and nations, likewise, are made up of component parts that are organized in some sort
of hierarchical manner; their ability to function properly (and for the
collective good of its component parts) largely depends upon the priorities of its hierarchy of command being respected and the demands of
its leadership being obeyed.

According to Hegel's biological metaphor, cultures achieve their true
essence and destiny only when people are obedient to their leaders. Hegel also assumes (in a flawed and simplistic way) that serving the needs
of the society/organism as a whole is inevitably in the best interest of
all individuals and subgroups.

Hegel can be justly attacked for his tendency to push the biological
metaphor too far. Nonetheless, as a metaphor (employed in guarded
ways), Hegel's vision of cultures/organizations as hierarchically oriented
conglomerates has much to commend it (as any professor of organization
behavior will quickly affirm). Like organisms, cultures are made up of
specialized parts that perform specific functions. Undeniably, a division
of labor exists. The success of both organisms and cultures depends upon
each specialized part being allowed to pursue its mission in appropriate
ways.

Hegel, furthermore, lived in the era that saw the rise of classical economics and he was both interested in and influenced by the economic
theories of his day. In this regard, Rudolf Siebert observes:

The [then] new science of economics is of great importance for Hegel as he develops the social scientific dimension of his [work]. . . . Economics provides for
Hegel the model by which he is able to connect the rational content of the the-
ological and humanistic anthropological sphere . . . with the highly irrational content of the social-scientific dimensions. (Siebert 1979: 94)

Adam Smith, in his *The Wealth of Nations* (1776), clearly makes reference to a division of labor and the efficiency of having specialized people perform specific tasks. This theory of the significance of a division of labor jives almost completely with the organism model of society that Hegel was simultaneously formulating. Thus, it was inevitable that these two concepts would become intertwined in Hegel's thought. According to this synthesis of biology and economics, nations are organizations that are made up of specialized subcomponents. This arrangement leads to more efficient functioning of the entire social/economic system. This more efficient functioning helps nations to achieve their destiny.

The implications of this metaphor led directly to the development of structural-functional social theory, the underpinning of modern social thought. This method is concerned with patterns of relationships that allow the culture or society to function; the collective society (not the individual) is emphasized.

In classic versions of the structural-functional model, social change and strife tend to be discounted or ignored (in a way that is reflective of Hegel's precedent) in order to more effectively deal with the implications of the interrelatedness and interdependency of various parts of the social system. This emphasis ultimately led to an embrace of what systems theorist Kenneth Boulding calls the "clockworks" model. According to Boulding, the most basic framework of analysis is what he calls "frameworks," which he describes as "that of the static structure" (Boulding 1956: 14). The next level of analysis, according to Boulding, is "clockworks": "that of the simple dynamic system with predetermined motions" (Boulding 1956: 14). The next level of analysis is what Boulding calls the cybernetic system; that "differs from the simple stable [clockworks] system in the fact that the transmission and interpretation of information is an essential part of the system. As a result . . . [behavior] is not merely determined by the equations [clockworks] of the system" (Boulding 1956: 14).

The particular issues explored by the classic structural-functionalist social scientists who embrace an organic metaphor of society tend to embrace Boulding's clockworks model. Researchers embracing the structural-functional intellectual tradition that stems from Hegel's work obviously conclude that the benefits of this limited clockworks analysis outweigh the costs and they embrace it accordingly. (And, editorially speaking, I often concur with them.)

After the "golden age" of structural-functional analysis, the complaint was increasingly made that the method tended to justify existing structures instead of explaining them. As might be expected, numerous critics lambasted classic social structural analysis accordingly. In an especially rhetorical example, Betty Friedan, in her polemical *The Feminine Mystique,* observes:

Functionalism began as an attempt to make social science more "scientific" by borrowing from biology the idea of studying institutions as if they were muscles or bones in terms of their "structure" or "function" in the social body. . . . [Unfortunately] "The function is" was often translated "the function should be"; the social scientists did not recognize their own prejudices in functional disguise. . . . [These social scientists] assumed an endless present [minimal social change] and based their reasoning on denying the possibility of a future different from the past. (Friedan 1964: 127–34)

Although Friedan's complaints reflect an oft-cited, and somewhat legitimate, critique of the structural-functional method, it is possible to establish a structural analysis that acknowledges change (a full discussion of these critiques and responses to them, however, will be postponed until later chapters, especially Chapter 14); here, my task is merely to provide an overview of Hegel's thought and what he strove to accomplish. Hegel used the metaphor of a living organism in order to deal with the history of culture and society. He combined this paradigm with the premise that cultures have unique spirits that must be understood on their own terms. Social structuralism is a powerful model even if it has limitations and, in the wrong hands, can be misused.

THE SPIRIT OF CULTURE

The social sciences often deal with the unique essence of specific cultures. Social scientists generally agree that the members of a specific culture are distinct from other people, while fellow members of the same culture tend to be somewhat homogeneous. Thus, social scientists commonly believe that each culture has its own unique spirit or style that makes it distinctive. Students of international business, for example, often affirm that people from Japan typically behave and respond in certain distinctive ways, while Americans, as a group, also have a cluster of traits that set them apart from others. Certainly, there is variation between the specific members of any culture and, of course, not all people fit the norms of their society; nonetheless, the concept of culture tends to be accurate enough to be useful, and it is employed for that reason.

This idea of "culture" or "national character" is so ingrained in us today that it is difficult to envision a world where this concept is not commonplace. Before Hegel, however, the concept of culture or national character (as used here) was not widely embraced. While later philosophers (such as Kierkegaard, Nietzsche, Sartre, and Derrida) focus primarily upon the individual, Hegel (and those who worked within his intellectual tradition) concentrate upon the nation-state or cultural tradition as a largely homogeneous collective entity.[1] Hegel is not concerned with specific people, but with the culture as a holistic entity comprised of interrelated parts. Much marketing/consumer research reflects this perspective.

Hegel's vision of the culture/nation as an interconnected, synergistic entity was influenced by German philosopher Johann Gottfried Herder. During the era of the Enlightenment, intellectuals tended to believe that one universal model of society could be established and universally applied to all people and all cultures. In some ways, this is similar to the notion of "globalization" that has been advanced by contemporary marketing theorists such as Theodore Levitt; Levitt theorizes that due to the impact of science and technology all of the world's cultures are evolving in homogeneous ways that are destined to reduce cross-cultural variation. As discussed above, the Enlightenment also focused upon rational thought and it tended (in the most chauvinistic of ways) to believe that its perspectives were inherently superior to all others and that the principles of the Enightenment were clearly the wave of an inevitable future.

Herder, however, rejected this position of the Enlightenment and he embraced an alternative model that is clearly in the tradition of cultural relativism. A classic statement of Herder's perspective is found in his *Auch eine Philosophie der Geschichte zur Bildung der Merschheit*, which translates to roughly "another philosophy of history for the education of humanity." Herder's alternative model is an overt attack upon the Enlightenment's premise that the history of mankind can best be depicted in terms of inevitable progress and as an evolution toward a predictable and homogeneous ideal.

These perspectives largely stem from Herder's excellent work as a literary critic. Herder's literary analyses emphasize that there are no universal models or patterns that can be applied to all literature because every society/culture possesses its own unique *volksgeist* (spirit of the people, national character). Thus, effective literary art tends to embrace the cultural essence of specific peoples and, therefore, no one artistic tradition is appropriate for all nations.

In the final analysis, Herder provided Hegel with the notion that specific cultures/nations must be evaluated on their own terms. Hegel's model clearly coincides with the modern concepts of culture and national character as used by contemporary social scientists. Cultures are holistic entities composed of various parts (language, art, literature, the spirit of the people) that are united in synergistic ways. Each culture has its own unique style.

There is a dark potential to these chains of thought, especially if they are embraced uncritically and if they are applied to the realm of ethical life in literal and unyielding ways. The whole thrust of Hegel's conservative philosophy emphasizes that individuals must subordinate them-selves to the will and demands of the larger collective group and accept the verdicts of its leadership. Thus, like the component parts of an or-ganism, individual members of society are encouraged to stick to their specialized tasks and not trouble themselves with issues that do not di-rectly concern them or question the decisions of their leaders. Ultimately, this kind of ethical model can, if carried to extremes, justify any kind of atrocity as long as the social actors who commit these acts are adhering to the norms of their culture and the dictates of their leaders. Since He-gel's time there has been a clear recognition that if individual members of society give their cultures and their leaders carte blanche to act in any manner they deem appropriate, and do so without recognition of human nature or universal codes of decency, moral leadership will be lacking. As a result, many thinkers, in Hegel's time and in ours, have been trou-bled with some of the implications of the *volksgeist* model especially when intertwined with theories of ethics. Still, the *volksgeist*/organic model has profound value and its continued use is clearly justified.

THE *VOLKSGEIST*-ORGANIC MODEL AND MODERN SOCIAL SCIENCE

Since Hegel's time, the organic metaphor has enjoyed a long history in sociology; it was a key component of the theory of Auguste Comte (1798–1857), the so-called father of sociology. It was clearly and forcefully present in the work of Herbert Spencer (1820–1903). Thus, when late 19th-century social thinkers, such as Emile Durkheim, employed the or-ganic metaphor, they were clearly working in a tradition that could be easily traced back to the era of Hegel.

It is useful to discuss various streams of thought in order to analyze various ways in which these ideas can be molded to fit the needs and temperaments of specific researchers. They include:

1. Spengler/Toynbee/Kroeber and cycles of history
2. Boas/Cultural Particularist Anthropology
3. Durkheim/British Structural-Functional Anthropology/Parsons
4. Reactions and alternative models

Each will be briefly discussed and traced to Hegel and his work.

Spengler/Toynbee/Kroeber and Cycles of History

As discussed above, a recurring, seductive, and useful theory of cul-ture and society affirms that particular cultures experience what can be viewed as a life cycle that is analogous to the career of a living being. It is commonplace to intuitively view specific cultures as growing, maturing, or declining as they respond to both internal or external pressures.

An opening salvo of this approach was provided by Oswald Spengler (1880–1936), a German intellectual who, in the days of defeat after World War I, published his *The Decline of the West* (1928). Spengler's basic thesis is that, although cultures are unique, definite and discernable laws determine the rise and fall of nations, societies, and cultures. As a result, Spengler argues that history is predictable. In his own way, Spengler, like the romantics, clearly rejects the theory (advanced during the Enlightenment and popular ever since) that cultures are constantly evolving toward some higher level of existence.

In a nutshell, Spengler argues that cultures begin with the life, beliefs, and essence of the peasants or folk. Eventually a rational religion takes hold that becomes the ethos of the culture. Borrowing from Herder, Spengler believes that art, science, and philosophy are reflections of this cultural ethos (that can be envisioned as a *volksgeist*). After this period, the culture reaches what Spengler refers to as "civilization," characterized by an effete existence and one where spontaneous behavior is discouraged or eliminated. Eventually, the culture collapses. Although Spengler acknowledges that many different cultures exist, he sees this pattern inevitably recurring in them all.

Spengler's theories became very popular in an era when the German people were searching to understand the defeat they had suffered in World War I. Although Spengler's basic perspective was one of resignation and inevitable defeat (since he believed that the cultures of Western Europe were in decline), many Germans sought ways to forestall this inevitable fate and used *The Decline of the West* as a means of understanding the flow of history in order to rechannel their culture in more productive ways. As a result, although Spengler himself was rejected by the Nazis because of his fatalism, many Spenglerian perspectives were sprinkled through the rhetoric of Hitler and other German leaders of the era. Because some of Spengler's ideas abound throughout Nazi propaganda, he has often been dismissed accordingly; in reality, this is not a legitimate critique.

Notably, Spengler looked at cultures as holistic entities, somewhat analogous to organisms proceeding through a life cycle. Reflecting the organic model, Spengler placed little significance upon individual people and, like Hegel, he concentrated upon the larger, more holistic cultural unit. Such ideas, of course, are clearly reflective of contemporary models in marketing/consumer research that deemphasize the individual and elevate the culture to primary importance in the analysis.

Arnold Toynbee (1889–1975) is a modern representative of the Spenglerian style of historical analysis. Like Spengler, Toynbee is concerned with the process by which cultures grow, mature, and decline. More general than Spengler, Toynbee depicted cultural growth as a response to the challenges faced. Cultures, he emphasizes, succeed when challenges are successfully met; when this does not occur, cultures decline. These models have a strong value both in marketing/consumer research, which seeks to explore how and why people change through time, and in international business, which seeks to interpret cultures on their own terms and with reference to the challenges faced, and how the resulting change leads to evolving patterns of consumption.

To my mind, the culmination of this general perspective is provided by Alfred Louis Kroeber, a noted anthropologist who explained cultures in historical terms. Like Hegel and Spengler, Kroeber was little concerned with the individual, he concentrated upon the culture as a holistic entity that responds to circumstances in its own unique way. Kroeber forcefully articulated this position in his seminal article "The Superorganic" (1917), which dismisses theories of a unilineal evolution that moved toward a homogeneous "progress." Kroeber also discounted the role of the individual in history.

Even before he published his superorganic manifesto, Kroeber had clearly indicated that anthropology (and cultural history) did not concern individual people, but social entities. Thus, in his "Eighteen Professions," Kroeber advanced his belief that "civilization, though carried by men and existing through them, is an entity in itself, and of another from life" and "The . . . individual has no historical value save as illustration" (1915: 283, 284). Kroeber's basic position, which spanned his long career, is that societies and cultures evolve and develop on their own terms, even if they use the works and efforts of specific people to achieve their ends. Kroeber repeatedly argues that people are basically identical; therefore, cultural differences cannot be explained merely in human or biological terms. Cultures, as holistic patterns, must be examined when explaining human behavior. This type of paradigm has a profound value in explaining how people react in the marketplace and elsewhere.

Boas/Cultural Particularist Anthropology

The pioneering phase of North American anthropology proceeded through the leadership of the German born and raised scientist/ethnographer Franz Boas. As Bunzl has observed: "It is a commonplace that Boasian anthropology was to a certain degree the product of his intellectual socialization in Germany" (1996: 18). And, of course, that intellectual pedigree includes a propensity to view things from a *volksgeist* perspective.

Being an informed scientist, Boas certainly believed in biological evolution. Nonetheless, when he studied human societies, he quickly discarded evolutionary theory and insisted that cultures must be evaluated on their own terms. Each society, he reasoned, was a product of long and sustained historical pressures that molded the culture in unique and particular ways. As a result, Boas' work is generally referred to as "historical particularism."

Boas influenced a number of noted anthropologists such as Ruth Benedict (1934), who refined the *volksgeist* model (while not using the term) and used it to explain the unique ethos of various cultures. Thus, a clear line between 19th-century romantic thought from Germany and 20th-century American ethnography clearly exists. Narroll and Narroll (noted cross-cultural analysts) observe:

The writings of Spengler (1928), Benedict (1934) and Morris Opler (1945) have led many anthropologists to believe that cultures characteristically contain certain thematic orientation elements. Such elements are reflected not only in purposive behavior and ideology, but also in cultural styles–art styles, games styles, and the like. These views have enjoyed substantial support from several recent holocultural studies. (1973: 338)

Although Boas and members of this basic method acknowledged the impact of biological evolution, they simultaneously believed that this paradigm had minimal value when analyzing culture. They, in contrast, viewed cultures as adjusting in unique ways to a particular set of circumstances, and that these various adaptations could not be effectively dealt with using evolutionary theory. As a result, the historical particularist model evaluated cultures on their own terms, and the model assumes that each culture is unique in important ways (even if diffusion and cultural borrowing takes place).

The values of this approach are many. As we all know, On many occasions it is important for marketing strategists to analyze a culture in order to discern ways in which it is specific and unique. By doing so, it becomes easier to assess the impact of cultural diffusion upon a particular culture; since the marketing of new products can be viewed as the diffusion of artifacts from one culture to another, the method has a significant value for our profession.

When applying this method, the observer simply wants to perceive the uniqueness of the particular cultural market and to nest various artifacts (products) within that context. This perspective, furthermore, has a clear practitioner focus that will be discussed in Chapter 9; marketing/consumer research can effectively and appropriately embrace this intellectual tradition.

Durkheim/British Structural-Functional Anthropology/
Parsons

By the late 19th century, organic models had become commonplace, and they were clearly embraced by Emile Durkheim, a seminal sociologist who greatly influenced both sociological and anthropological theory. Durkheim insisted that all social facts must be explained in terms of the society of which they are a part and not with reference to psychology or biology. He argued that society is itself an "organism" and that social life can be explained in terms of serving its needs. British anthropologist Alfred Reginald Radcliffe-Brown eventually embraced a position that was strongly influenced by Durkheim; he was also deeply influenced by and an eloquent spokesperson for the organic model. In one of his classic essays he observes:

The concept of function applied to human societies is based on an analogy between social life and organic life. . . . As the word function is here being used the life of an organism is conceived as the functioning of its structure. It is through and by the continuity of the function that the continuity of the structure is preserved. (1935: 394–95)

Not only that, Radcliffe-Brown argues that the society is an entity in its own right and that it functions in ways that parallel Kroeber's conception of the superorganic. He observes: "The social relationships, of which the continuing network constitute social structure, are not haphazard conjunctions of individuals, but are determined by the social process. . . . Thus . . . we find there are accepted rules" (1952: 10).

Similar patterns can be seen in American sociological theory of the same period. Talcott Parsons viewed society as a system whose parts fit together in functional and synergistic ways in order to maintain the system. He asserted that society is made up of three components: (1) the individual, (2) relations between people, and (3) the general culture. Change in one component triggers transformations in the entire system. If change occurs too quickly, stresses develop. Parson's classic work is *The Structure of Social Action* (1937); there he introduces the contributions of three pioneering sociologists: Emile Durkheim, Vilfredo Pareto, and Max Weber, and presents his own functional-structural synthesis that is, in part, based on his interpretation of their contributions. His later work, *The Social System* (1951), views society as a system of interrelated parts, each serving a specific function. This is the "classic" model of the social sciences and one that underlies much social theory that has influenced marketing/consumer research. Thus, it casts a long shadow and one which our discipline cannot legitimately ignore.

The basic point being made here is that in all these models of society, there is a strong affinity to the *volksgeist*/organic model that was provided by Hegel. These social structural models do have their limitations and no attempt to defend them is made in this discussion (although following chapters will do so as required and as appropriate).

REACTIONS AND ALTERNATIVE MODELS

The impact of Hegel (and the ideas that he embraced) are many. On the one hand, much social theory stems from the structural models that Hegel provides or suggests, perspectives that have much value to marketing/consumer research. Many of these theoretical options are discussed in later chapters. It is hoped that by being aware of the pioneering work of Hegel (and those who influenced him), these later adaptations can be discussed in a more robust and useful manner.

Besides providing a foundation for future work, Hegel presents a clearly articulated position that others have attacked and, thereby, their thoughts have been channeled in useful and productive ways. The next chapter deals with Karl Marx and Marxist analysis; there we will see how some aspects of Hegel are embraced by Marxism while others are clearly rejected. In essence, Marx focused upon conflict between people, not cooperation among them. As a result of this focus on dissension and conflict, Hegel's emphasis upon structure, harmony, and cooperation was largely eliminated from Marx's work and from models that stem from it. More contemporary views of conflict theory, furthermore, are considered in Chapter 14 and they more fully develop this area of scholarship and social theory. Since these perspectives do not focus on the culture, as an organism operating in mutually beneficial ways, they transcend Hegel in useful and compelling ways.

Hegel, furthermore, was primarily concerned with the collective culture, not with individual people. Indeed, it can be argued that Hegel underestimated the individual in order to develop his paradigm of social life, which was based on an organic model. Since Hegel's time, various schools of thought have arisen that are designed to more effectively deal with the individual. This thinking begins with the pioneering efforts of Søren Kierkegaard and Friedrich Nietzsche, progresses to existentialism, and is currently represented by poststructuralism and deconstructionism. Many of these developments are dealt within Part III of this book.

Hegel's influence is pervasive. Many thinkers embrace his basic position (even if they qualify it in some manner); their thoughts fall clearly within the Hegelian framework. Others actively reject Hegel; in their cases, Hegel has provided the stimulus upon which they have reacted in fruitful and insightful ways. In both cases, Hegel casts a long shadow.

HEGEL: A FINAL ASSESSMENT

Hegel greatly influenced social structural thought by employing the organic model of culture that drew an analogy between a living organism and social life. This model emphasizes cooperation and how the organism/culture functions for the collective good of all. Such a perspective (limited though it may be) has been usefully applied in many contexts. In terms of general systems theory, Hegel's model corresponds with what Kenneth Boulding calls the "clockworks model," since it deals with systems as homoeostatic devices that seek to stabilize the structure for the collective good.

Hegel developed his paradigm with reference to the *volksgeist* model, which assumed that specific cultures have their own unique ethos or essence. This perspective of Hegel has been usefully applied in various ways within the social sciences and especially within anthropology. The value of this perspective transcends evolutionary theory by dealing with cultures on their own terms. On many occasions, marketers need to apply such a culturally specific perspective; when they do so they follow the lead of Hegel.

Hegel provided a complex vision that simultaneously could influence both conservatives or radicals and justify the work of these rival camps. Marx provides a conflict theory that rejects Hegel's structural theory while preserving other aspects of Hegelian thought. Many of the philosophical and intellectual developments of the post–World War II era, furthermore, are reactions against a Hegelian view of society and they are best understood as such. Wherever one looks within social theory, the impact of Hegel can easily be found.

NOTE

1. Hegel concentrated upon the nation-state, while modern social scientists tend to focus upon the culture or social group. I follow the lead of modern social scientists and consider their vision to be a useful refinement of Hegel's seminal observations.

REFERENCES

Benedict, Ruth. (1934). *Patterns of Culture*. Boston: Houghton Mifflin.
Boulding, Kenneth. (1956). "Systems Theory: The Skeleton of Science." *Management Science* 2(3) (April): 197–208.
Bunzl, Matti. (1996). "Franz Boas and the Humboldtian Tradition." In *Volksgeist as Method and Ethic: Essays on Boasian Ethnography and the German Anthropological Tradition*, ed. George W. Stockington. Madison: University of Wisconsin Press.
Darwin, Charles. (1859). *On the Origin of Species*. A facsimile of the first edition,

with an introduction by Ernst Mayr. Cambridge, MA: Harvard University Press, 1964.

Friedan, Betty. (1964). *The Feminine Mystique*. Tenth Anniversary Edition. New York: W. W. Norton.

Hegel, Friedrich. (1959). *Reason in History*, trans. R. Hartman. Indianapolis, IN: Bobbs-Merrill.

Hegel, Friedrich. (1967). *Philosophy of Right*, trans. T. M. Knox. Oxford: Oxford University Press.

Hegel, Friedrich. (1977). *Phenomenology of Spirit*, trans. A. V. Miller. Oxford: Clarendon Press.

Herder, Johann. (1774). *Auch eine Philosophie der Geschichte zur Bildung der Merschheit*. Paris: Aubier, 1964.

Herder, Johann. (1778–1779). *Volksliender*. Reprint, Frankfurt: Deutscher Klassiker Verlag, 1990.

Kroeber, Alfred Lewis. (1915). "Eighteen Professions." *American Anthropologist* 17(2): 283–88.

Kroeber, Alfred Lewis. (1917). "The Superorganic." *American Anthropologist* 19.

Lamarck, Jean Batiste. (1809). *Philosophie Zoologique* [Zoological Philosophy], trans. Hugh Eliot. Reprint, New York: Hafner, 1963.

Montesquieu, Baron. (1748). *The Spirit of the Laws*, trans. Anne Cohler. Reprint, New York: Cambridge University Press, 1989.

Naroll, Raoul and Naroll, Frada. (1973). *Main Currents in Cultural Anthropology*. Englewood Cliffs, NJ: Prentice-Hall.

Opler, Morris. (1945). "Themes as Dynamic Forces in Culture." *American Journal of Sociology* 51: 198–206.

Parsons, Talcott. (1937). *Structure of Social Action*. Glencoe, IL: Free Press.

Radcliffe-Brown, Alfred Reginald. (1935). "On the Concept of Function in Social Science." *American Anthropologist* 37: 394–95.

Radcliffe-Brown, Alfred Reginald. (1952). "On Social Structure." In *Structure and Function in Primitive Society*. New York: Free Press.

Siebert, Rudolf. (1979). *Hegel's Philosophy of History*. Washington, DC: University Press of America.

Smith, Adam. (1762–1763). *Letters on Jurisprudence*, ed. R. L. Meek. Reprint, Oxford: Clarendon Press, 1978.

Smith, Adam. (1776). *An Inquiry into the Nature and Causes of the Wealth of Nations*. Reprint, Chicago: Encyclopaedia Britannica, 1955.

Spengler, Oswald. (1928). *The Decline of the West*, trans. Charles Francis Atkinson. New York: Knopf.

Textor, Robert B. (1967). *A Cross Cultural Survey*. New Haven, CT: HRAF Press.

Toynbee, Arnold. (1934–1961). *Study of History*. London: Oxford University Press.

Wood, Allen, W. (1990). *Hegel and Ethical Thought*. Cambridge: Cambridge University Press.

CHAPTER 4

Marxist Theory and Marketing/ Consumer Research: An Anthropological Perspective

VICTORY IN DEFEAT

In the late 1980s, I witnessed a "cocktail lounge debate" in which a wise old visiting professor provided a strong defense of Marxist theory. If I remember correctly, he taught at the University of Leipzig, which, due to the political reality of that era, was still known as Karl Marx University. The event took place during the declining years of the socialist bloc, and many of the American business scholars sitting around the table viewed the prevailing political currents and economic trends to be a validation of their anti-Marxist perspectives.

Various rhetorical questions pointedly emphasized the current disarray that existed within the Soviet bloc and the fact that the robust economies of the West clearly overshadowed their socialist counterparts. To the surprise of all, this besieged thinker, whose main pillars of intellectual support seemed to be toppling and stripped of their foundations, remained firm in his defense of Marxism and, with no sign of effort, he was able to persuasively rebuff the various attacks to which he and his ideas were subjected. Instead of being offended by this onslaught, he seemed to relish the fact that, in spite of the political and economic reversals within his homeland, a Marxist vision could still prevail in the great battle of ideas that takes place within the context of a friendly or, perhaps, not-so-friendly intellectual debate.

Marx, he emphasized, is simultaneously two different people in one. It can't be denied that Karl Marx was a passionate political activist who struggled to advance a partisan point of view. Marx's alter ego, however, is a major social theorist. And, in his social thought, Marx crystalizes, in a robust and easily understandable way, the impact of economic life upon the totality of human experience, ranging from the individual, to the society, to the grand flow of cultural history.

If we focus upon Marx's narrow political forays, his importance as an important social theorist will be overlooked; this potential must be resisted. That was the profound message that came from East Germany during the last days of the Soviet regime—presented by an old professor, with a sense of irony and a wink of the eye. And it was addressed to us, as marketers, in rather pointed ways. Could capitalistic business thinkers put aside their own narrow prejudices and embrace useful social theories, no matter what their origins might have been?

In closing his case, the Eastern bloc theorist suggested that the decline of Marxism in politics had, at long last, freed it from the shackles of partisanship and created a situation where all thinkers (even marketing researchers) can more clearly perceive what Marx has to offer. *As a result, there can be victory in defeat.*

In order to demonstrate the value of Marxist theory to marketing research, this chapter borrows heavily from Marxist anthropology. I present this analysis with the greatest respect for Karl Marx himself and those who have built upon his general social theory in ways that can be usefully employed by marketing/consumer researchers.

THE HERITAGE OF HEGEL

No analysis of Marxist theory is complete without discussing Marx's intellectual debts to Friedrich Hegel. Here, I will initially present a fairly straightforward comparison of Marx and Hegel and do so in ways that spotlight their differences. In general, Hegel gives marketing/consumer researchers a tool for viewing culture/society as a monolithic entity, while Marx provides ways to deal with divisions and tensions that exist within a specific culture/society. This discussion will be followed by an analysis of how Marx took the basic intellectual skeleton provided by Hegel and merged it with other useful concepts in order to forge his own system, typically known as "historical materialism." Useful models, based upon Marxist theory, that have value to marketing/consumer research are then spotlighted.

Hegel, as is generally known, was ultimately concerned with the nation or culture as a collective, homogeneous entity. Hegel's perspectives largely parallel the modern concepts of "culture" or "national character" that are embraced by many modern social scientists and humanists. On many occasions, scholars are primarily concerned with broad similarities that exist between most (or virtually all) members of a culture. Some of these models have been employed in marketing/consumer research; thus, in my study of the marketing of the cowboy story, I used the concept of the evolving "national character" of a people to discuss trends in the marketing and consumption of literature and popular culture (Walle 2000). By and large, however, marketing/consumer researchers have not forcefully embraced such methods of analysis.

When pursuing a Hegelian style of analysis, scholars certainly realize the obvious fact that the interworkings of society will never be totally harmonious or stress free; nonetheless, it is possible to view internal strife as abnormal and/or as detracting from more important and far-reaching implications stemming from the similarities and harmonies that are believed to dominate social life. Marx, as we shall see, rethought Hegel by concentrating upon conflict, not harmony. Thus, although Hegel centered upon how people are unified, Marx dealt with strife and rivalry. Nonetheless, Marx simultaneously made use of Hegel's dialectical model, and he went on to forge it into one of the great paradigms of social action and cultural history. That is our initial story.

MARX AND THE YOUNG HEGELIANS

In order to understand the process by which Marx rethought Hegel, it is necessary to remember that Hegel's theories can be interpreted either from a conservative or a radical perspective. Initially, Hegel was viewed in a conservative light. Indeed, in maturity, Hegel became increasingly reactionary and he insisted that all people should mold themselves in order to perfectly mesh with the priorities of their leaders. Hegel went so far as to insist that a meaningful and ethical life is only possible if people completely embrace their culture and its dictates. Hegel further insisted that all people must accept their niche within their culture and that most individuals inevitably do so intuitively, instinctively, and without great thought. It goes without saying that there is an obvious conservative thrust to all of these basic and pivotal ideas that are central to both Hegel and his vision.

Radicals, however, pointed to the fact that Hegel simultaneously recognized that cultures and nations are constantly evolving and striving to perfect themselves. Since this is true, a culture at any specific point in time is, by definition, flawed and in need of improvement. Since there exists a clear need for nations and cultures to improve themselves, people can and should actively oppose the shortcomings that currently exist and, thereby, strive for perfection. These radicals continued by insisting that when obvious and oppressive flaws in society exist, they cannot be tolerated. Such sentiments, of course, are clearly radical and potentially justify revolutionary action.

Thus, while conservatives used Hegelian logic to argue that the Prussian government was an edifice that should not be challenged or opposed, the "Young Hegelians" interpreted Hegel to be a clear advocate

of social change. While conservatives emphasized that society was a fulfillment of the rational thought of a great omnipotent mind, the Young
Hegelians responded that the only rational thing to do in Prussia was to
work to reform the nation or replace it with a more humane and equitable alternative. Marx, as the reader may have guessed, was one of the
Young Hegelians who actively opposed the Prussian status quo; his ideas
of revolution were spawned during this period of the reactionary sup-
pression of personal opportunity and freedom.

THE IMPACT OF FEUERBACH

Clearly distilling and embracing the progressive or revolutionary potential in Hegel's thought, Marx still needed a means of getting beyond
Hegel's idealism, which viewed culture as the work of a great mind
striving towards perfection, and Hegel's metaphor, which depicted cul-
tures/nations as living organisms, as great machines made up of inter-
working parts that inevitably serve the collective good in harmonious
and mutually beneficial ways.

As a means of overcoming these limitations within Hegelian theory,
Marx ultimately employed the work of Ludwig Feuerbach in order to
deal with the struggles and rivalries that occur between different members of a particular culture or nation. Feuerbach placed mankind within
the material world and his writing emphasized the impact of the "real
world" upon people, their thoughts, and their actions. Because people
are a part of nature, Feuerbach insisted that intellectuals need to envision
them as being nested within their environment. Instead of viewing humanity as distinct and unique, he envisions people as animals that, while
impressive and distinct, are still a part of the natural world; and being
a part of nature, people inevitably act in accordance with natural laws.

These perceptions are closely linked to Feuerbach's theories of religion
that are based, in part, upon the researches of David F. Strauss' provocative *Life of Jesus* (1835–1836). Strauss emphasized that religion and myth
reveal more about mankind and the inner-workings of the human mind
than anything else. Feuerbach's *Essence of Christianity* (1841) extended
that perspective and exerted a profound influence upon the Young Hegelians. Feuerbach's basic thesis is that religion is not a reflection of "the
almighty," but is an artifact of how people think about themselves. Thus,
the idea of God is the vision of mankind writ big. Karl Marx and Friedrich Engels saw Feuerbach's emphasis upon specific groups of people as
a way of dealing with actual dilemmas faced by distinct segments of the
population, not the needs of the nation as a whole. This perspective
provided Marx with a means of dealing with social conflict and a means
of avoiding Hegel's emphasis upon harmony.

Thus, Marx established his basic paradigm. From Hegel, Marx gained the view that history flowed toward "progress," even if it sometimes did so in slow and halting ways. Feuerbach contributed the orientation that mankind is a part of nature and needs to be dealt with from that context. Combining relevant aspects of Hegel and Feuerbach, Marx created one of the great theories of cultural history as well as a seductive call to revolution.

MARX AND DIALECTICAL MATERIALISM

In addition to combining and rethinking Hegel's and Feuerbach's views of mankind and society, Marx embraced Hegel's dialectical method, which argued that the flow of history could best be described as opposing forces competing against one another in ways that lead to a resolution or compromise position. This, of course, is Hegel's well-known "dialectical theory," in which an existing phenomena (the thesis) is confronted by its opposite (the antithesis), with a reconciliation (the synthesis) resulting. At that point, Hegel continues, the synthesis emerges as a new thesis and the process begins again as part of a never-ending cycle. This paradigm provided Marx with a theory of history and, on many occasions, Marx applied it to his vision of culture and cultural evolution. Thus, while "rallying the troops" in *The Communist Manifesto*, Marx and Engels observe: "What the bourgeoisie, therefore, produces, above all else, is its own gravediggers. Its fall and the victory of the proletariat are equally inevitably" (1848: 24). This is true, Marx and Engels suggest, because the economic system unleashes forces it cannot suppress: "A society that has conjured up such gigantic means of production and of exchange, is like the sorcerer who is no longer able to control the powers of the nether world whom he has called up by his spells" (1848: 11). While Marx and Engels are being partisan here, and although the model they developed is overly deterministic, it does employ Hegelian dialectical perspectives as a means of explaining social change. Since the underlying mainspring of evolution was materialistic, not idealistic, Marx's method is typically called "dialectical materialism."

According to Marx, the material and economic realms are paramount and primary in the flow of history and, ultimately, other aspects of culture and human activity are transformed to mesh with these impersonal materialistic forces. Such an observation probably doesn't seem to be particularly profound or noteworthy to us today; after all, the modern viewpoint is largely forged in Marx's image.

To fully appreciate the significance of Marx's breakthrough, it is useful to recall that during the era when Marx was forging these ideas, it was commonly thought that history was the legacy of a few "great men" who transformed history and society in their own image. Thus, revered historian Thomas Carlyle, a contemporary of Marx who died two years before him in 1881, became a celebrity after writing his *On Heroes, Hero Worship and the Heroic Way in History* in 1841, the same decade that gave us Marx's *The German Ideology* (1846) and *The Communist Manifesto* (1848). While Carlyle mused about the great achievements of the heroic few, Marx was fashioning a theory that explained how impersonal forces, not the visions of heroes, shaped our destiny.

Marx's transcendence of the "hero worship" tendencies of his age has proved to be a profound contribution to social theory. Although Marx presented his case in polemical and partisan ways, his basic insight has stood the test of time. And, as is the case with all great ideas, other talented thinkers stepped up to either collaborate with the pioneering innovator and/or to independently improve upon the innovation and the vision that a provocative intellectual trailblazer had provided.

MARX AND ANTHROPOLOGY: THE ROLE OF LOUIS HENRY MORGAN

Theories of historical materialism that parallel Marx's dialectical theory have a long and independent history within the social sciences. In the next three sections of this chapter, we will focus primarily upon some of the main currents of anthropological theory that intersect with and/or are influenced by Marx's social scientific thought. As a specific example of the value of these tools to marketing research, Marxist anthropological theory will be used to rethink the global vs. local dichotomy that is so crucial to marketing strategy. This will be followed by a brief discussion of Marx's humanistic thought and how it exerted a parallel, but distinct, impact upon the humanities in the West.

Strong currents of historical materialism stem from the work and influence of American ethnographer Louis Henry Morgan. Morgan's impacts upon classic Marxist thought (as well as his influence on post–World War II American anthropological thought) are crucial to the maturity of Marxist social theory. Due to this significance, Morgan will be discussed in some detail.

Although Morgan himself was not a Marxist, he independently came to conclusions that are very similar to those of Marx and Engles; as a result, Morgan's theories exerted a significant impact upon Marxist thought during its formative period and beyond. Living in upstate New York in the 19th century, Morgan developed an intense interest in the Iroquois Indians that lived there. Eventually, he began to develop theories of cultural evolution. His classic statement regarding the general flow of cultural evolution is found in his *Ancient Society* (1877).

Ancient Society is a speculative masterpiece that presents an evolutionary view of culture and society; in it, Morgan proposed a sevenfold typology of social systems ranging from "lower barbarism" on one extreme to "civilization" on the other. Arguing that "Each of these periods has a distinct culture and exhibits a mode of life more or less peculiar to itself" (1877: 12–13), Morgan saw each of these epochs as distinct. Ultimately, Morgan explained both material culture and social relations in terms of the underlying economic system and the means of production that are available to people.

This chain of thought clearly jived with the basic point of view being developed by Marx and Engels; as a result, Engels (relying on notes written by Marx before his death) wrote an influential book based on Morgan's *Ancient Society* entitled *The Origins of the Family, Private Property, and the State in Light of the Researches of Louis Henry Morgan* (1885). This book not only bolstered Marxist theory by providing a greater historical context, it also catapulted Morgan into the role of "father" of Marxist anthropology. Thus, writing in the *Great Soviet Encyclopedia*, A. I. Pershits observes:

Morgan . . . asserted the ideas of the unity of mankind and its progressive development . . . related to this were his theses of the development of property from collective to private forms. . . . Morgan was, in fact, able to move away from evolutionism and in the words of F. Engels, "within the bounds of his own field independently rediscovered, in Marxist fashion, the materialist understanding of history". . . . A number of Morgan's minor theses require greater clarification, but his theories about primitive society retain their significance and continue to be developed by Marxist science. (Pershits 1977: 565–66)

While Morgan rose to fame for ideological reasons within the Eastern bloc, in the West he was harshly criticized on methodological grounds and largely forgotten. Morgan was a general theorist who based his *Ancient Society* upon speculation, not hard evidence. As anthropology developed in the West, it became increasingly empirical and the canons of the discipline demanded that research be based on actual data gathered in the field, not merely upon "armchair" contemplation. British social anthropologist A. R. Radcliffe-Brown unceremoniously dismissed Morgan as a mere "conjectural historian," and the greater anthropological community of the West concurred. Until the era of World War II and after, Morgan's reputation in the West remained low and his work was generally ignored. In the East, however, Morgan's general theories were respected and they formed the basis of the general theories that developed there.

Morgan suffered a fate that is analogous to that of qualitative marketing/consumer researchers who fell from favor as scientific methods came to dominate in the post–World War II era. The issues that both Morgan and pre-1980 qualitative marketers dealt with were important, but they tended to be dismissed for methodological reasons.

THE REHABILITATION OF MORGAN IN THE WEST

During the first half of the 20th century, ethnography was concerned with understanding present-day cultures and how they functioned as holistic entities. Little time was spent contemplating the past, predicting the future, or proposing general theories (as Morgan had done). This model and research strategy also deemphasized strife and conflict and it dealt with cultures as machines with interconnecting and mutually reinforcing parts (in a way that parallels Hegel's model).

Broad evolutionary models, however, began to experience a renaissance in the 1940s; a key event in this process was the publication of Leslie White's "Energy and the Evolution of Culture" (1943). The basic point that White made is that the amount of energy per capita that is available to society has a profound effect upon the nature of its culture. Human life and achievements, White reasoned, would be extremely elementary until mankind was able to harness vast sources of energy that expanded significantly beyond mere human efforts.

Various technological advances (including the domestication of plants and animals, the harnessing of animal power as a source of energy, various inventions, energy generating devises, the industrial revolution, and so on) ultimately increased the amount of energy available per capita, and this eventually transformed culture and social life. An early discussion of White's basic chain of thought is *Science of Culture* (1949); his more mature magnus opus is *Evolution of Culture* (1959).

White's connections with Morgan, Marx, and Soviet anthropology are rather obvious. Trained as an anthropologist in the 1920s, White's professors harbored the usual prejudices against Morgan that were typical of that era. As a young assistant professor, however, White decided to read Morgan's writings on the 19th century Iroquois because he was teaching at the University of Buffalo (located in Iroquois territory). Confronting Morgan in a serious way for the first time, White was impressed and became converted to evolutionary theory. This led to "a tour through Russia and Georgia in 1929, during which he first made his acquaintance in any thorough way with the literature of Marx and Engels, particularly those portions dealing with the nature and development of civilization" (Barnes 1960: xxvi). After that, White's research was centered around cultural evolution in ways that extended the earlier work of Morgan and Marx by linking cultural transformations to economic factors.

In many ways, White's work cannot be considered to be "new," and White himself consciously refused to use the term "neoevolutionist" to describe his work; he insists, instead, that his efforts merely expand the theories of Morgan and Marx and other early evolutionists. He observes:

Neoevolutionism is a misleading term. . . . The theory of evolution [as I use it] does not differ one whit [from that of the 19th century evolutionists such as Morgan and Marx], although of course the development, expression and demonstration of the theory may—and does—differ at some points. (White 1959: ix)

As foreshadowed by his 1943 article, White increasingly concentrated upon examining the energy sources that are available to a society and his analyses habitually begin from that entry point. In a pivotal passage, he observes:

[Culture is] primarily a mechanism for harnessing energy and of putting it to work in the service of man and, secondly channeling and regulating . . . [people's] behavior. . . . Social systems are, therefore, determined by technological systems and philosophies and the arts examine experience as it is defined by technology. (White 1959: 390–91)

In order to perceive the degree to which White's basic model was Marxist, it is useful to compare the above quotation with a similar passage from the preface of Marx's *A Contribution to the Critique of Political Economy*:

The totality of these relations of production constitutes the economic structure of society, the real foundation on which rise a legal and political superstructure and to which correspond definite forms of social consciousness. The mode of production in material life determines the general process of the social, political, and spiritual processes of life. It is not the consciousness of man that determines their existence [, but, on the contrary,] their social existence determines their consciousness. (Marx 1970: 20)

While White's evolutionary work (based as it is on a theory of unilineal evolution) is useful, other anthropologists, such as Julian Steward, found that it possessed crippling blindspots. Because White focused upon the broad sweep of human and cultural evolution, Steward complained, White's research "is concerned with culture rather than cultures" (1955: 14). This kind of critique, incidentally, foreshadows the observation by Raymond Williams (1977) that White's analysis is unable to distinguish between what Williams labels "epochal" versus "historical" analysis. Epochal analysis deals with broad and sweeping flow of cultural history. Historical analysis, in contrast, considers the specifics of time and place.

When dealing with specific cultures, especially in a short-term perspective, the situation becomes increasingly complex and a total reliance upon a broad unilineal model becomes less and less appropriate. Thus, Steward embraces a multilinear evolution that acknowledges that evolution can take place in a number of ways. He observes: "Multilinear evolution, therefore, has no a priori scheme or laws. It recognizes that

the cultural traditions of different areas may be wholly or partly distinctive" (1955: 19). Steward, while recognizing that evolution takes
place, also realizes that this evolution might be channeled by specific
cultures in distinctive ways. He states his basic methodology:

First the interrelationship of exploitative or productive technology and the environment must be analyzed ... second, the behavior patterns involved in the
exploitation of a particular area by means of a particular technology must be
analyzed [and third] the extent to which the behavior pattern [exploits the environment must be considered]. (1955: 40–41)

In demonstrating how evolution can mold cultures in distinctive ways,
Steward employs what he calls the concept of "cultural core" which,
most basically, includes attitudes, activities, and relationships that are
closely linked to economic activities that are crucial to the society. While
these areas of the culture may be expected to evolve in line with the
means of production, other aspects of culture tend to have a greater
potential for variation. These activities, which are not directly tied to
economics and production, tend to provide a culture with its uniqueness
even if economic considerations mold the society in its own image in a
number of important ways.

As might be expected, White and Steward engaged in polemical exchanges since both were striving to advance their own evolutionary
agenda. Nonetheless, the two positions could be bridged. Thus, Marshal
Sahlins and E. R. Service, two scholars who had been students of both
White and Steward, observed: "Evolution moves simultaneously in two
directions. On the one hand, it creates diversity through adaptive mod-
ifications: new forms differentiate from old. On the other side evolution
generates progress: higher forms arise from and suppress [lower forms]"
(Salhins and Service 1960: 12–13).

Collectively, the works of White, Steward, Sahlins, and Service can be
viewed as the process by which the evolutionist theories of Morgan and
Marx were reintroduced into mainstream anthropological theory in the
West. In addition, Morgan's emphasis upon the materialist realm was
updated and put on a more rigorous footing. This can be viewed as the
first wave of Marxist theory in 20th-century American anthropology.

THE RISE OF CULTURAL MATERIALISM

From the 1960s on, a basic Marxist thrust in social anthropology, called
"cultural materialism," has largely been associated with Marvin Harris.
In the late 1960s, Harris published *The Rise of Anthropological Theory*
(1968), a book that appears at first glance to be an objective overview of
the history of anthropological thought. Nestled within the text, however,

was a provocative and polemical advocating of a specific brand of Marxist analysis that Harris dubbed cultural materialism.[1]

Most basically, cultural materialism suggests that a universal pattern exists in which cultures are comprised of three distinct components. The first is the infrastructure, which consists of the mode of production and the mode of reproduction. The mode of production deals with phenomena such as technology, systems of work, and relationships between technology and the environment, while the mode of reproduction can largely be equated with demographic issues.

Moving from the infrastructure to the structure, the concern shifts to the social structure and to political relationships. This includes kinship systems, social hierarchies, social structures, political organizations, warfare, and so on. Lastly, the superstructure is made up of mental structures such as ideological and cognitive patterns. Expressions of ideological and cognitive patterns (such as religion, art, music, dance, and sports) are also included within the superstructure. Ultimately, consumer preferences, habits, and behaviors also fit into this category.

Having described these elements, cultural materialism predicts causal relationships between them. In general, the underlying foundation of a culture is provided by its infrastructure, which, in turn, impacts the structure. Thus, the means of production and the demographic profile of society profoundly influence the social structure. Both the infrastructure and the structure, in turn, effect the superstructure. Note that this model is an almost complete restatement of the basic model of economic determinism that had been provided by Marx in *The German Ideology* (1846) and elsewhere. Cultural materialism, however, benefitted from over a century of sophisticated anthropological thought, and it is phrased in ways that can address the problems examined in more rigorous and scientific ways than classic Marxist analysis is able to accomplish.

Cultural materialism, furthermore, is useful because it is not as rigid as the more deterministic paradigm presented by Marx. Thus, cultural materialism tends to speak in terms of statistical frequency, not cut-and-dried inevitableness. Cultural materialism, furthermore, emphasizes that the typical dominance of the infrastructure upon the structure and superstructure only exists because human well-being, and even survival, ultimately depend upon the means of production coupled with demographic considerations. And, in important ways, cultural materialism recognizes that on some occasions, the superstructure and/or the structure may "reverse the flow" of determinism and exert a decisive impact upon the infrastructure.

Equally important is cultural materialism's rejection of Marx's notion of the inevitable nature of dialectical materialism: the theory that cultures are destined to evolve in a specific direction (toward a socialistic utopia).

Ultimately, it is that dialectical perspective, so strongly ingrained within classic Marxist thought, that has often prevented Marxist theory from being broadened in ways that went beyond partisan rhetoric. Strict Marxists who closely stuck to the dogmatic embrace of dialectical materialism, however, found themselves unable to explain how so many "capitalistic bosses" in the West had been able to reform themselves, accept unions, and provide decent wages and working conditions, thereby avoiding the revolution that Marx depicts as the inevitable flow of history.

Rejecting the dialectical paradigm, cultural materialism does not predict some universal and inevitable pattern of cultural evolution. Instead, it emphasizes that the economic base of society (infrastructure) exerts profound impacts upon everything that is built upon it. Using this paradigm, cultural materialism provides models and strategies of analysis that predict how cultures will function and how they can be expected to evolve. The infrastructure tends to be the "primary" variable that impacts the structure, a "secondary" variable. The structure, in turn, emerges as a primary variable, in its own right, and goes on to influence the superstructure, its secondary variable.

For our purposes here, cultural materialism can be viewed as a revised and updated Marxist vision that provides a wide range of tools for predicting how cultures evolve and why they do so. In many situations, marketing research has a profound interest in such transformations; the health and success of all organizations are typically linked to an ability to understand how needs and wants are transformed and why specific cultural changes occur; and cultural materialism provides a sophisticated model that forcefully deals with these issues.

In recent years, anthropology as a discipline has become increasingly fragmented and general theories, such as cultural materialism, have ceased to be "hot topics" of research. Today, many anthropologists (influenced by models such as mental structuralism and poststructuralism) are more concerned with the interworkings of individual cultures and/or individual people, not with examining broad patterns of cultural development and evolution. Nonetheless, cultural materialism continues to be a powerful and respectable school of thought and a useful methodology. And, as we shall see, it can be profoundly adapted to the needs of marketing/consumer researchers. Those seeking a useful overview of the application of the cultural materialist model will find it in Harris' *Cultural Materialism* (Harris 1979: 77–114).

MARKETING AND MARXIST ANTHROPOLOGY

The basic flow of thought from Marx, to Morgan, to modern cultural materialistic anthropology provides focused, rigorous, and relevant tools for examining the impact of economic and technological patterns (infra-structure) upon the culture and the social system (structure). The result-ing structure of society, in turn, impacts the superstructure that triggers and/or channels much buyer behavior.

Marketing/consumer research has independently, and in its own way, embraced a similar set of concepts; marketers are aware that the flow of cultural history typically impacts societies and their patterns of behavior in ways that are relevant to marketing. Two widely acknowledged per-spectives are the so-called "global" and the rival "local" theories of cul-ture and marketing strategy that, in recent years, have impacted our field in provocative, polemical, and useful ways. Here, we will discuss both global and local theories in terms of cultural materialism; this will be followed by a more general discussion of the potential of cultural ma-terialistic methods within marketing/consumer research.

Global Theories

Especially since the publication of Theodore Levitt's *The Marketing Imagination* (1983b) and Levitt's much-discussed "The Globalization of Markets" (1983a), much marketing thought has been devoted to an anal-ysis of what might be described as "unilineal cultural evolution." In es-sence, Levitt encourages marketers to abandon the marketing concept (giving specific people what they want in the here and now) in order to respond to cultural changes that, he asserts, are making all people (and their consumer behavior) increasingly similar cross-culturally. Cultural homogeneity, he asserts, is the inevitable wave of the future and pro-gressive marketers should respond to this trend, not to the circumscribed strategies of the past that focus on responding to the unique demands of specific cultures.

Although it is impossible to provide a full review of literature regard-ing global theories and methods, Levitt's "The Globalization of Markets" was quickly followed by a wealth of articles that refined Levitt's position while generally embracing it. Noted strategic analyst Michael Porter (1986), for example, drew a distinction between what he called multi-domestic vs. global industries and, thereby, attempted to augment the global paradigm. A number of other contributions (many of them ap-pearing in *Harvard Business Review*, where Levitt's seminal article was published) expanded the global vision (Hamel and Prahalad 1985; Quelch and Hoff 1986; Bartlett and Ghoshal 1986).

In many ways, this kind of evolutionary vision echoes the model pro-vided by Leslie White because both depict technology as leading man-kind in specific and predictable directions. Although differences between cultures exist and will continue to exist, the global theory views these variations as becoming increasingly weak and insignificant because an emerging cultural homogeneity (triggered primarily by technological advances) is rising to paramount importance.

The basic point being made by Levitt is that advances in transportation, technology, mass communication, and other technological innovations are causing different societies, their demands, and their consumer behavior to become increasingly homogeneous. As this occurs, all cultures are viewed as following a single stream of cultural evolution that is triggered and fueled by technological change. This model continues by arguing that all people, no matter what their cultural heritage, will increasingly resemble each other in their marketplace behavior. Of special interest to marketing/consumer researchers is the fact that as a result of these emerging similarities, the world's population, in general, is predicted to want the same products and be predisposed to consume them in parallel ways.

Asserting that a pattern of unilineal evolution exists, Levitt and the globalizers insist that marketing strategies should embrace the notion of cultural homogeneity (and the inevitable wave of homogeneous cultural evolution) and, as a result, marketing strategists should forge campaigns that mesh with the inevitable future. To do otherwise, Levitt insists, is to live in the past and, as he has often affirmed, a reliance upon yesterday's strategies will ultimately backfire and potentially prove to be the kiss of death to non-progressive marketers.

A problem with the global paradigm is that even if it is correct in the long run, in the short term it may be incapable of dealing with the situations that marketers face in the here and now.

A neo-Marxist cultural materialist model, however, provides a method of analyzing the culture in ways that can deal with how, why, and when various kinds of transformations will take place. By looking at the infrastructure, the structure, and the superstructure as separate but interrelated components of society, marketing researchers can begin to envision ways in which various parts of the culture either encourage or discourage certain types of behavior that, in turn, have the potential to impact marketing and consumer response.

Local Theories

While Levitt's theory of globalization has had a legitimate impact on marketing thought, critics have noticed that the reality often observed in the international marketplace does not jive with theories of unilineal cultural evolution that predict the inevitable molding of all cultures into a homogeneous worldwide pattern. Kashani (1989), for example, warns, "beware of the pitfalls of global marketing."

Specific cultural differences persist and they impact consumer response. Thus, when critiquing Levitt's globalization model years ago, I pointed out that although facing profound threats in America, a distinctive Afro-American culture was able to survive and thrive. That analysis concluded when I rhetorically asked:

If Afro-American culture can resist 400 years of depravity, forced illiteracy, and slave drivers beating down traditions can other cultures survive the onslaught of Coke and Pepsi? And if today's cultures can survive such relatively trivial threats, will global marketing apply only in some rather specialized cases where homogeneous products are easily translated into different lifestyles? (Walle 1985: 87)

Most basically, those who embrace the localized theory, while not necessarily denying the long-term implications of global tendencies, insist that (at least in the short term) cultures continue to be distinct and marketing strategies must recognize that fact.

A good review of the pros and cons of globalizaton is presented by Aaker (1992: 305–20). Within that discussion, he observes:

The reality is that a standardized global product and marketing effort is not always desirable or even possible. In general, each element of a marketing program needs to be analyzed to determine whether or not the advantages of standardization outweigh the gains in effectiveness amassed in tailoring the program to local markets. (Aaker 1992: 313)

And some writers call for more flexible strategies that tailor global strategies to circumstances. Thus, Quelch and Hoff observe (1986: 59):

Too often executives view global marketing as an either/or proposition—either full standardized or local control. But when a global approach can fall anywhere on a spectrum from tight worldwide coordination . . . to loose agreement on a product idea, why the extreme view? In applying the global marketing concept and making it work, flexibility is essential.

Clearly, marketing/consumer researchers need a means of acknowledging the potential for different streams of evolution to exist; the work of anthropologists such as Julian Steward provide the tools needed to do so. Cultural evolution will be different from one culture to the next; these differences are best conceptualized in terms of models of multilineal evolution that acknowledge the culture and its traditions. As a result, in some marketing/consumer research such models are preferable to the global model that emphasizes unilineal evolution. The stream of thought stemming from multilineal evolutionary theory provides the lens by which cultural variation can be most efficiently analyzed by marketing/consumer researchers.

Nonetheless, changes in the infrastructure of a culture can impact the structure and the superstructure in ways that lead to concomitant changes in consumer response. By understanding how these changes in the infrastructure impact a culture (and consumer response) and by considering how their influence travels though a society, the impact of global trends can be predicted, as well as how cultures may maintain a distinctiveness that impacts their responses as consumers.

Since cultural materialism acknowledges that, in a reversal of the usual flow of influence, it is possible for the superstructure to impact the structure and that the structure, in turn, can trigger changes in the infrastructure, a more flexible and robust model of cultural change is presented. This is exactly the kind of analytic paradigm that marketing/consumer researchers need when they deal with the massive social and technological changes that are remaking the world in its own image. The tendency toward globalization (homogeneous cultural evolution and its impact upon consumer response) needs to be recognized, on the one hand, while the power of tradition must also be factored into the equation, on the other. Theories of multilineal evolution are able to do so.

Ultimately, Marxist thought deals with the impact of the means of production (material/economic considerations) upon other facets of life. Marxist analysis asserts that the economic/technological realm is primary and that other forms of human behavior are secondary and based upon the foundation created by economics and technology.

Indeed, in recent years there has been a recognition of the value of Marxist models within economic and business research. Thus, William Jackson has recently observed:

A Marxist approach is . . . more amenable than neo-classicism to cultural ideas: it avoids individualistic reductionism and insists on the historically specific nature of . . . [the events being considered]. Some Marxian authors have sought to redress the balance between economics and culture . . . with a more complex interplay between culture and the economy. (1996: 222)

Jackson continues by speaking specifically of Marvin Harris' cultural materialism methods (which have been spotlighted in this chapter: "Marvin Harris introduced the term 'cultural materialism' in the 1960s to describe his explicitly materialist outlook . . . the motivation behind cultural materialism is to demonstrate that all cultures are adapted to . . . their material" (1996: 226–27).

By using the paradigm of cultural materialism as a jumping-off point, marketing/consumer researchers will have a series of testable hypotheses that they can poise when investigating specific phenomena that concern them. Because Marx developed his classic model over 150 years ago, certain of his perspectives are, understandably, dated. Nonetheless, the notion that, in most cases, the economic and technological realm impacts other aspects of culture in its own image continues to be a viable working hypothesis, and it is an idea that has independently been invented within marketing/consumer research as represented by the theory of the globalization of markets. By refining Marxist thought with models such as cultural materialism, a more robust paradigm of cultural evolution results that possesses great potential value for marketing/consumer researchers.

ALTERNATIVE MARXIST PARADIGMS

So far we have dealt with what are usually referred to as the works of the "mature Marx," although I disavow that label because it seemingly belittles his earlier accomplishments. Nonetheless, the "mature" phase of Marx's thinking is very different from his earlier work because it systematically attempts to place the study of society and mankind upon a "scientific" footing.

The basic chain of thought presented by the mature Marx was first visible in his *The German Ideology* (1846). Once formulated, these ideas were repeated and refined in subsequent writings such as *The Communist Manifesto* (1848), *A Contribution to the Critique of Political Economy* (1859), and *Capital* (1867). We saw how Friedrich Engels edited the notes that Marx had compiled about Louis Henry Morgan's evolutionary theories of society and presented them in *The Origins of the Family, Private Property, and the State in Light of the Researches of Louis Henry Morgan* (1885). This cluster of ideas led to the development of a Marxist social science that culminated in the cultural materialist model of anthropology, which has been our primary topic of discussion.

There is, however, another phase of Marx's thinking that has had a different kind of impact. Although Marx thought of his work as scientific (and even called it "scientific socialism,") he was also a humanist. And when thinking in humanist terms, Marx was largely concerned with the needs of individuals, not merely the flow of collective history evaluated in scientific terms. Thus, much of Marx's thinking largely hinges around concepts such as "the alienation of the individual," and it concentrates upon the process by which people become estranged from themselves, others, and society. This writing has exerted a strong impact, but it has largely influenced humanists while not being as attractive to members of the social scientific community.[2]

In the United States, this brand of Marxist humanist/thought became a powerful intellectual force during the 1960s and 1970s and was further influenced by the impact of the Frankfurt School of Marxist thought (and the body of work it produced, collectively known as "critical theory," and the works of writers such as Herbert Marcuse, Theodor Adorno,

Lew Lowenthal, and Max Horkheimer). Useful anthologies and interpretations include Arato and Gebhardt (1978), Ingram and Simon-
Ingram (1990), Jay (1973), and Wiggershaus (1994).

In the 1960s, furthermore, French philosopher Jean-Paul Sartre embraced Marxist thought as the "philosophy of our time," an event that
opened the door for existentialism (and later developments, such as
poststructuralism and deconstructionism) to more fully embrace humanistic Marxist thought. This stream of critical analysis was introduced to
the United States in the 1970s and it has exerted a profound impact ever
since. Thus, what can be viewed as "humanistic Marxism" is exerting a
powerful force within the humanities, but one that is very different from
the "scientific Marxism" discussed above.

These humanistic contributions, of course, are important and they deserve to be recognized and discussed. And various well-respected marketing scholars (such as John Sherry, Fuat Firat, and Alladi Venkatgesh
are concerned with models such as poststructuralism that have links to
the humanistic traditions of Marxist theory. I have the greatest respect
for these scholars and their work. Nonetheless, Marx's influence as a
humanist is distinct from his role as a major social scientist. As a result,
discussions of Marx's humanistic theories represent a different stream of
thought that has not been addressed here.

A CONCLUDING STATEMENT

Marx's social theory assumes that economic pressures exert a primary
influence upon human behavior and cultural evolution. While much
Marxist theory is centered around unilineal evolution, which envisions
a universal overarching trend in cultural history, alternative multilineal
models acknowledge that different cultures evolve in distinct ways. Both
of these variants of Marxist social theory are profoundly important to
marketing thought because they provide robust models of social change
that project how economic forces can trigger concomitant changes in behavior, including consumer response. As a result, both unilineal and
multilineal evolution have significant contributions to make to marketing
research; they, furthermore, can be linked to the current "global" vs.
"local" theories with marketing research.

Marx's basic writings, however, were composed over 150 years ago;
as a result, his thinking is, understandably, dated in a number of significant ways. Marxist theory, however, did not stop evolving when Marx
died in 1883. Instead, his model of economic determinism has continued
to evolve and it has become a staple of social (not merely socialist)
thought. Here, I have focused upon the Marxist tradition within anthropological theory in order to demonstrate the significance of that specific
body of Marxist thought to marketing/consumer research. The modern

cultural materialist model, as a particularly well-developed and useful example, breaks cultures down into their component parts and then analyzes how cultural transformations take place. This technique provides viable and practical research designs that have profound significance for marketing/consumer research.

Due to the political realities of the times, until recently, Marxist theory tended to be viewed in partisan and polemical ways. As a result, Marxist thought was not viewed in objective ways by either friend or foe. Today, as Marxist thought ceases to be a powerful political dogma, we can come to know and appreciate Karl Marx, the detached and impartial social theorist. And, from Marx and those who have embellished his ideas, marketing/consumer researchers can learn important lessons from a polemical antagonist who thought of himself as the great foe of business.

NOTES

1. There is also a humanistic movement known as cultural materialism, but this is not specifically related to it.

2. Although the current vogue of existential-based methods within the social sciences is making these aspects of Marx more attractive to some scholars.

REFERENCES

Aaker, David A. (1992). *Strategic Marketing Management.* New York: John Wiley.

Arato, Andrew and Gebhardt, Eike, eds. *The Essential Frankfurt School Reader.* New York: Urizen Books.

Barnes, H. E. (1960). "Foreword." In *Essays in the Science of Culture,* ed. G. Dole and R. Carniero. New York: Thomas Crowell.

Bartlett, Christopher and Ghoshal, Summantra. (1986). "Tap Your Subsidaries for Global Reach." *Harvard Business Review* (November/December): 87–94.

Carlyle, Thomas. (1841). *On Heroes, Hero Worship, and the Heroic in History.* Reprint, New York: J. W. Lovell, 1885.

Child, V. Gordon. (1942). *Man Makes Himself.* Reprint, New York: New American Library, 1951.

Child, V. Gordon. (1946). *What Happened in History.* New York: Penguin.

Engels, Friedrich. (1885). *The Origins of the Family, Private Property, and the State in Light of the Researches of Louis Henry Morgan.* Reprint, New York: International Publishers, 1942.

Feuerbach, Ludwig. (1841). *The Essence of Christianity,* trans. George Eliot. Reprint, New York: Harper, 1957.

Firat, Fuat and Venkatesh, Alladi. (1995). "Liberatory Postmodernism and the Reentrenchment of Consumption." *Journal of Consumer Research* 22(3) (December): 139–267.

Hamel, Gary and Prahalad, C. K. (1985). "Do You Really Have a Global Strategy?" *Harvard Business Review* (July/August): 139–48.

Harris, Marvin. (1968). *The Rise of Anthropological Theory*. New York: Thomas Crowell.

Harris, Marvin. (1979). *Cultural Materialism: The Struggle for a Science of Culture*. New York: Random House.

Ingram, D. and Simon-Ingram, J., eds. (1990). *Critical Theory: The Essential Readings*. New York: Paragon House.

Jackson, William A. (1996). "Cultural Materialism and Institutional Economics." *Review of Social Economy* 54(2) (Summer): 221–24.

Jay, M. (1973). *The Dialectical Imagination*. Boston: Little, Brown.

Kashani, Kamran. (1989). "Beware the Pitfalls of Global Marketing." *Harvard Business Review* (September/October): 91–97.

Levitt, Theodore. (1983a). "The Globalization of Markets." *Harvard Business Review* 61(3) (May/June): 92–102.

Levitt, Theodore. (1983b). *The Marketing Imagination*. New York: Free Press.

Marx, Karl. (1846). *The German Ideology*. Parts 1 and 3 by Karl Marx and Friedrich Engels. Reprint, New York: International Publishers, 1947.

Marx, Karl. (1867). *Capital*. Reprint, Chicago: Encyclopaedia Britannica, 1955.

Marx, Karl. (1970). *A Contribution to the Critique of Political Economy*, trans. S. W. Ryazanskaya, Moscow: Progress Publishers.

Marx, Karl and Engels, Friedrich. (1848). *The Communist Manifesto*. Reprint, New York: Monthly Review Press, 1964.

Morgan, Louis Henry. (1877). *Ancient Society, or Researches in the Lines of Human Progress from Savagery, through Barbarism, to Civilization*. Reprint, Cleveland: World Publishing Co., 1963.

Pershits, A. I. (1977). "Louis Henry Morgan." *Great Soviet Encyclopedia* 16: 565–66.

Porter, Michael. (1986). "Changing Patterns of International Competition." *California Management Review* 28 (Winter): 9–40.

Quelch, John A. and Hoff, Edward J. (1986). "Customizing Global Strategies." *Harvard Business Review* (June/July): 59–68.

Sahlins, Marshall and Service, E. R. (1960). *Evolution and Culture*. Ann Arbor: University of Michigan Press.

Sherry, John (1991) "Postmodern Alternatives: The Interpretative Turn in Consumer Research." In *Handbook of Consumer Behavior*, ed. Harold H. Kassajarian and Thomas Robertson. Englewood Cliffs, NJ: Prentice-Hall.

Steward, Julian. (1953). "Evolution and Process." In *Anthropology Today: An Encyclopedia Inventory*, ed. Alfred Louis Kroeber. Chicago: University of Chicago Press.

Steward, Julian. (1955). *Theory of Culture Change: The Methodology of Multilineal Evolution*. Urbana: University of Illinois Press.

Strauss, David F. (1835–1836) *Das Leben Jesu* [Life of Jesus]. Reprint, Gottingen: Vandenhoeck and Ruprecht, 1975.

Walle, Alf H. (1985). "Review of Theodore Levitt's *The Marketing Imagination*." *Journal of Macromarketing* 5(1) (Spring): 85–88.

Walle, Alf H. (2000). *The Cowboy Hero and Its Audience: Popular Culture as Market Derived Art*. Bowling Green, OH: The Popular Press.

White, Leslie. (1943). "Energy and the Evolution of Culture." *American Anthropologist* 45: 335–56.

White, Leslie. (1949). *Science of Culture*. New York: Grove Press.
White, Leslie. (1959). *Evolution of Culture*. New York: McGraw-Hill.
Wiggershaus, Rolf. (1994). *The Frankfurt School: Its History, Theories, and Political Significance*, trans. Michael Robertson. Cambridge, MA: MIT Press.

CHAPTER 5

The Intellectual Ancestors
of Modern Qualitative Thought

In the previous chapters, three important intellectual ancestors of contemporary thought (Kant, Hegel, and Marx) are discussed and evaluated on their own terms. Each of these prominent visionaries exerts a profound influence upon the way contemporary people envision the world and society. Thus, Kant, Hegel, and Marx exercise a powerful influence when their ideas are both embraced and repudiated. In both circumstances, however, contemporary thinkers typically distort the intellectual heritage of the 18th and 19th centuries in order for it to mesh with the tastes, needs, and dilemmas of the contemporary scene. Thus, Kant, Hegel, and Marx tend to be viewed from our perspective, not their own.

The purpose of the cluster of chapters presented above is to provide an evenhanded view of these powerful intellectual ancestors in ways that help marketing/consumer researchers to more effectively envision the work of these seminal thinkers. Since my comments are, themselves, contemporary interpretations, I hope that they do not fall into the trap of being so locked into their own time and place that they lack an ability to present these intellectual giants on their own terms.

By looking at these thinkers in an objective and open-minded way, various issues can be more readily appreciated and factored into marketing/consumer research. These issues include Kant's, Hegel's, and Marx's perspectives regarding:

1. The limitations inherent in scientific thought
2. The benefits of qualitative thought
3. The nature of humanity and culture
4. The nature of society

Each of these issues will be discussed below. It is hoped that by dealing with these topics individually, the fuller implications of Kant, Hegel, and Marx can be more fully appreciated.

THE LIMITATIONS INHERENT IN SCIENTIFIC THOUGHT

The modern intellectual tradition can best be interpreted as a reaction to the age of the Enlightenment that preceded it. The Enlightenment was a rational movement in which intellectuals believed that science and rational thought could answer the world's riddles, solve any question, and mitigate all human misery. Kant, Hegel, and Marx, each in their own way, temper this optimistic vision of the Enlightenment. In doing so, they collectively point to the limitations inherent in the scientific method and in rational thought.

In Chapter 2, we saw how Kant convincingly ripped the crown of intellectual superiority from the brow of scientific thought and how he reaffirmed that there are other ways of knowing besides formal scientific experimentation and quantitative analysis. Kant pointed out an obvious reality that (during the age of science and the Enlightenment) had been largely overlooked and ignored: in the final analysis, Kant affirms that the human mind thinks in patterned ways and in a manner that precedes actually empirical knowledge. According to Kant, these processes of the human mind (working independently of science and empirical observation even while collaborating with them) are vital and indispensable prerequisites of knowledge.

Coming to focus upon the human mind, its innate analytical powers, and how it operates is generally known as the "Kantian turn" in philosophy. And since the era of Kant, this inward focus has dominated the thought of intellectuals (especially in the West).

As we have discussed, the vision provided by Kant went on to influence and encourage the romantic era and the self-reflective focus that typified the movement and can be represented by Keats, Shelley, Byron, Wordsworth, and Coleridge (merely to mention English-speaking romantic writers). And, as also discussed above, the romantic era spawned romantic nationalism, in which people actively sought their cultural essence and, in the process, rejected the universal notion that, culturally speaking, one well-constructed prototype of society could serve all people with equal effectiveness.

Although the Kantian turn in philosophy and the priorities of the romantic era came to dominate the intellectual life of the West, the basic premises of the Enlightenment continued to survive and exert a powerful impact. In many ways, the emergence of the theory of evolution bolstered the core ideas of progress that the Enlightenment so fondly and dogmatically embraced. Social Darwinists viewed cultures and societies as evolving toward perfection and leading to a better world for all (a world that many depicted as a technologically driven utopia).

The aftermath of World War I, however, burst that "bubble" of Enlightenment thinking. The horrors of the conflict led to (among other things) what has come to be called "the lost generation": a group of American expatriate intellectuals who settled in Paris after World War I and lived and worked there during the 1920s and the 1930s. The term "lost generation" was originally introduced by the American writer Gertrude Stein (1874–1946); it was also used by Ernest Hemingway in *The Sun Also Rises* (1926). The lost generation provides a specific example of the rejection of the last vestiges of optimism and rationality that typified the Enlightenment. Instead of embracing a comforting belief in progress, the lost generation spoke in terms of broken dreams, false hopes, and the decline of Western civilization.

Almost exactly a century earlier, German philosopher Arthur Schopenhauer had argued an equally disillusioned thesis in his *The World as Will and Idea* (1818); he, furthermore, wrote in an era that parallels the world of the lost generation: the blighted years after the end of the Napoleonic era (another epoch of destruction and exhaustion in Europe that corresponds, in many ways, to the post–World War I era). Schopenhauer embraced a profound pessimism because he believed that the nature of the "human will" exerted inevitable tragic influences upon people. In specific, Schopenhauer asserts that the human will relentlessly encourages people to seek an endless array of goals, none of which provide permanent satisfaction, fulfillment, or happiness. As a result, the power of the will inevitably leads to pain, suffering, and death. Schopenhauer suggests that this endless cycle of misery can only end when people resign themselves, via reason, and accept the world as it is. Thus, while Schopenhauer denies that rational thought has the power to create a better world, he nonetheless affirms the value of rational thought in helping people to cope with the plight they face. The lost generation, in addition to being as pessimistic as Schopenhauer, placed little faith in rational thought and viewed the world as irrational and, perhaps meaningless. Thus, rational thought was increasingly discredited. (This theme, of course, is a crucial component of existentialism and its analogues; they will be discussed in later chapters.)

While Kant's focus upon irrationality has been pervasive, Hegel's reworkings of Kant are more influential, even though Hegel and his thought are distinctive. Hegel employed the ideas of Kant by thinking of nature as a great mind and, as a corollary, by suggesting that smaller subunits, such as cultures, are manifestations of this universal and omnipotent force. Fortifying this perspective with the findings of the emerging disciplines of biology and economics that were arising in the late 18th and early 19th century, Hegel created a structural model of great explanatory value. Ultimately, Hegel embraced the idea of *volksgeist* (spirit of the people, national character); his ideas profoundly impacted the social sciences, especially the ideas of social structural analysis. In his work, Hegel struggled to find the "ethos" of a people, and he did so in intuitive and non-scientific ways. Hegel, like Herder before him, did excellent work in literary and cultural criticism; his strategy resulted in a powerful method of conceptualizing a culture. Having done so, Hegel forged interpretations of people and their culture. Ultimately, this method of analysis parallels modern anthropological fieldwork methods, another intellectual system that rejects the scientific method in order to better examine the truth.

The work of Karl Marx and his rejection of science and the Enlightenment are more complex than those of Kant and Hegel because Marx thought of himself as being scientific. While Hegel focused upon how cultures work in systematic ways for the betterment of all, Marx presents an early conflict theory, and this perspective of strife and disunity is more complex than Hegel's emphasis upon harmony and cooperation. Marx's conception of antagonism and controversy between people provides a clear alterative to models that explored how people fit into what Hegel envisioned as a mutually beneficial pattern: the social system. Marx affirms that the social system does not inevitably work for the universal betterment of all members of society. This perspective invariably leads to an analysis of the thought and priorities of individual people/circumscribed groups and how their thinking influences social action; such perspectives possess an inevitable Kantian twist because they center upon the worldview of social actors and because they transcend scientific or rational analysis.

Although, in a macro and long-term sense, Marx envisioned a march toward progress, and whereas he placed this achievement within the flow of history, Marx's vision of progress is somewhat different from that of the leaders of the Enlightenment. Marx embraced the dialectical model with its emphasis of thesis, antithesis, and synthesis, not a typical scientific theory that tended to make a straight line toward progress (even if and when occasional reversals may occasionally be observed).

Kant, Hegel, and Marx, each in their own way, provide a frontal attack upon the methods of science and the ethos of the Enlightenment. While powerful individually, collectively their critique of the scientific method and their impact of upon later thinkers is profound and pervasive.

THE BENEFITS OF QUALITATIVE THOUGHT

Rejecting scientific and rational thought, however, will be a purely negative activity until positive and constructive alternatives are offered. In this spirit, Kant, Hegel, and Marx each provide constructive options that usefully transcend rational thought and the scientific method.

Kant emphasizes that science and rational thought do not reflect reality in all its complexity and, therefore, alternatives to it are legitimate and needed. Human thought, Kant affirms, goes beyond the scope of rationality and the techniques of scientific/quantitative methodologies. Kant emphasized that there are other inherent ways of knowing; focusing upon the innate functioning of the human mind, Kant demonstrated that, to truly understand people, it is first essential to acknowledge that human thought is more than the passive processing of empirical information that is received by the senses. Instead of being passive, the human mind processes empirical data using modes of thought that are inherent within all normal people. As we have discussed, this focus upon the inherent structuring and functioning of the human mind is generally known as the Kantian turn in philosophy, a perspective that has profoundly influenced later generations of thinkers.

Hegel, for example, took the ideas that Kant presented and forged them into a unified vision of mankind and culture. Hegel can best be understood as a part of and as a contributor to the romantic movement as it existed in the early 19th century. In addition, Hegel combined the romantic vision with the perspectives of the then-emerging disciplines of biology and economics. In doing so, Hegel created a powerful qualitative model of mankind and social action. As discussed above, Hegel's combining of the *volksgeist* model with the emerging theories of biology and economics led to the foundation of the basic underpinnings of the modern structural theories of the social sciences. As with all great theories, social structuralism is a simplification (and can be attacked accordingly). Nonetheless, it is one of the most powerful theories available for social analysis, even if it is not particularly fashionable today.

Marx, in contrast to Hegel, focused upon conflict. Today, much social theory is more concerned with conflict than with cooperation, and Marx can be pointed to as a seminal thinker who provides an early and powerful version of this chain of thought.

Kant, Hegel, and Marx each pointed to the benefits of qualitative thought, which transcended the rational and scientific thinking that typified the Enlightenment. Since the era of Kant and the rise of the Kantian turn in philosophy, scholars and intellectuals have increasingly looked inward. Although the methods of science survive as ad hoc techniques, contemporary scholars and intellectuals struggle to understand how people actually think; this focus (essentially non-scientific in method and spirit) increasingly impacts marketing/consumer research.

THE NATURE OF HUMANITY AND CULTURE

Today, the theory of the "psychic unity of mankind" prevails as the dominate paradigm of human nature. This perspective is paramount in our global age, where businesses must deal with diverse people that stem from different cultural origins. Kant, Hegel, and Marx each deal with these issues in their own ways. Combined, they collectively point to the psychic unity of mankind: the theory that all normal people tend to think in identical ways. Nonetheless, the perspectives that stem from this core position can also acknowledge significant differences between people, even if the nature of human thought is homogeneous. These differences stem from divergences between various subgroups of society and/or tensions that exist between members of different social classes.

Kant pointed to inherent and universal abilities that are collectively possessed by all people. According to Kant, these ways of thinking are universal and shared by all normal people. Hegel coupled Kant's theory of the universal nature of human thought with an acknowledgment of the uniqueness of specific cultures. As a result, human thought (universal though it might be) is largely conditioned by cultural variations. Those embracing this perspective can (1) affirm that all people, as members of the same species, operate and think in a parallel way while (2) acknowledging that history and cultural influences can channel these universal processes in unique and divergent ways.

Hegel also insisted that all members of a specific culture are unified by their culture and that they all equally benefit from participation in it. As a result, Hegel's theory of society and later models that stem from it are not inherently designed to deal with social change and conflict. Marx, in contrast, added a theory of conflict, and he convincingly argued that different members of the same culture are often in significant conflict with one another. Marx, of course, was primarily concerned with economic influences that centered around an analysis of who controlled the means of production. More generally, Marx affirmed that vested interests create conflicts between various groups within society and that this strife is a fact of life. Hegel's "clockworks" model, which largely ignores conflict, is a simplification of reality and it must be accepted as such, even if it is useful in various contexts.

Kant, Hegel, and Marx each embrace a somewhat similar theory of mankind. Each, however, is distinctive. These variations offer a wide range of alternatives that marketing/consumer researchers can usefully embrace.

THE NATURE OF SOCIETY

Not only is the nature of humanity and culture a major issue, the nature of society is also a matter of significant concern. In this regard Kant, Hegel, and Marx are in significant disagreement, and they embrace important differences regarding the degree to which society serves the needs of all members of society. Both Kant and Marx embrace theories of social conflict, while Hegel tactically avoids conflict in order to deal with cultures as collaborative and mutually beneficial.

Although Kant tended to think in terms of a universal force, and although he envisioned some kind of internal harmony within nature, this theory did not dominate his concept of society. Instead, Kant's thinking somewhat parallels the theories of Thomas Hobbes (1158–1679), who insisted that people were typically in conflict with one another. Hobbes, as the reader may recall, developed a theory of politics, society, and ethics which asserted that, because people fear each other, they submit to the supremacy of the state; thus, Hobbes envisioned a world of conflict where people make political choices to protect themselves. In a similar way, Kant insists that individual people possess and act in accord with their own goals; Kant, however, suggested these individualistic tendencies could be harnessed for the general good. Kant stated this premise in his *Metaphysical Foundations of Natural Science* (1784). In essence, Kant argues in a way that parallels Adam Smith's theory of the "invisible hand" of economics, which points to an impersonal force that channels individual self-interest in ways that achieve social needs. Such ideas are more fully developed in Hegel, although Hegel tended to sidestep theories of social conflict.

Hegel embraced Kant's emphasis upon a universal spirit, and he built upon Kant's view that the desires of individuals unwittingly contribute to the general good. Hegel refers to this process as "the cunning of reason"; this concept or metaphor can also be viewed in a way that is parallel to Adam Smith's concept of the invisible hand. Hegel goes on to discuss both hurtful events and human selfishness in terms of the fulfillment of the grand design for society and nature.

Hegel, as we have seen, deemphasizes conflict in order to concentrate upon the social system functioning as a mutually beneficial system. The key tool that Hegel used when doing so was the conception of the *volksgeist*, which he envisioned as a unifying principle or orientation that all people in a society inevitably embrace. As a result of this perspective, Hegel tended to ignore the conflicts within society that Kant acknowledged and, in doing so, Hegel concentrated upon cooperation and the mutual benefits inherent in collective social life.

Marx, in turn, reaffirmed social conflict and focused upon the economic competition that exists between different segments of society. In developing his model of strife and competition, Marx suggested that economic tensions related to the means of production created conflicts, and that those who controlled the economic system dominated and exploited other social groups and classes, even though they were all part of the same cultural or social system.

Ultimately, mankind is a social animal. As a result, it is important to embrace some coherent view of society. Although Kant, Hegel, and Marx are similar in some ways, they offer alternative views of society; these visions are parallel in some ways and distinct in others. We, as intellectual borrowers, need to be aware of these differences and the options they facilitate.

ANCESTORS OF MODERN QUALITATIVE THOUGHT: A DISCUSSION

Kant, Hegel, and Marx each possess an inward focus and, as such, they are concerned with how people think; these models seek to analyze people and their thought on their own terms. Kant, Hegel, and Marx analyze the inward thought of people, not merely their outward (and empirically observable) actions. This focus leads to methods, models, and strategies of analysis that are very different from scientific analysis, which objectively gathers empirical evidence, looks for statistically significant patterns, and generates conclusions accordingly. The basic modus operandi represented by Kant, Hegel, and Marx is distinct from science and it provides an alternative to scientific thought and analysis. This basic and distinct strategy has proved to be a fruitful method of thinking and researching; today's qualitative marketing/consumer research stems from this intellectual tradition.

Kant, Hegel, and Marx each reject the scientific method and empirical analysis as developed and employed by the leaders of the Enlightenment and by later, scientifically oriented researchers. Collectively, they demonstrate that there are a number of ways to transcend science and empiricism. They include:

1. Focus upon the individual as distinct from culture (Marx, existentialism).
2. Focus upon society as a collective mental construct (Hegel).

Qualitative marketing/consumer researchers have tended to focus upon the first option: centering upon the individual/circumscribed group. In doing so, they have, seemingly, not fully emphasized the value of the second approach.

In the final analysis, however, society and culture are collective entities. The concept of *volksgeist* is powerful and can be usefully applied in a variety of contexts. For obvious reasons, such concepts are often used in business and marketing (especially within international business). Nonetheless, this model seems to be far removed from the work of many contemporary qualitative marketing/consumer researchers. And following the lead of fashionable models from the liberal arts and humanities, some marketing/consumer researchers seemingly treat structural analysis as passe.

Nonetheless, a dual path stems from Kant; one focused on the individual, the other on the society. We, as marketing scholars, need both methods. Suggestions of how to appropriately use each method is the concern of later chapters.

REFERENCES

Hemingway, Ernest. (1926). *The Sun Also Rises*. Reprint, New York: Scribner's, 1956.

Kant, Immanuel. (1784). *Metaphysical Foundations of Natural Science*, trans. James Ellington. Reprint, Indianapolis, IN: Bobbs-Merrill, 1976.

Schopenhauer, Arthur. (1818). *The World as Will and Idea*, trans. R. B. Haldane and J. Kemp. Reprint, London: Trübner & Co., 1883–1886.

PART II

The Structural Paradigm and Its Variants

The basic orientation of all varieties of structural analysis is that distinct structures and patterns in human life and thought exist, and that analyzing these structures is useful and productive. Opponents or detractors may assert that what seems to be a structure is actually an illusion and/or that these structures are not particularly important and, therefore, do not deserve much attention; nonetheless, structuralists emphasize these patterns and the pervasive impacts they exert. To acknowledge my own bias, I am an unmitigated social structuralist, both in my thinking and in the research strategies I employ. This does not mean that I look disparagingly at other kinds of analysis, but merely that I affirm that structural analysis has a legitimate role to play in research.

In today's world, at least two specific (although non-contradictory) structural models share the stage. One (which we will call "mental structuralism") deals with the internal workings of the human mind. The second (which we will call "social structuralism") focuses upon the structures of society and culture.

Mental structuralism deals with the universals of the human mind and can be envisioned as parallel to Kant's basic research and analytic agenda. Today, the term "structuralism" is most often identified with French anthropologist Claude Levi-Strauss, whose work clearly focuses upon the functioning of the human mind (albeit within a cross-cultural perspective). More generally, however, various other influential thinkers can also be depicted as mental structuralists. Carl Jung, for example, spoke in terms of "archetypes"; being analogous to inherent instincts, they are best viewed as part of the structure of the human mind. And Sigmund Freud's model of the ego, id, and superego triumvirate (as well as his social theories) can be viewed in mental structural terms.

Social structuralism, in contrast to mental structuralism, deals with how the culture and society are structured and how these structures help meet the needs of both society and individual people. In many ways, social structuralism can be seen as an extension of the thought of Hegel, and, especially, as an elaboration of his view of the *volksgeist* and its impact.

While I have a firm respect for mental structuralism, this book primarily deals with social structuralism. Social structural analysis is a complex and multifaceted phenomenon. Three representative schools of thought will be discussed in order to demonstrate this diversity. They are the "culture at a distance" method, the "presentation of self techniques" associated with Erving Goffman, and the "myth and symbol method" (which has long been a staple of literary analysis and American studies). Each of these methods will be considered in chapter-length discussions and are presented as illustrative; thus, this book makes no attempt to provide an exhaustive review of all available structural techniques.

Various structural methods are powerful tools. Nonetheless, in today's scholarly world they have largely become unfashionable, a situation stemming from contemporary research tastes and research agendas and not due to any "fatal flaw" in these methods. It is hoped that the discussions provided here will help restore various forms of structural analysis to their rightful place both in marketing/consumer research and within the liberal arts disciplines.

CHAPTER 6

Mental Structuralism: The Nature of the Human Mind

A basic orientation of this book is that two very different structural methodologies (mental structuralism vs. social structuralism) are commonly used to investigate mankind and society. One can aptly be called "mental structuralism" because it focuses upon the inherent structure of the human mind. My use of the term "mental structuralism" can be viewed as distinctive from but somewhat related to the concept of "structural" vs. "functional" psychology. The work of William James, for example, is a classic representative of functional psychology because he was concerned with the goals or purposes that underlay people's behavior. Structuralists, in contrast, are concerned with the inherent structure of the human mind. For a particularly readable (although somewhat dated) overview, see the chapter on structural psychology in Edna Heidbreder's *Seven Psychologies* (1933).

Mental structuralists are aware of the profound impact of cultural and social structures upon human thought and that social structures exhibit profound variations within different cultural contexts. Nonetheless, mental structuralism deals with the social environment primarily as an extension of innate mental structures. Ultimately, and most basically, mental structuralists focus upon (1) the universal nature and functioning of the human mind and (2) the influence that innate mental structures exert upon social life and the human decision-making process.

Social structuralism, in contrast, focuses upon specific cultures and their uniqueness. Typically, social structuralists do not reject the premise that the human mind possesses an inherent structure; they do, however, deal with social structures as their primary unit of investigation. Doing so is legitimate.

This socially oriented research agenda is often needed and appropriate. Both intuitively and empirically, we realize that people who are raised in Japan or China think and behave very differently from those who are raised in the United States or Canada. And, of course, the Japanese are distinctive from the Chinese, while Canadians diverge in some important ways from their closely related southern neighbors. Thus, there is a clear recognition that universal patterns or potentials of human thought pass through a cultural or social filter and are transformed accordingly. And, as researchers who specialize in cultural diversity will attest, these differences are profound.

The research interests of mental vs. social structuralists is somewhat analogous to the old "nature/nurture" dichotomy that has long existed in the social sciences. The "nature" paradigm centers upon the human animal and its innate potentials of response; behavior is explained accordingly. Thus, some researchers analyze the behavior of men vs. that of women in terms of the inherent "nature" of the sexes.[1] The "nurture" argument, in contrast, focuses upon human behavior (such as stereotyped patterns of sex-role behavior) in terms of culture, society, and socialization; thus, researchers such as Margaret Mead argue that, to a large extent, patterns of response are learned and not innate. Both the nature and the nurture paradigms continue to exist as legitimate; they, furthermore, are not inherently mutually exclusive.

The primary focus of this book concerns social structural (nurture) models as powerful analytic methods that currently seem to be underutilized by the qualitative research stream that currently prevails in marketing and consumer research. Nonetheless, this book would be incomplete without a discussion of mental structuralism; as a result it will be dealt with here.

In order to deal with the diversity that exists in various mental structural models, three different approaches are considered. This is a convenient sample of analytical techniques and is not meant to be an exhaustive list. They are represented by Claude Levi-Strauss, Sigmund Freud, and Carl Jung. Each of these notable scholars (and the schools of thought that they represent) seeks to examine the inherent structure of the human mind; in doing so, each has performed a profound service. In providing a thumbnail sketch of each (and relating their methods to marketing/consumer research), both the power of these models and their applicability to our profession are presented.

CLAUDE LEVI-STRAUSS

Today, when scholars speak of structuralism, the name of French anthropologist Claude Levi-Strauss immediately comes to mind. It is useful, therefore, to begin our analysis of mental structuralism with a discussion of Levi-Strauss and the intellectual traditions in which he was raised and those that he transcended.

Starting with Claude Saint-Simon (1760–1825) and Auguste Comte (1798–1857), France has long been a center of sociological thought. This tradition was continued in the late 19th/early 20th century by Emile Durkheim, a major social theorist who focused upon the needs and behaviors of cultures/societies, not individual people or the general characteristics of mankind as a species. In this vein, Durkheim observes: "[Behavior is] caused not by . . . the consciousness of individuals but by the conditions in which the social group is placed" (Durkheim 1895: 136).

This is the socially centered focus in which Levi-Strauss was trained and against which he ultimately rebelled. His alternative position came to center upon the underlying and innate mental processes of mankind that give rise to culture and social life. He, for example, observed in the early 1940s: "[Levi-Strauss looks for] Hidden fundamental elements which are the true components of [social life. This] trying to reduce the concrete [empirical evidence] into more simple and elementary structures is . . . the fundamental task of sociology" (Levi-Struass 1945: 525).

The implications of this shift in thought and research agendas are significant. Under Levi-Strauss, social science becomes more of a study of innate and universal human nature than an analysis of culture and society. Levi-Strauss moves from studying society as the primary topic of investigation to dissecting the innate psychological and mental background inherent in cultures and cultural artifacts. Ultimately, Levi-Strauss uses the empirical evidence provided by specific cultures in order to bolster his theories regarding the nature of the human mind/thought; thus, Levi-Strauss' primary focus is the innate psychological nature of mankind, not specific variations exhibited by individuals and/or cultures. This kind of analysis is useful, but it is very different from focusing primarily upon culture as the primary phenomena being analyzed; Levi-Strauss' research agenda, while augmenting the techniques of social analysis, does not replace it.

In order to deal with the universal psychic structure of the human mind, Levi-Strauss relied upon linguistic theories coupled with psychology. Praising linguistics as the most advanced of the social sciences, he observed early in his career: "Modern sociologists and psychologists solve such problems [concerning social structures] by calling upon the activity of the unconscious mind; but at the time when Durkheim was writing the main results of modern psychology and linguistics were lacking" (1945: 518). Here, we will deal with how Levi-Strauss used the methods of structural linguistics in order to place anthropology within a more scientific framework, and we will consider the implications of doing so.

Due to World War II, Levi-Strauss found himself a displaced person and he settled in the United States until the hostilities in Europe were over. This twist of fate resulted in Levi-Strauss meeting and working with structural linguist Roman Jakobson (1896–1982), another intellectual who moved to New York City after being uprooted by the war (although Jakobson went on to permanently settle in the United States). Jakobson was a leader in structural linguistics, and Levi-Strauss was greatly influenced by him and the paradigm of structural analysis that he represents. Levi-Strauss was also influenced by the "Russian formalist" folklorists, such as Vladimar Propp, who focused upon the study of recurring patterns in folktales and literature. As a result, Levi-Strauss came to concentrate upon patterns of behavior and response that were universal in all people; he also developed a strong professional interest in mythology and folklore. Although Levi-Strauss is aware of the uniqueness of specific cultures, he tends to search for parallels and similarities between them and/or for patterns and structures in cultural complexes such as mythological systems.

Perhaps the most readily available discussion of these principles of analysis is provided in Levi-Strauss' "Language and the Analysis of Social Laws," which appears in his *Structural Anthropology* (1963: 55–66). There, Levi-Strauss argues that it is possible to study human behavior scientifically. He then points to the fact that scholars can extrapolate beyond observed empirical behavior in order to explore what lies below the surface. In phonemics, for example, the scholar takes observed empirical evidence (studying actual utterances: phonetics) and teases out underlying patterns that cannot be directly observed. Having made this observation, Levi-Strauss goes on to suggest that other social phenomena, cultural artifacts, and human behaviors (ranging from social structures to folktales) can be examined in analogous ways in order to better understand the nature of the human mind and the behavior that stems from it (Levi-Strauss 1963: 58–59). In doing so, Levi-Strauss links himself to the structural linguistics of Nicolas Troubetzkoy, who, Levi-Strauss suggests, provides a "programmatic statement" regarding how to abstract the structural method into four basic operations:

First, structural linguistics shifts from the study of *conscious linguistic* phenomena to the study of their *unconscious* infrastructure; second, it does not treat *terms* as independent entities, taking instead as its basis of analysis the *relations* between terms; third, it introduces the concept of *system*—"Modern phonemics does not merely proclaim that phonemes are always part of a system; it *shows* concrete phonemic systems and elucidates their structure"; finally, structural linguistics aims at discovering *general laws*, either by induction "or . . . by logical deduction, which would give them an absolute character." (1963: 33)

As time went on, Levi-Strauss came to focus upon mythology. Reduced to its most basic elements, Levi-Strauss' techniques of analyzing a myth begins with an examination of the available examples of the myth. The next step is to abstract the myth into its various component parts, which Levi-Strauss calls "mythemes": the various events and motifs that can be found in the myth. These mythemes can be analyzed diachronically (historically) and synchronically (structurally). The specific myth is interpreted diachronic/historically while, more generally, the structure of the myth can be explicated from a structural or synchronic perspective.

These ideas are developed in Levi-Strauss' *The Raw and the Cooked* (1969), a classic and seminal example of structuralist anthropology and mythology. Initially, Levi-Strauss begins with a look at various examples of Bororo mythology and ends up examining the structure of a broad array of South American mythology. Levi-Strauss' goal is to showcase a methodology and the basic principles of a structural approach that can be used to apply it.

Levi-Strauss' premise is that myths cannot be understood in isolation and that they need to be interpreted in structural or systemic ways. Using this structural approach, the researcher can identify shared features of different myths and the various linkages and transformations that unite them.

Levi-Strauss uses the concept of the binary opposition to explain how the human mind works and how human thought and behavior are structured. A binary opposition is set up in a way that parallels a "yes" or "no" question. Thus, since an animal may be "living" or "dead," living can be viewed as a binary opposition regarding its status. Additional "yes/no" questions can further refine the analysis: Is the animal edible or inedible? Is the animal raw or cooked? And so on. Ultimately, a subtle array of binary oppositions can portray any situation.

According to Levi-Strauss, the dichotomy "raw vs. cooked" equates with "nature vs. culture"; a key point Levi-Strauss makes is that the structures of binary oppositions can be extended to encompass all categories of human thought. He attempts to demonstrate this potential via his studies of culture, folklore, and mythology.

These relationships and transformations, viewed in terms of the cultural context, make it possible to see how various myths (or different examples of a myth) reveal an underlying cultural or social structure. Levi-Strauss' goal is to create a structural methodology that provides insights both into mythology, as a discipline, and into various specific examples of myth that are examined.

Centering on structures of the human mind and how human behavior/artifacts are reflections of it has exerted a profound impact upon literary criticism and folklore. Essentially literary products/folklore traditions are viewed as artifacts somewhat deriving from (or operating according to the constructs of) the inherent structure of the human mind.

Having made this assumption, literature/folklore is examined for clues regarding the binary oppositions that significantly impact the author and/or the culture. By analyzing these clues, a better understanding of the culture and the mainsprings that drive it can be extrapolated.

Sidney Levy (1981) has provided a clear example of how this mental structural model can be applied to marketing and consumer research. Levy, in essence, provides an example of how the mental structural model of Levi-Strauss can be used to better understand how consumers view products and choose to consume them. Unfortunately, later "qualitiative" marketing scholars, who are concerned with literary theory and mythology, tend to be more identified with models that derive from the existential tradition, and little expansion of the method proposed by Levy has occurred. Nonetheless, Levy's approach is legitimate.

Arising in the post–World War II era, the mental structural models of Claude Levi-Strauss initially exerted a powerful influence upon the humanities. The analytic options provided by linking Levi-Strauss' structuralism (stemming from anthropology) with other humanistic disciplines (such as literary criticism and folklore) furnished a new way to envision the essence of a culture by assuming that human thought operates according to the principle of binary oppositions. As we shall see in later chapters, the structural model has largely fallen from fashion as methods such as deconstructionism, which stem from the existential intellectual tradition, have come to dominate the critical scene. Nonetheless, Levi-Strauss and his mental structuralism have played an important role in modern critical theory; since qualitative marketing research often employs humanistic theories such as those stemming from literary criticism, Levi-Strauss' efforts have a valuable contribution to make to marketing/consumer research.

SIGMUND FREUD

Most basically, Freudian analysis points to the fact that on many occasions people are not totally aware of the true mainsprings that motivate their behavior. In stating this position, Freud suggests that the human mind is structured in a way that pits different mental forces against each other, and that by being aware of this innate mental framework the behavior of individual people and of cultures becomes more predictable. Because classic Freudian analysis focuses primarily upon the structure of the human mind, the paradigm can be viewed as a form of mental structuralism.

While Levi-Strauss focused upon rational models that are inspired by linguistics, however, the mental structures that are of primary interest to Freud and Freudian analysis tend to be irrational and emotional, not rational and thoughtful. Essentially, Freud argues that the human mind is structured in a way that juxtaposes an animalistic nature with more cultural and civilized components. Freud believes that these two forces are constantly in combat with one another, jockeying for power and position. Although people may believe that they rationally and consciously know what they want and why they act in the way they do, Freud argues that behavior is actually triggered by irrational forces that lie below the level of consciousness.

Freud's model is basically a form of mental structuralism. Essentially, this structure consists of the ego, the superego, and the id. The ego, according to Freud, is the conscious self of which people are overtly aware. The ego of a person is typified by conscious thought, it has opinions, and it feels that it "understands" its needs and wants. Nonetheless, this seemingly freestanding and free-willed ego is largely controlled by the superego and the id.

The superego can be envisioned as the internalized rules and priorities that are provided by the culture. Society has its own sets of rules that exist in order to facilitate social and economic life. These rules, however, tend to force unwanted controls on individual people that inhibit them in significant ways. By inculcating people to believe that these rules are inherently good, however, the culture encourages people to conform, even if doing so is not truly in the (short-term or long-term) interest of the individual. On many occasions, the dictates of the superego may be so internalized that the individual does not consciously recognize their impacts upon the ego.

The id, the third member of the triumvirate of personality, is the animalistic forces within the individual. According to Freud, although much behavior is motivated by the id, the individual tends to be unaware of the true genesis of these motivations. This is because the dictates of the culture provided by the superego routinely redefine the desires and goals of the id in its own terms. Thus, perhaps a man wants a shiny new car because his id wants to attract females in order to have sex (an animalistic goal); nonetheless, on a conscious level, the ego may believe he wants this expensive sex symbol for other reasons that the culture accepts as "legitimate" (perhaps related to dependability, gas mileage, and so on). Thus, according to Freud, much behavior is motivated by forces stemming from the id, even though the ego is largely unaware of these influences.

The concept of repression is crucial to Freudian analysis. As indicated above, the animalistic id exerts a powerful force upon behavior; nonetheless, people tend to disavow these influences, especially when such motives conflict with the moral dictates of society. Consciously ignoring these motivations is what Freud depicts as repression. As a result of the mechanism of repression, people are often deeply motivated by forces that lie below the level of consciousness.

Working in 19th-century Europe, a culture area that embraced strict codes of sexual conduct, many of Freud's patients suffered from mental problems that were related to sexuality. As a result, Freud tended to focus upon sexuality as the major unconscious force impacting people and their behavior. Today, however, it is generally realized that Freud mistook certain characteristics of 19th-century European culture (and/or the class of people from which his clients came) for human universals. Thus, Freud created a general model of the structure of the human mind that was closely linked to sexuality. Later researchers, however, have come to recognize that sexuality exerts a variety of different pressures in diverse cultures, and that those documented by Freud are but one example.

In addition, social structuralists have accepted that specific cultures have their own areas in which they tightly control people and their actions. This broader vision led to the establishment of the neo-Freudian movement, which preserved concepts such as repression while affirming that each culture is distinct and needs to be analyzed as such.

There is an obvious value of this kind of model to marketing/consumer research. Freud suggests that people are motivated by forces that lie below the level of consciousness. As a result, people cannot rationally tell marketing/consumer researchers what they want. In addition, since people tend to be unaware of what truly motivates them, the marketer may need to recognize subtle cues that influence consumer behavior, even though the ego may be consciously unaware of them.

Emphasizing Freudian techniques has a long tradition in marketing. An early exposé of this tendency is Vance Packard's *The Hidden Persuaders* (1957), which made ample use of Freudian theory and asserted that marketing researchers and advertising strategists were significantly involved with Freudian depth psychology.

According to this orientation, people repress their actual motivations and what they truly seek in social interactions (including the buying and consumption of products). Regarding this tendency, Markin observed in the late 1960s:

The last thing the motivation researchers would do would be to ask the consumer. For it is argued, the consumer is the least reliable index the marketer can have on what he ought to do to win customers. First, the customer does not know the meaning or ramifications of his motives; therefore, how can he possibly know what products or services are required to satisfy them? Secondly, the consumer is not at all likely to admit his motives. (Markin 1969: 42–43)

During this era, Ernst Dichter became a tireless advocate of a Freudian style of research that relied upon depth psychology (psychology concerned primarily with the unconscious functioning of the human mind) in marketing/consumer research. In this regard, a specific example in his influential *Handbook of Consumer Motivation* observes: "Soup is a profoundly emotion-charged food. It has become identified with the positive symbols of abundance, security, warmth, comfort, and friendliness. . . . Highly emotional associations with soup center around family ties, especially mother's love" (Dichter 1964: 67).

Dichter's techniques can be easily abstracted; he places a high value on in-depth interviews that are designed to extend below the level of conscious and rational thought. He uses these techniques in order to discern subtle and repressed motivations. Dichter went on to dabble in projective techniques, such as word association methods and sentence completion exercises, with his informants. On occasion Dichter used pictures in order to elicit the responses that immediately came to the minds of his informants. The basic strategy of all these techniques is to get below the level of conscious thought; and the rationale for doing so is based on the premise that people are motivated by phenomena of which they are but dimly aware, if they recognize these motivations at all.

Thus, Freudian analysis has cast a long shadow upon marketing/consumer research (as it did in the scholarly world in general). In a vintage text written in 1970, Waters and Paul observe: "Although the validity of much Freudian theory has been questioned in recent years, the basic structure of personality analysis is still to a significant extent Freudian and he has greatly influenced all the behavioral sciences" (Waters and Paul 1970: 331). Although this quotation is over 30 years old, it continues to be an accurate analysis of the role of Freudian analysis and its influence.

While practitioners were making use of Freudian theory, scholars were also taking notice. In this regard, Philip Kotler observed in the *Journal of Marketing*:

The guilt or shame which man feels towards some of his urges—especially his sexual urges—causes him to repress them from his consciousness. Through such defense mechanisms as rationalization and sublimation these urges are denied or become transmuted into socially approved expressions. . . . Perhaps the most important marketing implication of this model is that buyers are motivated by symbolic as well as economic-functional product concerns. (Kotler 1965: 41)

Speaking in general regarding Freudian analysis, Kotler observes: "An important marketing application of Freudian motivation theory is that buyers are motivated by psychological as well as functional product concerns. . . . [Thus, marketers] should be aware of the role of visual and tactile elements in triggering deeper emotions that can stimulate or inhibit purchases" (Kotler 1980: 146). This kind of perspective was echoed by George Fisk in his seminal text *Marketing Systems: An Introductory*

Analysis, where he observes: "Man, as Freud saw him, was . . . endowed with a biological heritage of unconscious drives and impulses . . . [the id] which is always at war with the ego. Only his cultural history, represented by the superego is available to guide [his behavior]" (1967: 111). Fisk goes on to explain the failure of the Edsel automobile in the 1950s in such terms:

> The marketing analyst attributes the failure of the Edsel to poor timing and to the offer of a product ill suited to the desired of the upward-mobile social strainers. Psychiatrists point out that the Edsel was designed to appeal entirely to the id of the neighbors of the people whose demands were studied. By emphasizing questions about other people's desires instead of the prospective buyer's, the decision makers overlooked the participation of the ego. (Fisk 1967: 111)

Without doubt, Freudian analysis has proved to be of significant value to marketing/consumer research. Nonetheless, as demonstrated by the Edsel example, much care needs to be exerted when using such techniques.

This basic strategy of analysis, of course, has never died. Today, however, some marketing/consumer researchers use elaborate hardware designed to measure brain waves to better understand what goes on in people's minds below the level of their consciousness.

The functioning of the unconscious continues to draw the attention of marketing researchers. Thus, in the fall of 2000 there was much talk about the assertion that Chrysler's "retro-look" PT Cruiser car reminded people of the gangster Al Capone who, apparently, drove a similar-looking automobile in the 1930s. Arguing that people want power and respect on the highway, the ghost of Al Capone (reflected in the style of the car) was asserted to be an unconscious trigger of consumer motivations.

Freudian analysis is clearly a form of mental structuralism. It argues that the human mind possesses a specific structure. Freud tightly centered his analysis around sexuality, although later thinkers (the neo-Freudians) rejected sexuality as a universal mainspring and acknowledged that different cultures have their own subliminal influences. Nonetheless, the neo-Freudians preserve Freud's recognition of the significance of repression and the belief that people are often motivated by forces of which they are consciously unaware. The value of such perspectives to marketing/consumer research is immense.

CARL GUSTAV JUNG

The last basic paradigm of mental structuralism to be discussed derives from the work of Carl Gustav Jung. Like Freud, Jung did not base his mental structural models upon theories of linguistics, relying instead upon depth psychology. Indeed, for a number of years, Jung was Freud's prized pupil. Over their period of professional association, Freud and Jung exerted multiple influences upon one another.

Jung, however, eventually broke away from strict Freudian analysis because he rejected Freud's rather unyielding emphasis upon the impact of sexuality. The key breakthrough in Jung's rejection of strict Freudian analysis was the publication of his *Psychology of the Unconscious* (1916).[2] In this seminal analysis, Jung dealt with myths and pointed to parallels between myths and the fantasies and delusions that people experience. And significantly, these fantasies transcended sexual themes.

Most basically, Jung suggested that during the process of human evolution people have inherited a propensity to respond to specific phenomena in predictable and structured ways. Thus, in addition to being influenced by their own personal experiences, people are also impacted by what Jung calls "archetypes" that he depicts as "racial memories" or innate patterns of reaction that influence all people. These archetypes are not learned, Jung insists; instead, they are inherent in all people.

This perspective, of course, is reflective of the basic paradigms developed by Immanuel Kant. As the reader will recall from earlier discussions, *the Critique of Pure Reason*, Kant's definitive statement, dealt with inherent ways of thinking that all people possess and that exist before people experience the empirical world. Therefore, according to Kant, pure reason (or patterns of human thought) exist independently of individuals and their experiences. Jung, in his own way, points to a cluster of propensities to respond that are also inherent in the human psyche and are not the result of learning or experience.

Jung builds upon this premise of innate knowledge or tendencies of response by suggesting that due to this shared collective unconscious, certain symbols, images, and themes are invented and reinvented time and time again because people find them to be inherently attractive and interesting. And, as indicated above, Jung traces this collective interest back to inherited characteristics of humanity that result from the impacts of evolution.

In specific, Jung calls these inherent predispositions "archetypes." He felt that these archetypes are worked and reworked in many ways in accordance with the specific cultural context. Although the response to these archetypes are impacted by culture and personal experience, however, Jung maintains that a limited number of archetypes exist. Thus, although human behavior is outwardly very different in various and distinct contexts, it is still impacted by a limited number of inherent archetypes. As a result, subtle universal patterns can be discerned. In addition, this limited array of archetypes impact and influence all people in similar ways, even though the specific cultural context simultaneously exerts its own unique influences.

Jung suggests that archetypes exist for phenomena such as birth, death, the devil, the wise old man, the earth mother, and so on. Most significant to literary critics and mythologists who embrace a Jungian analysis is Jung's identification of what he feels is a universal "heroic pattern" that is believed to provide a universal cycle or plotline that is theorized to exert a cross-cultural influence, even in situations where cultural diffusion or borrowing has not taken place.

Jung's focus upon a universal heroic cycle was popularized by Joseph Campbell, who, in a number of books (the most distinguished of which is *The Hero with a Thousand Faces*), presents a widely acknowledged presentation of world mythology in terms of the Jungian archetype method. Besides Campbell, the fields of literary criticism and mythology have made significant use of archetypical analysis.

In some cases, an attempt has been made to utilize the concept of archetype in ways that divorce it from the model of "racial memory" that Jung embraced. Thus, some critics, such as Leslie Fiedler, speak in terms of culturally specific archetypes. This strategy can be viewed as paralleling the neo-Freudian attempt to dismiss sexuality as a universal mainspring of behavior while preserving other aspects of Freudian analysis such as repression, the ego/superego/id paradigm, and the focus upon unconscious motivations.

This kind of analysis has a clear role to play in marketing/consumer research. Thus, a few years ago I published an article that provided a Jungian interpretation of a number of advertising campaigns that dealt with sports heroes. Essentially, I argued that certain athletes' careers closely resemble what Jung depicts as the archetype of the heroic cycle. I found that these athletes were more popular and more able to influence consumer response than other athletes whose careers did not reflect the archetype of the heroic cycle. Thus, replicating an archetype is, in some ways, more powerful and compelling than athletic ability and achievement.

Thus, Jungian analysis provides an alternative to the methodologies and theories of both Claude Levi-Strauss and Sigmund Freud. All three, however, are best viewed as mental structural theories because they explain phenomena in terms of the inherent structure of the human mind. And as we have seen, this perspective has strong precedents in the work of Immanuel Kant.

MARKETING'S STAKE IN MENTAL STRUCTURALISM

Marketing/consumer research has long embraced large segments of the mental structural model and reworked these theories for its own purposes. This is true both of the legacy of Sigmund Freud and of Claude Levi-Strauss. Relatively little use has been made of the work of Carl Gustav Jung, although a brief suggestive literature points to possible uses.

While these theories point to a universal tendency for people to respond in uniform ways that are inherent and innate within all people, mental-structural methods, nonetheless, possess a flexibility that allows them to deal with the responses of specific cultures, not merely universal patterns. As a result, these models have a great power and they can be employed accordingly. Although more fashionable methods often overshadow mental structuralism, the method survives as a valuable and respectable analytic technique.

NOTES

1. A position not embraced here.
2. The later edition is known as *Symbols of Transformation* (1962).

REFERENCES

Dichter, Ernst. (1964). *Handbook of Consumer Motivation*. New York: McGraw-Hill.

Durkheim, Emile. (1895). *Rules of the Sociological Method*, trans. J. Mueller. Reprint, New York: Free Press, 1938.

Heidbreder, Edna. (1933). *Seven Psychologies*. New York: Century.

Fisk, George. (1967). *Marketing Systems: An Introductory Analysis*. New York: Harper and Row.

Jung, Carl Gustav. (1916). *Psychology of the Unconscious: A Study of the Transformations of the Libido, a Contribution to the History of the Evolution of Thought*, trans. Beatrice M. Hinkle. New York: Moffat, Yard, and Company.

Jung, Carl Gustav. (1962). *Symbols of Transformation: An Analysis of the Prelude to a Case of Schizophrenia*, trans. R.F.C. Hull. New York: Harper.

Kant, Immanuel. (1781). *Critique of Pure Reason*, trans. Norman K. Smith. Reprint, New York: St. Martin's Press, 1961.

Kotler, Philip. (1965). "Behavioral Models for Analyzing Buyers." *Journal of Marketing* 29 (October): 36–45.

Kotler, Philip. (1980). *Marketing: Analysis, Planning, and Control*. Englewood Cliffs, NJ: Prentice-Hall.

Levi-Strauss, Claude. (1945). "French Sociology." In *Twentieth Century Sociology*, ed. G. Gurvitch and W. Moore. New York: Philosophical Library, pp. 503–37.

Levi-Strauss, Claude. (1963). *Structural Anthropology*, trans. Claire Jacobson and Brooke Grundfest Schoepf. New York: Basic Books.

Levi-Strauss, Claude. (1969). *The Raw and the Cooked*, trans. John Weightman and Doreen Weightman. New York: Harper.

Levy, Sidney. (1981). "Interpreting Consumer Mythology: A Structural Approach to Consumer Behavior." *Journal of Marketing* 45(3): 49–61.

Markin, Rom. (1969). *The Psychology of Customer Behavior*. Englewood Cliffs, NJ: Prentice-Hall.

Packard, Vance. (1957). *The Hidden Persuaders*. New York: David McKay and Company.

Raglan, Lord. (1936). *The Hero: A Study in Tradition, Myth, and Drama*. Reprint, New York: Vintage, 1956.

Waters, C. Glenn and Paul, Gordon W. (1970). *Consumer Behavior: An Integrated Approach*. Homewood, IL: Irwin.

CHAPTER 7

Classic Social Structuralism:
An Overview

INTRODUCTION

In Chapter 3, we discussed a number of specific social structural theories and how each resonates from ideas that were clearly articulated by Friedrich Hegel in the early 19th century. Especially influential was the concept of the *volksgeist* (or national character), presented by Herder and Hegel, which argues that culture molds people (and peoples) in unique and specific ways that profoundly influence the entire essence of their society, including the thoughts, the feelings, and the artifacts of the individuals who comprise it.

As we shall see in this discussion of classic social structuralism[1] and the cluster of chapters that follows it, the basic idea that the culture is a synergistic entity casts a long shadow, and it has emerged as a key premise of the social sciences; this basic orientation, however, can be articulated and modeled in a variety of ways. One such analytic option is what can be called "classic social structural theory"; this chapter focuses upon that specific orientation. In some ways, the issues, dilemmas, and assumptions embraced by classic social structuralism are incorporated into all social structural models; where this is true, this chapter can be viewed as a general primer. The classic social structural model, in addition, is somewhat distinct; as a result, other paradigms offer alternative visions (or methodologies) that either supercede the classic social structural model and/or provide a more appropriate paradigm to employ in specific circumstances. Many of these options are discussed in later chapters.

In any event, classic social structuralism provides a model that focuses upon society as a structured and functioning entity that operates according to its own rules and needs; this is the primary universe of discourse pursued by the social structural research strategy and by parallel modes of analysis. Embracing this intellectual tradition involves the acceptance of both strengths and weaknesses of the structural model. Thus, social structuralism represents a specific form of analysis that accepts certain important tradeoffs. This chapter begins our discussion of these strengths and weaknesses.

HOW ADAPTABLE ARE PEOPLE?

A key issue that must be resolved when entering into any discussion of the nature of culture/society (and its influence) centers around the degree to which people can be molded by the culture. In other words, to what degree can people be groomed to think, feel, and act in specific ways? To what extent do cultures fashion people in their own image? To whatever extent people are viewed as being products of their culture and society, a social structural model will rise to prominence. In contrast, to whatever degree people are viewed in universal ways, the social structural model must be subordinated to a more generic study of human nature.

The previous chapter focused largely upon human universals, not the specifics of the particular culture. The "mental structural" model discussed here centers upon the nature of mankind and deals with cultures primarily as particular manifestations of a universal human nature. Without doubt, this kind of analysis is legitimate. In pursuing such a point of view, however, it becomes easy to ignore the uniqueness of specific cultures and the distinctive impacts that particular cultures exert upon people and their behavior.

Social structural orientations, in contrast to mental structural models, emphasize the adaptability of humanity. The impact of the culture is emphasized and people are viewed as responding to these influences and adjusting themselves accordingly. Thus, while mental structuralism concentrates upon the universal nature of humanity, the social structural perspective centers upon how human nature allows cultures a high degree of leeway.

In this chapter and in the cluster of chapters that follows, we will focus on the premise that the human species (and individual people) are very moldable and adaptable, and that cultures groom their members accordingly. This flexibility gives cultures a great latitude in adjusting people to fit circumstances. And since culture is a basic (albeit multidimensional) tool that helps to ensure human survival, the ability of people to adapt to circumstance ultimately promotes the well-being of mankind, even if it can be argued that in various situations specific individuals may not always be "well served" or "fairly treated" by a particular cultural arrangement.

It is generally accepted (by philosophers, biologists, and social scientists, among others) that mankind is the most versatile member of the animal kingdom. People have the ability to adjust to a wide variety of cultural and physical environments. Due to this adaptability, people have options and capabilities that other animals lack, and it is the adaptability created by cultures that gives mankind a competitive edge. Social structuralism centers upon how this adaptability of mankind (and the diverse cultural arrangements that stem from it) performs valuable functions that work on behalf of mankind.

CULTURE, NOT PEOPLE, AS A UNIVERSE OF DISCOURSE

As has been indicated above, social structuralism is not concerned with the nature of the human mind. Instead, the human mind is merely viewed as one of the preexisting constraints that impacts culture. Thus, although social structural models tend to assume (either overtly or covertly) that some kind of human nature exists, this assumption is merely viewed as one of the building blocks that leads to and facilitates social life. Analyzing the specific characteristics of human nature, however, is beyond the universe of discourse typically pursued by social structuralism.

Although social structural researchers may informally be curious about human nature, and even though they may have some fairly detailed views or theories of the essence of mankind, these scholars center upon the corporate/collective nature of social life, not mankind as a species or specific people as individuals. As a result, social structuralism studies the culture/society, its needs, and how it functions. Other considerations (such as those that explore human nature or the uniqueness of the individual) fall outside of the range of questions pursued.

According to such a culture-centered focus, the needs and behaviors of society, not those of individual people or the generic responses of the human species, emerge as the paramount topic under investigation. When pursuing this course of analysis, the culture is viewed as distinct from people and it is conceptualized and studied accordingly. In addition, the culture is viewed as having its owns needs, rules, and vulnerabilities that must be considered and taken into account. And due to the adaptability of the human species, individuals are seen as being molded in ways that reinforce the culture and allow it to more effectively function as a structural entity in its own right.

From a marketing/consumer research point of view, the social structural approach assumes that what people want to consume (and how they acquire and evaluate the products they buy) falls into the realm of learned behavior prompted by the cultural tradition. While mental structuralism concerns itself with human universals (even if these universals are channeled by the culture in specific ways), social structuralism focuses upon the cultural tradition, even if it is underlaid or influenced by some kind of generic or universal human nature.

THE SOCIAL STRUCTURAL MODEL IN ANTHROPOLOGY

One of the most pervasive trends of 20th-century scholarship and research was the growth of the structural perspective in general and in the social sciences in particular. Although alternatives to structural models have been presented (such as poststructural models, conflict theory, or more general pronouncements such as chaos theory and the research of Mitchell Feigenbaum), the structural model has long served as a vital paradigm that can be usefully embraced both intuitively and formally. One way of envisioning the structural model is through the lens of general systems theory, as presented by Kenneth Boulding (1956). According to Boulding:

General systems theory lies somewhere between the highly generalized constructions of pure mathematics and the highly specialized theories of specific disciplines.... One approach is ... though the arrangement of theoretical systems and constructs into a hierarchy of complexity of the explained fields. This approach [leads] to a system of systems. (Boulding 1956)

As seen in Chapter 3, one component of this system of systems is called the "clockworks" model. Boulding observes: "[A level] of systems analysis is that of a simple dynamic system with predetermined motions. This might be called the level of clockworks" (Boulding 1956). As we will see, this clockworks level of general systems theory corresponds (more or less) to structural models of society that are typified by British social anthropology (1930s–1950s) and with the classic/mainstream models of American sociology (late 1930s–1960s). We will first deal with structural anthropology, and will consider structural sociology in a later section.

As we have already discussed, Herder and Hegel called attention to the distinctiveness of specific cultural traditions and they advanced the proposition that cultures and societies possess their own unique characters. This orientation was followed by the theories of Auguste Comte, who in the first half of the 19th century more fully developed an organic model of society. Comte's work was followed by additional evolutionary theories, such as that of Karl Marx, which were further bolstered by the evolutionary models stemming from biology and identified by Charles Darwin. Darwin's evolutionary theories, in turn, led to the vogue of social Darwinism that applied the paradigm of biological evolution to the social realm. A key social theorist who advanced such a proposition was Herbert Spencer. In time, however, the prestige of Spencer (as well as structural theories inspired by social Darwinism) declined.

In the late 19th century, French sociologist Emile Durkheim picked up the intellectual torch by embracing a structural model of society that focused upon social structures on the one hand while rejecting a social Darwinistic orientation on the other. In addition, Durkheim focused upon empirical evidence and he did not merely base his theories upon conjecture. It was upon this form of social structural analysis that British social structural anthropology was built.

Having presented this prologue, it is useful to briefly review the classic structural model that first emerged in British social anthropology in the first half of the 20th century.

First, social structuralism conceptualizes specific cultures as structured entities. At least in its initial stages, social structural anthropology began as a quest for increased scientific rigor within the social sciences. The late 19th and early 20th centuries was an era when the theory of evolution exerted a great influence and social scientists sought to use evolutionary theory to extrapolate earlier forms of social organization. Since the ancient cultures being analyzed no longer existed, the resulting theories were not based on empirical evidence. As a result, these methods fell from favor as researchers became increasingly concerned with rigor and empirical evidence.

As a means of dismissing and going beyond this ascientific "armchair anthropology," British structural-functionalists (lead by Alfred Radcliffe-Brown and Bronislaw Malinowski) emphasized conceptualizing cultures as highly structured systems comprised of interrelated and mutually reinforcing parts. In order to see how these various components of a culture meshed with one another, a fieldworker needed to visit the society and interact within it long enough to be able to intuitively conceptualize the culture as a holistic entity.[2]

Eventually, British structural anthropology divided into two groups. The one led by Malinowski (1949, 1954, 1962) focused up on the needs of individual people; this school came to be known as "functionalism." Radcliffe-Brown and his students concentrated upon the social unit and its requirements (1952), which were seen as being distinct from actual people and their needs; this movement became known as "structuralism."

In Radcliffe-Brown's mind, the society (at a macro level) is the appropriate unit of investigation; human nature and psychological phenomena are viewed as universal facilitators of culture that, while constituting important prerequisites for social life, were not explicitly investigated. (This focus, of course, meshes with Herder and Hegel's concept of the *volksgeist* as transformed by social theorists such as Emile Durkheim.) Here, we will focus upon Radcliffe-Brown and his students because their method ultimately dominated over Malinowski's functionalism, and since it provides a classic example of the social structural approach.

The Radcliffe-Brown position was strengthened by the embrace of the theories of French sociologist Emile Durkheim (1893, 1912, 1964, 1975).[3] Crucial to Durkheim's thought was the idea of the "collective conscience," (sometimes referred to as "conscience collective" (Parsons 1968: 314). According to Talcott Parsons, Durkheim felt the collective conscience

was a "system of beliefs and sentiments" held in common by the members of a society and defining what their mutual relations ought to be. . . . [Its] focus seems to be what we have come to call the values common to the members of any relatively well integrated social system; the sharing of common values. (Parsons 1968: 314)

This concept, of course, closely parallels Herder's and Hegel's *volksgeist*.

Although this idea of a collective consciousness can be subjected to severe attack (including those of the poststructuralists, who feel that society is made up of many different groups that structural arguments ultimately fail to address), the concept calls attention to the social system or culture as a distinct and unique entity, as well as pointing to the shared values and beliefs that many members of a society routinely accept (typically in a covert way). These phenomena are of value to marketing/consumer researchers who examine the overarching impacts of a national character and how it can influence consumption. This kind of model is especially useful in situations where marketing/consumer researchers are concerned with mass marketing and where most (or all) of the society are assumed to respond in similar ways to a product or marketing campaign. It is also useful in exploring how macro cultural forces can significantly impact marketing and consumption.

The value of this model to marketing/consumer research is rather obvious. To the extent that a culture has an identifiable *volksgeist* that is homogeneous and shared by the population at large, the attitudes, beliefs, and propensities embraced by the national character can be used to predict and influence consumer response. Thus, the British social structural anthropologists present a means by which marketing/consumer researchers can operationalize Hegel's concept of *volksgeist*.

Social structural anthropology deals with the culture or society as a structured entity and, as emphasized above, it does not directly concern itself with human nature or psychological universals, such as the structure of the human mind.

THE AMERICAN STRUCTURAL SOCIOLOGISTS

As indicated above, the seminal thinker in the development of what came to be known as modern social structural thought is Emile Durkheim. Thus, the basic intellectual push toward modern sociology stems from the European intellectual tradition in general and France in particular.

Although sociology emerged out of the European intellectual tradition, in the first half of the 20th century it came to fullest flower in the United States. Before World War II, the center of sociological thought was the University of Chicago. Inspired by the work of George Herbert Mead (1863–1931), the University of Chicago research agenda focused upon what has been called "microsociology" (i.e., the analysis of small groups of people in intimate social contact with one another). Mead, a pragmatist philosopher (along with William James and John Dewey) as well as a social scientist, was a major force in social theory during the first third of the 20th century, and he continues to exert a significant impact.

While the torch of leadership eventually passed to others, this "social interaction" approach typified by the University of Chicago intellectual tradition continues to be a fruitful method. Thus, Erving Goffman's dramaturgical approach is closely identified with the Chicago social interaction tradition; since Goffman is dealt with in a separate chapter, however, he and his work will not be discussed here.

By the late 1930s, the avant-garde of American sociology was beginning to emphasize more social structural ambitions. In 1937, for example, Talcott Parsons introduced the ideas of three sociological pioneers (Emile Durkheim, Max Weber, and Vilfredo Pareto) in his seminal *The Structure of Social Action*; in so doing, Parsons increasingly drew attention toward the macro social structure as an overarching entity that serves various functions and impacts all members of a culture in profound and parallel ways. This style of analysis turned attention away from the more micro-oriented studies that are typified by the University of Chicago intellectual tradition.

The basic premise of structural sociology is that the structure of a society serves various functions and achieves various goals that bolster the culture as a social entity while satisfying the needs of specific people. From an evolutionary point of view, cultures are seen as evolving in order to make their members better able to adapt to circumstances and to achieve their goals. Thus, a well-structured and functioning society is viewed as providing an advantage to both individuals and to the social organizations of which they are a part. This observation led to the prevailing belief among structuralists that, as in biological evolution, the structures of society must either adapt (in order to remain functional) or they will become extinct.

In today's world, for example, computers have emerged as crucial to the functioning of society. As this process has deepened and widened, the amount of prestige that accrues to those who possess computers and computer skills has grown. As a result, much consumer response is hinged around computers, flaunting their power, and mastering their operation; status and power walk hand in hand with gaining computer expertise. Society needs and values computer capabilities and the status system, and consumption patterns triggered by society have evolved accordingly. Older skills, such as blacksmithing, are no longer as highly valued within the mainstream culture, and respect for them has atrophied accordingly.

As the structural/functional paradigm came to dominate sociology, Harvard University and Talcott Parsons (1902–1979) and (at a slightly later time) Columbia University, the professional home of Robert Merton (1910–), an early student of Parsons, came to dominate. Parsons on the faculty of Harvard University from 1927 until 1974, was an important advocate of the structural/functional method in sociology. One of his major premises is that people cooperate because they share common goals and values; this "common dominator" (or *volksgeist*) helps to reinforce the culture and perpetuate its existence as a going concern. Parsons' major works include *The Structure of Social Action* (1937), *The Social System* (1951b), and *Sociological Theory and Modern Society* (1967).

In Parsons' often-discussed model there are four distinct but interrelated "action systems" that can be recognized and discussed. They go from the purely social to the specific individual. They include (1) the culture as a system, (2) the social milieu, (3) the personality of people, and (4) behavior traits of the human organism. This situation of multiple influences and "players" within a social system results in a very complex model, and Parsons has often been criticized on the grounds that his paradigm is unwieldy and unworkable. Nonetheless, Parsons does demonstrate the complexity of human behavior and social life.

The essential model that was advanced by Parsons embraced the organism analogy that goes back to Hegel and Comte. Society was viewed as an overarching entity in which the various parts are controlled by some sort of hierarchy; in addition, cooperation and collaboration for the common good prevail. When these conditions were not met, the system was typically viewed to be breaking down or (to revert back to an organic analogy) "sick." The value of such an approach is that it facilitates an analysis of the existence, evolution, and operation of social systems in terms of mutual self-interest. And Parsons believed that the shared values, norms, and beliefs of members of society (*volksgeist*) were key elements in this process of cooperation.

It was George C. Homans (1950) who expanded Parsons' perspectives by pointing out that, from a social structural point of view, there exists both "manifest" factors (which are overtly built into a social system and generally understood and recognized) and "latent" factors (that are unintentional or covert side effects and are often unrecognized). For our purposes as marketing/consumer researchers, certain recurring consumer desires or propensities to consume in specific ways may reflect the structured ethos and orientations of a culture; where this is true, these tendencies may be viewed as important latent functions or factors, triggered by manifest factors, that impact the consumption process.

In my monograph on the marketing and consumption of the cowboy story (Walle 2000), for example, I linked the evolution of the cowboy story (and its consumption) to evolving worldviews that have been held by the American people during different eras. Ultimately, I argued that in the late 19th and first half of the 20th century, "rugged individualism" was a prized characteristic because this trait served the needs of a society that was rapidly growing and expanding on an uncharted frontier. As the frontier era closed, however, our society became more collective and bureaucratic. After World War II, as the implications of this transformation came to be felt, a more collective orientation became a "manifest" factor that served the needs of society by providing personnel who were appropriate for the tasks that needed to be performed in order to maintain society.

As this transformation took place, new plotlines that viewed the cowboy hero as representative of an obsolete personality type became popular. This analysis envisions the consumption process of popular culture as a latent factor that changes in tandem with the evolution of the structure of society.

Another example of latent factors that impacts the consumption process is what classic sociologically oriented economist Thorstein Veblen (1857–1929) calls "conspicuous consumption." According to Veblen (1899), the social elites are interested in maintaining their position and privilege. One way in which specific members of the elite can maintain their position is to display their wealth. One way to display wealth is to constantly spend money in ways that are obvious, self-evident, and demonstrate power/status. From a marketing/consumer research point of view, conspicuous consumption can be viewed as what Homans would call a latent function—an unintended consequence of a manifest function. And, as is also self-evident, the consumption decisions associated with this latent function exert a profound impact upon our economy and our society.

Thus, consumption can often be viewed in terms of the social structure and the attempts of people to fit into (or rise to the top of) the social hierarchy. Thus, studying these latent influences may be of profound value to marketing/consumer research.

A common complaint of the social structural approach is that it does not adequately account for social change. In reality, this complaint is not completely valid; although social structural analysis does emphasize homeostasis (self-regulation in order to maintain stability), sophisticated social structural models clearly recognize social tensions and the fact that social change is a fact of life. A discussion of the concept of anomie will demonstrate how social structural analysis can acknowledge change.

The concept of anomie initially stems from the early work of pioneering French sociologist Emile Durkheim and it was introduced in Durkheim's *Suicide*, a classic account of how social change can result in unhappiness, despair, and (as a result) lead to a growing suicide rate (Durkheim 1893). Discussed in layman's terms, anomie has sometimes been equated with "normlessness," although a more theoretical definition indicates that it "signifies the state of mind of one who . . . has no longer any sense of continuity, of folk, of obligation. The anomic man has become spiritually sterile, responsive only to himself, responsible to no one" (MacIver 1950: 84). As a result, individuals who experience anomie become alienated and cut off from their heritage. As Dressler observes: "To put it allegorically, the anomic individual has lost his past, foresees no future and lives only in the immediate which is virtually nowhere" (Dressler 1969: 251).

According to Merton, a key cause and source of anomie is a disparity between the goals that society gives to people vs. their means of achieving them; when this unhealthy situation arises, anomie is the likely result (Merton 1957: 121–94). Specifically, Merton argues that the mores and norms of the society provide individuals with goals to which they should aspire on the one hand and the socially acceptable methods of achieving these goals on the other. Over time, however, the social structure (or the socioeconomic milieu in which society exists) may change to such a degree that its members are no longer able to achieve sanctioned and honored goals in socially acceptable ways.

Merton, then, suggests that when people cannot achieve their goals in socially acceptable ways, the propensity for deviant behavior increases (and deviant behavior can involve consumption decisions). Thus, in the case of mainstream upper-middle-class people (who have a relatively good chance of achieving their goals in socially acceptable ways), there is a greater chance that they will make consumption decisions according to culturally provided norms (dress in a conservative "preppy style," for example, even if some individuals, especially rebellious youth, break this dress code). People who have less of a stake in the status quo and people who exist largely outside of the status hierarchy, in contrast, may be more prone to embrace fads, quickly evolving styles, and non-conformist patterns of behavior.

According to this model, tensions and deviance occur when certain people feel that they are somehow cut off from the benefits that derive from participating in the mainstream culture. When this occurs, they seek alternatives. By seeking alternatives, they help to further evolve the culture (i.e., transform the social structure). The resulting innovations can either become mainstream over time or provide a place of refuge for individuals who, choosing new options where they can be evaluated on their own terms, cease to be in disruptive conflict with the system. The concept of anomie provides a viable social structural theory that is useful in this regard.

It is of special interest to us as marketing/consumer researchers that the innovative deviance that can stem from anomie has profound implications for consumption. This is because there are various ways in which people can respond to anomie; each option potentially impacts the consumption of goods and services among specific segments of the population in specific ways. Thus, Merton provides a typology of responses to anomie that includes (1) conformity, (2) innovation, (3) ritualization, (4) retreatism, and (5) rebellion (Merton 1957). They can be described as:

1. *Conformity*: a situation in which the person embraces the goals of the society and seeks to achieve these goals in socially acceptable ways.

2. *Innovation*: a situation where the person embraces the goals of society by employing methods of achieving these goals in socially unacceptable ways.

3. *Ritualization*: a situation where the person acts according to the norms of society but loses track of the goals to be achieved.

4. *Retreatism*: a situation where the person rejects both the cultural goals and the institutionalized methods of achieving them.

5. *Rebellion*: a situation where the person rejects the goals and means of achieving them and substitutes an alternative.

Graphically, they can be juxtaposed as shown in Figure 7.1. In recent years, there has been an attempt to use Merton's model of anomie to deal with the consumption of popular music (Hemmens 1999); thus marketing/consumer researchers are in a position to tap this emerging intellectual tradition.

The concept of anomie, therefore, provides a concrete and well-developed means of dealing with how consumption patterns change through time and offers a menu of specific responses that are available to people. Although the social structural approach focuses on macro cultural units, and although this method centers upon self-regulation and the maintenance of the system, social change is not ignored by the social

Figure 7.1
Anomie and Consumption Patterns

Response	Description	Relevance
Conformity	Goals and means accepted	People who are successful within the accepted prevailing social order tend to consume products that reinforce and mesh with the status quo.
Innovation	Goals accepted, means rejected	People who are underserved by the status quo can retain the goals of society while rejecting the means of achieving them.
Ritualization	Means retained, goals forgotten	Some people maintain the conventions of society while losing touch of why they are doing so. They will consume products in conventional ways even though they do not know why.
Retreatism	Goals and means rejected	Some people may reject both the goals of society and the means of gaining them. They offer no alternative and may choose consumption styles that lampoon the status quo.
Rebellion	Goals and means replaced	There is a complete break with tradition, consumption is motivated by new mainsprings, and the products consumed are different.
Discussion	A number of alternative tools exist for researchers who are dealing with how people respond to the pressures and precedents provided by society. By understanding how specific individuals and groups respond, it becomes easier to predict the kinds of products they will consume and why they will do so.	

structural approach. By dealing with social change, profound clues about the consumption process and its transformation over time can be integrated into the analysis.

BEYOND STRUCTURES

Earlier in this chapter we dealt with the "clockworks" model of general systems theory and suggested that classic social structuralism basically embraces such a perspective. In view of the fact that the clockworks model is not specifically designed to deal with change, disruptions, and tensions within a culture, the social structural model often needs to transcend this static focus; one way of doing so is to embrace what Boulding calls a "cybernetic system" of general systems theory that he defines as: "that of the control mechanism of the cybernetic system . . . this differs from the simple stable system in the fact that the transmission and in-

terpretation of information is an essential part of the system. As a result
. . . [behavior] is not merely determined by the equations of the system"
(Boulding 1956: 14).

The discussion of anomie presented above provides one example of
how a structural model can be coupled with a cybernetic orientation so
that behavior is not viewed as merely "determined by the equations of
the system"; so reformulated, structural analysis can usefully deal with
stress, evolution, and change.

Scholars who are seeking to go beyond the clockworks model have at
least two different strategies from which to choose:

1. Expand the existing structural model so that it can adequately deal with more
   complex situations involving differences, tensions, rivalries, and communication.
2. Abandon the structural model and replace it with an alternative method that
   is able to deal with a wider range of phenomena.

Although the second option (abandoning the social structural model)
has often been employed, the first option (adjusting the structural model)
is an equally viable alternative. Indeed, the structural model can be expanded and adapted. As a result, it does not need to be discarded.

In the 1950s and 1960s, for example, innovative social structural anthropologists[4] began to critique the traditional Radcliffe-Brown methods
of a relatively static structural anthropology and acknowledge that this
approach unduly discounted and ignored conflict and change. A classic
statement of this emerging research stream was provided by Fredrik
Barth.[5] Barth attacked the Radcliffe-Brown variety of structuralism for
encompassing only static rules of behavior: "The [Radcliffe-Brown]
model does not depict any intervening social processes between the
moral injunction and the pattern. There is indeed no science of social life
in this procedure, no explanation of how actual forms, much less frequency distributions in behavior come about" (1966: 2).

Barth feels that social scientists must study people in action, not merely
investigate the social rules and the social structure: "[Researchers must
study] people exercising choice while being influenced by certain constraints and incentives. Indeed, once one admits that what we empirically observe is not "customs" but "cases" of human behavior, it seems
to me that we cannot escape the concept of choice in our analysis" (1966:
1).

Indeed, Barth concludes that it is necessary for social structural
method to transcend the old clockworks model and to adopt a more
cybernetic posture. He observes: "I believe that the study of social anthropology cannot today be advanced much by sophistication and refinement of the current stock of concepts and ideas" (1966: iv). Other

anthropologists, such as Clifford Geertz (1973), have presented similar arguments, but Geertz's work seems more in tune with poststructural analysis and will not be considered here.

At approximately the same time, Edmund Leach in his *Rethinking Anthropology* (1961) was arguing that British social anthropology needed to expand beyond the static social structural models if it was to continue as a vital intellectual force.

While Barth and Leach were theorizing about the inherent weaknesses in the clockworks orientation of British social structural anthropology, others anthropologists, such as Victor Turner, were actively developing methods and techniques that were designed to overcome these limitations. Turner's concept of the "social drama" comes close to meeting the criteria of a cybernetic system. Turner realized (as Barth had) that what the anthropologist observes is "not customs but cases" and he observes:

On a number of occasions during my fieldwork I became aware of marked disturbances in the social life of the particular group I happened to be studying at the time. The whole group might be radically cloven into two conflicting factions. . . . These eruptions which I call "social dramas" [consist of] (1) breach, (2) crisis, (3) redressive action, (4) reintegration or recognition of schism. (1957: 91–92)

By studying the social dramas of a society, the anthropologist is able to get beyond the static clockworks model in order to analyze both social change and tensions within the cultural system:

In the social drama, latent conflicts become manifest, and kinship ties, whose significance is not obvious in genealogies, emerge into key importance. . . . If we examine a sequence of social dramas arising within the same social unit, each one affords us a glimpse . . . of the social system. . . . Through it we are enabled to observe the critical principles of the social structure in their operation and their relative dominance as successive points in time. (1957: 92–93)

Indeed, some forms of consumer behavior (and their evolution over time) may be interpreted in terms suggested by Turner's conception of the social drama. In this regard, I will consider each component of the social drama with reference to the consumption process. In doing so, Turner's model will inspire an overview of the consumption of Rock and Roll music, how it is consumed, who consumes it, and how its consumption has evolved over time.

Breach

In the 1950s, Rock and Roll music emerged as an innovative form of musical expression that jointly stemmed from the musical traditions of rural Blacks and Whites from the Southern region of the United States. Initially, this form of music was viewed as merely a passing fad that would quickly fade, exerting little long-term impact. There was a breach, but initially no real crisis was perceived. At this point, the consumption of Rock and Roll music was confined to a relatively small group of people and the status-quo musical traditions (extensions of the musical tastes of the World War II era) continued to dominate.

Crisis

In 1954, the song "Rock Around the Clock" (released a year earlier to lukewarm sales) was part of the soundtrack of the movie "High School Confidential"; the film clearly linked Rock and Roll music with juvenile delinquency and deviant behavior on the part of rebellious youth. In addition, as time went on, various Rock and Roll stars flaunted an overt sexuality that challenged the norms of a society which, at that time, were sexually conservative. A crisis emerged as the music that was embraced by youth overtly rejected by the values of the older generation. At a later period, Rock and Roll became identified with social change, civil rights, drugs, and the anti-war movement.

Redressive Action

In the 1950s various "clean-cut" performers, such as Pat Boone, began to transform Rock and Roll music into a form of music that would be acceptable to the conservative and traditional elements of society. Throughout the history of Rock and Roll, there have always been those who bowdlerized its musical innovations in ways that accommodate the conservative element in society; some Rock bands (such as Stryper, for example) consciously cater to the conservative Christian element of society while having the outward persona of a typical "heavy metal" band.

During the 1960s, however, Rock and Roll again became controversial due to the emergence of the counterculture and the "sex, drugs, and Rock and Roll" mentality of the era. Due to the power massive numbers and economic clout of the baby boom generation, however, Rock and Roll emerged as a norm.

Reintegration or Recognition

Eventually, Rock and Roll music emerged as an international form of musical expression and it is consumed accordingly; thus, it has been reintegrated back into mainstream society. Today, Rock and Roll has largely emerged as a status quo form of musical expression and it is consumed as such.

Nonetheless, there continues to be distinctive groups in American society that feel alienated from the mainstream of society. One such segment of the population innovated "Rap," "Hip-Hop," and "Gangstra" music. Initially, this music signaled a breach within society and a potential crisis. Today, however, these forms of musical expression (and the clothes and personal styles that go with them) are increasingly becoming reintegrated into the mainstream. Even some "Gangstra" movies with their Rap or Hip-Hop soundtracks ("Original Ganstras" is an excellent example) celebrate what are best described as "traditional" and "family" values. Graphically, this process can be described as shown in Figure 7.2.

Thus, evolving styles of popular music and their consumption (as well as many other consumer products) can be viewed in terms of Turner's social drama. This model, while having strong roots in social structural analysis, acknowledges both tensions within society and social change. As demonstrated above, this structural model has significant contributions to make to marketing/consumer research.

There, incidentally, is a key difference in how marketing/consumer researchers use social theories and how they are employed within the theoretical social sciences. Social theorists seek to analyze empirical reality and to explain how the structures of society operate. Marketing/consumer researchers, in contrast, are primarily interested in using social theory in order to predict how people will purchase and consume particular products in specific circumstances. By focusing on how crises percolate through a social system, it may become easier to understand how consumers are likely to behave over time and how their responses may evolve. Thus, this kind of model can be used to supplement the hoary old truisms of our discipline (such as the adoption curve and the product life cycle), and this "social drama" model can be used in tandem with a social structural analysis.

Besides Turner's work with social dramas, other British social anthropologists such as Rodney Needham (1987) attempt to redefine "oppositions" by suggesting that every culture tends to deal with oppositions in their own way. So arguing, Needham seeks to bring the social context of behavior back into focus. And we, as marketing/consumer researchers, are often interested in the social context of behavior.

Thus, even though the classic model of British structural anthropology may lean toward a static clockworks model, it can be expanded and elaborated in dynamic ways in order to deal with change and conflict.

A BROADER PERSPECTIVE

The emphasis upon stability or change differentiates "clockworks" and "cybernetic" structural models. Classic social structuralism tended to deal primarily with static structures. As time went on, however, ex-

Figure 7.2
Musical Consumption as Social Drama

Component	Description	Discussion
Breach	Rock and Roll is a significant breach in musical styles and demonstrates a breach in lifestyle. Initially no crisis is perceived.	Rock and Roll was a fusion of Black and White music. Initially seen as a short-lived fad among a small segment of youth.
Crisis	Crisis emerges as Rock and Roll becomes popular and is identified with social taboos (juvenile delinquency, overt sexuality) and, later, the counterculture.	Rock and Roll becomes identified with juvenile delinquency. Overt sexuality and the counterculture add to crisis mentality. Links to social activism fans flames of crisis.
Redression	Various performers translate Rock and Roll in ways that are acceptable to the mainstream.	Various opportunistic marketers of music bowdlerize Rock and Roll and showcase "clean cut" performers (the "Dick Clark Syndrome").
Reintegration	Through time, Rock and Roll emerges as mainstream. New forms of music (Hip-Hop) begin the process of the social drama once again.	Over time, changing tastes and the power of the baby boom generation transform Rock and Roll into status quo music. Tensions, however, remain.
Recognition	Hip-Hop initially signals a recognition of a division in society, but in time it (and the personal style associated with it) also becomes mainstream.	There are always groups that are at odds with the mainstream of society. Thus, there is always a recognition of some breach and/or the potential of crisis. Nonetheless, styles of musical expression that start as social dramas can also become mainstream.

panding the static paradigm in dynamic ways has become important. There is a profound value in preserving the social structural paradigm. It is self-evident that social structures exist and that they exert profound influences upon society. This fact does not deny the equally important truth that much behavior must be viewed in terms of individuals and circumscribed groups. Nonetheless, social structures do exist. This fact needs to be recognized because, on many occasions, the social structure provides a key to understanding consumer response.

Ultimately, structural models can be either static or dynamic. Historically, much of the research performed by social structuralists has been static in nature. This was not due to any inherent limitation in structural analysis but is merely an artifact of the research agendas that existed in an earlier era.

It is clearly possible to supplement static structural models with more dynamic alternatives. Doing so opens up valuable options; it also eliminates the need to reject the structural model and to "inevitably" replace it with some kind of poststructural alternative. Marketing/consumer researchers need to remain aware of these valuable options.

SPECIALIZED SUBDISCIPLINES AS TAILORED TOOLS: A CONCLUSION

Much of what we have been talking about here falls within the realm of general social theory. The tendency for marketing/consumer researchers to embrace the general theoretic themes of outside fields has long been a common strategy of marketing/consumer research; doing so has provided a number of exciting research agendas and prevented us from having to constantly "reinvent the wheel." While not discounting the value of general theory, it is worthwhile to mention that modern sociology has multiplied into a number of specialized subdisciplines, each of which has a well-defined universe of discourse. While many of these subdisciplines have a structural component, general theory is largely subordinated to a particular area of substantive interest.

Long-established subdisciplines of sociology include marriage and the family, rural sociology, social structure, social problems/deviance, race and ethnic relations, and the sociology of organizations. Subdisciplines that have emerged more recently include gerontology and the sociology of sex and gender. As a result of this degree of specialization within contemporary sociology, it is often useful to go directly to these subdisciplines because specialists in these fields often have more in common with like-minded marketing/consumer researchers than with fellow sociologists who embrace other specialities.

Thus, it is not necessary (or even an optimum strategy) for marketing/consumer researchers to go straight to "general social theory" and "work up" applications and theoretic models from that point. Instead, much of the groundwork and refinement needed by marketing/consumer researchers has already been accomplished by specialists working within rather self-contained subdisciplines. Building upon this preexisting work can save time and increase the sophistication of a final research project.

Since the 1980s, furthermore, a new and revived interest in structural analysis has emerged that is typically referred to as neo-functionalism (Alexander 1985; Mouzelis 1999). As a result, by examining specialized subdisciplines of sociology (such as neo-functionalism), marketing/consumer researchers can make good use of these exciting research streams.

NOTES

1. Various people label this school of thought in different ways. Perhaps the most common label is "functionalism." It is also known as "functional-structuralism." Here I will call it "structuralism" because this general model exists both in anthropology and sociology. Since A. R. Radcliffe Brown, a leader of British social anthropology, called the method "structuralism" in order to distinguish it from the work of Bronislaw Malinowski (that was called "functionalism"), we will use the term "structuralism" to deal with the work of both the anthropologists and the sociologists.

2. This eventually led to charges of a lack of rigor since analysis was based on subjective impressions, not replicable evidence. In its own time, however, it was a methodological advancement and many anthropologists continue to feel it is the ideal way to conduct research.

3. Durkheim reacted against the didactic and methodological agenda of the utilitarian philosophers (such as John Stuart Mill). In addition, Durkheim embodied the ethos of pioneering French social scientists such as Auguste Comte.

4. As a matter of personal taste and interest, in this section I will focus upon solutions forged by a number of noted social anthropologists. This discussion presents a non-exhaustive convenience sample of useful perspectives.

5. Edmund Leach, in his *Rethinking Anthropology* (1961), provides an earlier critique. Since Barth is slightly later and his critique is more to the point, he will be used as representative of this phase of the development of the structural method.

REFERENCES

Alexander, Jeffrey C. (1985). "Toward Neo-Functionalism." *Sociological Theory* 3(2): 11–23.

Barth, Fredrik. (1966). *Models of Social Organization*. London: Royal Anthropological Institute.

Boulding, Kenneth. (1956). "General Systems Theory: The Skeleton of Science." *Management Science* 2(3) (April).

Dressler, David. (1969). *Sociology: The Study of Human Interaction*. New York: Alfred A. Knopf.

Durkheim, Emile. (1893). *Suicide*, trans. John A. Spaulding and George Simpson. Reprint, New York: Free Press, 1966.

Durkheim, Emile. (1912). *The Elementary Forms of Religious Life*. Reprint, New York: Macmillan, 1926.

Durkheim, Emile. (1964). *The Rules of the Sociological Method*, trans. Sarah A. Salovay and John Mueller. New York: Free Press.

Durkheim, Emile, with W.S.F. Pickering. (1975). *Durkheim on Religion: A Selection of Readings with Bibliographies*. London: Routledge and Kegan Paul.

Geertz, Clifford. (1973). *Interpretation of Culture: Selected Essays*. New York: Basic Books.

Hemmens, Craig. (1999). "There's a Darkness on the Edge of Town: Merton's Five Modes of Adaption in the Lyrics of Bruce Springsteen." *International Journal of Contemporary and Applied Criminal Justice* 23(1–2): 27.

Homans, George C. (1950). *The Human Group*. New York: Harcourt Brace Jovanovich.

Kroeber, Alfred Louis. (1917). "The Superorganic." *American Anthropologist* 19: 41–54.

Kroeber, Alfred Louis. (1948). *Anthropology*. New York: Harcourt Brace.

Leach, Edmund. (1961). *Rethinking Anthropology*. London: University of London Press.

MacIver, Robert. (1950). *The Ramparts We Guard*. New York: Macmillan.

Malinowski, Bronislaw. (1949). *The Dynamics of Culture Change: An Inquiry into Race Relations in Africa*. Edited by Phyllis M. Kaberry. New Haven, CT: Yale University Press.

Malinowski, Bronislaw. (1952). *Sex, Culture, Myth*. New York: Harcourt, Brace, World.

Malinowski, Bronislaw. (1954). *Magic, Science, and Religion and Other Essays*. Garden City, NY: Doubleday.

Merton, Robert. (1957). *Social Theory and Social Structure*. New York: Free Press.

Mouzelis, Nicos. (1999). "Neo-Functionalism and After." *Sociological Forum* 14(4): 721–33.

Needham, Rodney. (1987). *Counterpoints*. Berkeley: University of California Press.

Parsons, Talcott. (1937). *The Structure of Social Action*. Glencoe, IL: Free Press.

Parsons, Talcott. (1951a). *Towards a General Theory of Action*. Edited with Edward Shils. Cambridge, MA: Harvard University Press.

Parsons, Talcott. (1951b). *The Social System*. Glencoe, IL: Free Press.

Parsons, Talcott. (1967). *Sociological Theory and Modern Society*. New York: Free Press.

Parsons, Talcott. (1968). "Emile Durkheim." In *International Encyclopedia of the Social Sciences*. New York: Macmillan and Free Press.

Radcliffe-Brown, Alfred R. (1952). *Structure and Function in Primitive Society: Essays and Addresses*. Glencoe, IL: Free Press.

Smith, Grafton Eliott. (1927). *The Evolution of Man*, 2nd ed. Oxford: Oxford University Press.

Smith, Grafton Eliott. (1929). *The Migration of Early Cultures*. Manchester: Manchester University Press.

Turner, Victor. (1957). *Schism and Continuity in an African Society: A Study of Ndembu Village Life*. Manchester: Manchester University Press.

Veblen, Thorstein. (1899). *The Theory of the Lesiure Class*. New York: Macmillan.

CHAPTER 8

Social Structures and Consumer Response: The Culture at a Distance Method

ALTERNATIVE STRUCTURAL THEORIES

The last chapter dealt, in almost generic ways, with the mainstream of social structural theory and analysis. The basic orientation of that method is largely akin to Herder's and Hegel's concept of the *volksgeist*, which suggests that each culture or society has its own unique spirit or national character. Extending that premise, the method extrapolated the essence of specific social structures and analyzed their functions accordingly.

While there exists what can be viewed as the "mainstream" of social structural thought (which starts with Herder and Hegel, proceeds to Durkheim, and culminates in the British structural anthropologists and the social structural sociologists of North America), splinter groups and alternative orientations have also made their mark. In the heat of intellectual debates, however, the champions of these alternative visions have sometimes failed to emphasize their deep structural orientations, just as more mainstream social structuralists dismissed them. Nonetheless, these alternative approaches embrace their own structural vision and, in retrospect, the kinship between mainstream structuralism and various other orientations can be recognized.

Here, one such model and school of thought—the "historical particularism" school centered around American anthropologist Franz Boas—is analyzed. After an introduction to Boas and his work, further refinements in Boas' method are discussed. This chain of thought is especially relevant because, as it evolved, much of the effort of this group became oriented around practitioner issues and, therefore, it provides a refreshing alternative to much "ivory tower" social theory. Although that method is currently dated and unfashionable, it can be and should be updated, revised, and returned to useful service.

BOAS AND HIS METHOD

The evolution of American social anthropology bears the imprint of focusing upon the uniqueness of specific societies and dealing with them as distinct entities that function according to their own rules and internal logic. Instead of seeking general theories, these scholars were interested in the interworkings of specific cultures viewed, more or less, in isolation.

To a large extent, this distinctively American approach to social analysis is the lengthened shadow of Franz Boas, who (after coming in contact with Eskimo culture) moved from Germany to the United States, joined the faculty of Columbia University, and went on to become the father of North American anthropology. Although, in the heat of the moment, the Boasian contingent and the social structuralist movement tended to view each other as "rival camps," each emphasized social structures in their own specific manner. And, as we shall see, in America these pervasive structures tended to be called "configurations." In order to flesh out the situation that developed, a brief overview of Boas' career and influence is useful.

The late 19th century was an era in which broad and general theories of cultural evolution (social Darwinism) dominated the intellectual landscape. Although Boas clearly believed in biological evolution, he did not feel that evolutionary theory was the appropriate lens with which to examine cultures and societies. Instead of focusing upon general evolutionary models (as social Darwinists such as Herbert Spencer had done), Boas and his students concentrated upon how cultures developed in specific ways due to the unique pressures that they faced. These cultural adaptations, Boas emphasized, did not necessarily reflect the general theories of evolutionary development that were popular in the late 19th century.

As a result, the Boasian school is typically referred to as "historical particularism" since it was primarily concerned with the specific and isolated developments of distinct cultures/societies, not with universal evolutionary patterns or general trends that effected all cultures and mankind as a whole. The connection between this position and that of Heder's and Hegel's concept of the *volksgeist* is hard to miss. This type of analytic strategy, furthermore has much to offer marketing/consumer researchers who seek to understand the specific kinds of responses that can be expected from the members of certain cultures and/or organizations.

Originally trained as a physical scientist, Boas was a stickler for details and he emphasized gathering voluminous empirical evidence. Indeed, anthropologists often use the term "Boasian" to describe (in disapproving terms) the tendency to spend so much time collecting facts that they are never synthesized into an adequate and coherent interpretation. Nonetheless, there was a theoretical underpinning to Boas and his work; members of the historical particularist school tended to believe that (1) circumstances impacted specific cultures; (2) cultures, therefore, evolved in particular ways; (3) due to the flexibility of human nature, this variation is possible; and (4) the job of anthropologists is to focus upon the distinctiveness of specific cultures and social groups.

While historical particularism offered a useful alternative to general evolutionary theory, some of the movement's leaders eventually began to realize that Boas' preoccupation with material culture left gaps that potentially compromised his method (Boas 1940). Noted anthropological linguist Edward Sapir (1949), for example, complained that historical particularism did not deal with the emotional lives that people experienced. This limitation led to the development of a school of anthropology that is usually referred to as "culture and personality," a subdiscipline that, building upon Boas' paradigm, combines the theories of anthropology and psychology in order to develop a more robust theory of mankind and social life (and one that acknowledges people's emotional and spiritual lives). In essence, this method combined psychology with social structural perspectives in a substantial and useful manner, the method that Sapir advocated.

Eventually Ruth Benedict (a student of both Boas and Sapir) developed a sophisticated and eclectic method in which social structures and psychological responses are usefully intermingled. Benedict, incidentally, came to anthropology late in her intellectual development (she had previous training in writing and literary criticism). As a result, she possessed a diverse outlook—one that was profoundly influenced by the broader humanistic tradition, not merely by the social sciences. Indeed, her approach is strikingly similar to that of modern marketing researchers, who seek to merge marketing/consumer research with the humanities and social sciences. Thus, Benedict is a "kindred spirit," and many avant-garde marketing/consumer researchers will feel comfortable with her and her approach.

A key premise unifying Benedict's method is the emphasis that the human spirit is very adaptable and pliable; she argued that due to this flexibility, successful cultures could emphasize a wide variety of orientations. Nonetheless, Benedict affirmed that each culture could be fully embraced by its members.

BENEDICT, MEAD, AND THE CONFIGURATION METHOD

A classic statement of this potential is found in Benedict's article "Anthropology and the Abnormal" (1934a), where she argued that what is "abnormal" is defined as such by the culture and does not constitute an objective diagnosis to which all "normal" people will inevitably concur. In other words, what constitutes "sane" and "insane" behavior is culturally defined, and these definitions ultimately reflect the degree to which behavior reflects the norms of the culture. Those who act according to the rules and the perceived needs of society are viewed as normal; others are dismissed accordingly.

Benedict's *Patterns of Culture* (1934b) is the tour de force of the cultural configuration method; here, Benedict affirms that cultures can best be envisioned as holistic and synergistic "patterns" that orient their members to think, feel, and behave in predictable ways. By understanding the overarching cultural pattern or configuration, a wide variety of behaviors can be more effectively predicted and/or explained. The value of this approach to marketing/consumer research is self-evident.

A basic premise of *Patterns of Culture* is that, at birth, people are very flexible and that they have the potential to develop in innumerable ways. Benedict argues, however, that each culture possesses a particular "configuration" and that members of that culture are socialized to behave and respond in accordance to it. Thus, patterns and structures of personality and responses to them are, in large measure, artifacts of the culture. By understanding the influences of the culture upon its members, the future responses of both the individual and the collective society can be more accurately predicted. Again, this method has obvious value in predicting consumer response.

In *Patterns of Culture*, Benedict presents sketches of three cultures—the Zuni of New Mexico, the Dobu of Melanesia, and the Kwakiutl of the western coast of North America. In the process, Benedict also provides her visions of the inherent cultural configurations of the different cultures she analyzes. Benedict goes on to argue that these cultural patterns, in turn, impact both the personalities of specific people and their reactions to circumstances. Thus, Benedict saw personality and human response as historical products and she viewed the culture as a structured response to particular historical pressures. Benedict is very clear about how the culture and the individual are intertwined: "There is no proper antagonism between the role of society and that of the individual. . . . Society . . . is never an entity separable from the individuals who compose it" (1934b, 1959: 251).

Quickly following Benedict's *Patterns of Culture* was Margaret Mead's *Sex and Temperament in Three Primitive Societies* (1935), which suggested that aspects of personality that had often been linked to the biological fact of one's sex (such as aggressive behavior among males verses passive responses among females) are actually learned by children during the socialization process and, therefore, are based on the structures provided by the culture, not upon an innate propensity to act in a specific manner. Studies such as Mead's (connected, as they are, to the historical particularist perspective) point to the impact of culture upon the human personality; as a result, they underscore the fact that the structure of human response varies widely in different cultures. These insights regarding the flexibility of mankind (and the fact that people are largely products of historical circumstance) have a clear value to marketing/consumer researchers since they point to patterned responses that are not "rational" and calculated in a strategic or game theoretic sense. And yet, these underlying structures are often the mainsprings driving actual behavior.

Since people's actual responses may not be "thought out" in rational and tactical ways, they constitute structured reactions that are dictated by the underlying patterns of a culture. Investigating these overarching influences can provide marketing/consumer researchers with invaluable insights. The work of the historical particularistic anthropologists and culture and personality specialists (such as Benedict and Mead) provide a systematic means of dealing with this phenomena.

During World War II, these scholars (and the methods they represent) attracted the interest of the U.S. State Department, which commissioned Benedict and Mead (among others) to provide advice on how to conduct the war effort. The result of their efforts is a test of the practitioner value of the configurational theories proposed by Boas and his students. The result of this collaboration was a major case study regarding the contribution that the theoretical social scientist can make to the practitioner world.

CULTURE AT A DISTANCE

The essentials of the culture at a distance method can be easily stated; by comprehending cultures as structured and homogeneous entities, Benedict, Mead, and their colleagues were able to predict how people would react to certain circumstances, such as internal and external pressures and the propaganda with which they were bombarded. The basic technique was to extrapolate the "national character" of a particular people and then predict their responses. Certainly, cultures are complex and the core of the culture may be elusive; some researchers (such as those whose theoretical base stems from existentialism), furthermore, may deny that a basic uniformity within cultures exists. While the rhetoric of these naysayers may be convincing, it is hard to deny the fact that cultures are patterned and structured, even if this fact clashes with the cherished ideologies that some intellectuals hold dear.

Although much anthropological work was purely theoretical and dealt with small-scale hinterland cultures, the threats and needs of World War II created the necessity of analyzing complex societies and organizations, not rustic tribes and vestigial enclaves. Acclaimed anthropologist Margaret Mead states the situation as it appeared to her in 1942:

Six times in the last seventeen years I have entered another culture, left behind me the speech, the food, the familiar postures of my own way of life and sought to understand the patterns of life of another people. In 1939, I came home to a world on the brink of war, convinced that the next task was to apply what we [anthropologists] knew as best as we could, to the problems of our own society. (1942: 83)

Mead's strategy was to apply anthropological fieldwork methods and analytic techniques to her own culture and to the developed, industrial world in ways that are clearly centered around the needs of practitioners (i.e., those who were conducting the war effort). Anthropology was striving to become a policy science capable of dealing with the contemporary mass/industrial society.

The end result of Mead's efforts was her highly acclaimed *And Keep Your Powder Dry* (1942), a book that provided a strategically oriented analysis of American culture. Her monograph was delivered in the belief that by understanding the "cultural configuration" of the United States, it would be possible to predict the response of its citizens to both internal and external pressures. The value of this general approach to marketing/consumer research is obvious.

In her analysis, Mead distilled key aspects of the American psyche that have emerged as conventional wisdoms. Americans, we are told, are forward looking and they have little concern with the past (1942: 37). Mead, in addition, was also able to point to differences in the response of Americans when compared to their European counterparts. Mead argued, for example, that: "The point of a negotiated peace [for traditional Europeans] is so that everybody can stop, have a breathing spell, and fight more effectively in the future. War to the finish is never the slogan" (1942: 215). Mead goes on to suggest, however, that "leaving the job undone" does not make sense to the average American. Instead, she observes:

And we must see it as our duty—if we are to call ourselves good—to fight for the right to do this next big job uninterrupted [by a negotiated peace]. . . . It lies within the American character to see a job as so important [that it must be completed] . . . we can only win the war if we fight it in terms that do make sense to Americans. (1942: 215–16)

In essence, *And Keep Your Powder Dry* was a national character study that provided decision makers with the insights and tools that they needed in order to effectively control and lead the members of a modern industrial society. Dealing with American society in cultural particularist terms, Mead extrapolated the underlying structures of American culture, the resulting American psyche, and patterns of response that stemmed from both. As indicated, these efforts clearly parallel the work of many contemporary marketing/consumer researchers who employ the social sciences in order to understand why people behave the way they do and how their behavior can be strategically modified.

While Mead's *And Keep Your Powder Dry* has justifiably won high praise, the actual writing was probably relatively easy for her. First, Mead was writing about her own culture. Second, she was free to conduct research as she saw fit. As a result, Mead faced minimum obstacles when conducting her research and fieldwork.

Other researchers, however, were not as lucky. Those directing the U.S. war effort did not merely need to understand it own citizens; in addition, they also needed to strategically envision the culture of its enemies and probable patterns of response that stemmed from these cultural traditions. These societies, however, could not be investigated using the usual anthropological research techniques of participant observation. Because enemy cultures were obviously closed to analysts who worked on behalf of their foes, alternative techniques of investigation had to be developed. With direct fieldwork impossible, researchers began to broaden the array of evidence that they used when analyzing other societies. Films, literature, and other cultural products were analyzed. Informants (prisoners of war, expatriates, etc.) were interviewed on a "catch as catch can" basis. Any and all sources of information were examined and gleaned of the information they could provide. Due to the fact that researchers could not actively visit the cultures being examined, this type of research eventually came to be known as the "culture at a distance" method. Note how this method parallels the strategies of today's qualitative marketing/consumer researchers who employ naturalistic and humanistic analytic strategies.

The classic example of this method is Ruth Benedict's *The Chrysanthemum and the Sword* (1946). Written and researched during the war, the book provided insights to decision makers. After the war, the public developed a fascination with Japan and the book emerged as a best-seller and as a classic cultural analysis. Essentially, Benedict returned to the methodology that she had developed in *Patterns of Culture* and she sought to distill the unifying principles (or cultural configuration) that underlay Japanese society.

Early in the book, Benedict indicates the importance of understanding the culture of the enemy and how culture influences the behavior of its members:

The Japanese are the most alien enemy the United States had ever fought in an all out struggle. In no other war with a major for had it been necessary to take into account such exceedingly different habits of acting and thinking. . . . We were fighting a nation fully armed and trained which did not belong to the Western cultural tradition. Conventions of war which Western nations had come to accept as facts of human nature obviously did not exist for the Japanese. It made the war in the Pacific more that a mere series of landings on island beaches, more than an unsurpassed problem of logistics. It made it a major problem in the nature of the enemy. We had to understand their behavior in order to cope with it. (1946: 1)

Some of Benedict's observations have become conventional wisdoms regarding Japanese culture. Most of us, for example, are familiar with the notion that the Japanese tend to be "collectively" oriented (while Americans are more "individualistic") and that the Japanese want to "fit into" their society and not stand above or sink below it. We are familiar with Japanese proverbs such as "the nail that sticks up is nailed down" and the metaphorical message that people should fit into their culture and not attract attention to themselves.

Benedict dealt with these phenomena by observing that while people in the United States tended to be concerned with abstract concepts of "right" and "wrong," the Japanese were more preoccupied with other people's opinions of them, and these feelings tended to dictate their behavior. As a result, Westerners had difficulty understanding the Japanese and their behavior, and vice versa. According to Benedict, however, once the cultural configuration was understood, it becomes possible to understand the Japanese and to accurately predict their behavior.

Although *The Chrysanthemum and the Sword* is a classic study of Japan, certain flaws and limitations do exist. For one thing, Benedict tended to rely primarily upon information provided by members of the upper middle classes and her work was not based on a true cross-section of society. As a result, certain patterns of behavior were over (or under) emphasized and the distinctions between specific social classes were blurred or ignored. Benedict, furthermore, depicted Japanese culture at a specific snapshot in time; as a result, the implications of social change were not addressed. And when working "at a distance" Benedict inevitably made numerous errors and oversimplifications.

Nevertheless, Benedict was able to produce a useful cultural analysis under inhibiting conditions. Her work, furthermore, was accurate enough to provide decision makers with a decided edge when forming strategies and tactics.[1] Critiques of Benedict's analysis notwithstanding, she provided invaluable insights and she did so using readily available sources of information and "catch as catch can" interviews. This is exactly the type of information that is often analyzed by today's marketing/consumer researchers who employ naturalistic methods.

During World War II and immediately thereafter, the culture at a distance method thrived. After the war, however, those who had developed the method left government service and returned to their universities, and an emerging generation of scholars began to question the ability of the cultural configuration model to usefully serve in situations where complex cultures are composed of many (and often conflicting) segments. As a result, the use of the method eventually declined.

CULTURE AT A DISTANCE: THE GREAT QUALITATIVE SYNTHESIS

As indicated, during World War II the culture at a distance method embraced the qualitative social sciences and humanities in a profound and robust way. In addition, the method was especially geared toward the use of secondary, "open source" information. Various other forms of information (although, perhaps, compromised) were used in a "catch as catch can" way. The whole agenda of the 1940s culture at a distance research stream was to examine society using diverse types of qualitative information.

The example of the culture at a distance method is particularly relevant to contemporary qualitative marketing/consumer researchers because it provides relevant clues regarding strategies and tactics to use when conducting research and analysis. By understanding the issues involved in the culture at a distance method, we can better understand the situation that currently faces qualitative marketing/consumer researchers.

Here I will briefly examine key aspects of the culture at a distance method and discuss marketing/consumer research with reference to them. It is hoped that, by doing so, the reader will be able to better perceive both available options and the challenges faced by the field. Specifically, five separate issues will be discussed including:

1. Marketing/consumer research often takes place at a distance
2. Marketing/consumer researchers must often rely upon "open source information"
3. Cultures/organizations can often be viewed as systems
4. Systems often exhibit uniform and patterned responses
5. Individual responses can still occur in cultural/organizational systems

Each of these issues will be discussed separately before a general analysis unites them.

Marketing/Consumer Research Often Takes Place at a Distance

For a variety of reasons, qualitative marketing/consumer researchers often gather information at a distance. Thus, researchers often lack a full range of information and they must deduce probable patterns of response using whatever information is available. As a result, many of the techniques that are used center around using judgments to interpret diverse sets of data. Qualitative marketing/consumer research tends to conduct research at a distance and apply intuition to the data that is available.

This situation and strategy parallels the situation faced during World War II when qualitative social scientists were unable to conduct primary research involving their enemies. During that period, elaborate methods of viewing cultures at a distance and extrapolating actionable information from afar were developed. The problems facing the World War II social researchers and those facing today's qualitative marketing/consumer researchers are essentially the same. By embracing and updating the techniques that served so well in World War II, qualitative marketing/consumer researchers can significantly augment their toolkit.

Marketing/Consumer Researchers Must Often Rely Upon "Open Source Information"

In view of the fact that much primary research is either too costly/time consuming and/or unethical/illegal, secondary and open source information (including that available over the Internet) must often be substituted. As with any other uses of secondary information, researchers typically employ existing data in ways for which it was not intended. As a result, the data may need to be massaged and interpreted with intuition and insight.

The established tools emerging within qualitative marketing/consumer research often employ literary analysis (such as the "myth and symbol method" and "deconstructionism"). These techniques offer suggestions regarding how to interpret communications in ways that tease insights and perspectives from documents in order to gain information about the communicator and/or about the audience. Since qualitative marketing/consumer researchers routinely examine and interpret secondary/open source information, they require organized and systematic methods for doing so. Humanistic tools that build upon (and/or offer alternatives to) the culture at a distance method are particularly useful in this regard.

Cultures/Organizations Can Often Be Viewed as Systems

The responses of cultures/organizations are not random. Instead, they are (to a large degree) artifacts of cultural patterns that underlie behavior. If qualitative marketing/consumer researchers can isolate these relevant patterns of response, future behaviors can be more effectively predicted.

Existing secondary/open source data provides examples of how the culture has responded in the past. If these responses can be abstracted into routine responses, the underlying system that impacts decision making can be extrapolated. By viewing cultures as patterned systems, this kind of generalized analysis can best be pursued. Marketing/consumer researchers have long employed this technique. They, however, can enhance their toolkit by embracing the techniques of the culture at a distance method. By incorporating these techniques into their toolkit, qualitative marketing/consumer researchers can more effectively pursue their agendas and mesh their work with a wide array of social perspectives that have important clues to provide when analyzing consumer response.

Systems Often Exhibit Uniform and Patterned Responses

Marketing/consumer researchers are often interested in isolating recurring patterns of behavior that will continue to impact future behaviors. Although much marketing/consumer research is geared toward answering particular ad hoc questions, attention can (and should) also be centered around more general considerations. Understanding the underlying structure of society and how it impacts future behavior is one such general body of valuable information. Marketing/consumer researchers often need to interact with diverse colleagues in order to deal with broad systematic issues (as well as ad hoc concerns). By pursuing this general work, qualitative marketing/consumer researchers will be in a position to provide information and predictions that have long-term value to both theoretic scholarship and to clients from the practitioner world.

Individual Responses Can Still Occur in Cultural/ Organizational Systems

While societies exhibit patterned responses, different segments of society may have their own patterns of response. On some occasions, understanding variations, not merely similarities, is most useful to the research agendas of marketing/consumer researchers and to their practitioner-oriented clients.

When these variations occur, they also tend to exhibit patterns. Thus, both similarities and differences in the behavior of specific groups can be viewed as structured and predictable behavior. These patterns can often be extrapolated by consulting secondary/open source information.

Marketing/consumer researchers need to master both (1) the techniques of recognizing homogeneous patterns and (2) methods of isolating distinctive responses by specific subgroups. By analyzing both sets of information, marketing/consumer researchers will be able to pursue complex and robust analysis. Presented in tabular form, these issues can be presented as shown in Figure 8.1.

The example of the culture at a distance method, therefore, has much to contribute to qualitative marketing/consumer research. Although there are significant differences between the cultural analysts of World War II and today's marketing/consumer researchers, there are also profound similarities. These similarities provide suggestive clues regarding how our profession can best adjust to future needs.

EDWARD T. HALL: EXTENDING THE CONFIGURATION METHOD

As documented above, during the 1940s, anthropologists were given positions of authority in international relations, but after the war their power waned. Margaret Mead reports that the decline of anthropology in international affairs was followed by a rash of international "boners." Novels such as the *The Ugly American* (Lederer and Burdick 1958) can, perhaps, best be seen as a commentary on the low point of international interaction that occurs when qualified social scientists are purged from the decision-making process.

The achievements of qualitative marketing/consumer research demonstrate a recognition of the value of diverse research strategies. Humanistic and social scientific methods are gaining respect within marketing/consumer research and such tactics can help expand our understanding of the consumption process.

Edward T. Hall is a pioneer in applying anthropological perspectives to business. Hall provides a definitive statement of his method in his *The Silent Language* (1959). In that pioneering work, and in his others books, Hall emphasizes that careful attention must be paid to subtle clues, customs, and habits that have been internalized by people as members of their culture. He also underscores that customs can become so ingrained within the characters of people that individuals may be oblivious to them or assume they represent aspects of "human nature" that are shared by all people. Hall's general, theoretical books, which include *The Silent Language, The Hidden Dimension* (1966), and *Beyond Culture* (1976), have been interspaced with and amplified by a number of specific studies regarding

Figure 8.1
Culture at a Distance: Key Considerations

Issue	Characteristic	Discussion
Research at a Distance	Research must often be conducted at a distance. As a result, analysts cannot ask many important questions and they are denied many important sources of data.	It is a fact of life that when conducting qualitative research, analysis typically takes place at a distance. As a result, tools of analysis that anticipate this reality must be employed.
Open Source Information	Open source data must often be the prevailing source of information when analyzing the internal workings of organizations.	Due to the nature of much qualitative research, diverse forms of gathering information are used. Using eclectic methods and diverse forms of information is the trump card of qualitative marketing/consumer research.
Culture/ Organizations as Systems	Cultures/organizations are not random. Instead, they exhibit patterns. If these patterns can be extrapolated, a greater understanding of the culture/organization results.	Since cultures/organizations are not random, they exhibit patterns. These patterns, if identified, are of great value to qualitative marketing/consumer researchers.
Patterned Responses	The behavior of cultures/organizations is often a reflection of underlying patterns. By understanding the underlying pattern, future behavior becomes more predictable.	Patterns within cultures/organizations lead to patterned responses. By understanding the pattern, responses that stem from the pattern become more predictable.
Individual Responses	While cultures/organizations exhibit homogeneous patterns, various subgroups may have their own distinctiveness. These differences are also the result of patterns that can be discerned by competitive intelligence analysis.	Qualitative marketing/consumer researchers often need to isolate subgroups and how their responses are distinct from the larger culture. Doing so can be a valuable contribution to understanding the consumption process.

the customs and lifeways of specific peoples, and he has written widely for the business community.

Hall has long been deeply involved in applied social anthropology, and he worked with and studied under the same anthropologists that had helped the U.S. government during World War II. Long before the publication of *The Silent Language*, therefore, Hall was an established anthropologist who studied communication and miscommunication between members of different cultures. In doing so, Hall worked with many of the analysts who made the World War II era a "golden age" of applied anthropology.

Transcending the theories of some of his teachers while embracing the work of other mentors, Hall emphasizes a basic theory of culture that stems primarily from linguistics. This paradigm begins by suggesting that the human ability to use symbols makes mankind and the actions/artifacts of mankind unique. Embracing this perspective, all human actions are viewed in terms of symbolism, using methods of interpretation that are influenced by linguistics. The theoretical implications of Hall's model of culture are open to debate, but Hall's professionalism and his ability to translate the habits and customs of one culture to another are generally acknowledged. His ability to mesh his work with the needs of the business community is equally important.

Ultimately, however, Hall's paradigm came under attack from within the anthropological community. Part of this attack stemmed primarily from the bureaucratic priorities of the university establishment. According to Hall's vision, linguistics can be viewed as the primary discipline, with social anthropology forming a subordinate discipline beneath it. Although this is not the only way in which these fields can be intertwined, doing so is legitimate and defensible. Over time, however, the power of anthropology grew and it increasingly came to dominate linguistics. According to the organizational scheme that resulted, anthropology emerged as the mother discipline with a number of subdisciplines nested under it. These subordinate disciplines included fields such as cultural anthropology, archaeology, physical anthropology, and linguistics. This arrangement, of course, eliminated linguistics as the primary theoretical bedrock of anthropology.

I personally witnessed a particular example of this transition while a graduate student at the University at Buffalo in the 1960s. Historically, Buffalo had been a university in which linguistics was the dominant discipline, and the anthropology program grew out of and was nested under linguistics. At the time I was at Buffalo, the anthropology department was making the painful break with linguistics and setting itself up as a freestanding department. As a result, I had "a foot in both camps."

I remember a particular graduate seminar, taught by Henry Lee Smith, that dealt with linguistic theory and cultural analysis. It had a theoretical structure that was powerful and compelling. Smith had been involved in the World War II experiments that were discussed above (he devised, among other things, innovative ways of quickly teaching languages) and his accomplishments were impressive and undeniable. And yet, even though he could vanquish all rivals in debate and outdistance them in his accomplishments, the cards were stacked against the basic paradigm that he embraced.

In Smith's seminar, students were introduced to Hall's linguistically based paradigm as a method that could be used when viewing all of mankind's cultural achievements, and yet Smith argued that this model was being sacrificed in order for anthropologists to structure themselves in ways that gave them greater clout within academe. Smith saw the handwriting on the wall; what was happening at Buffalo was a reflection of a general trend, one that could not be reversed. Nonetheless, Smith emphasized the costs of making decisions based on bureaucratic priorities instead of theoretical concerns. Ultimately, positions such as Hall's lost out, in part, due to the evolving structure of academic bureaucracies, not because of any inherent weakness in the method.

Years ago, Hall's work was highly regarded by business thinkers. This influence, however, seems to have cooled. I believe this is true because Hall's approach is no longer fashionable within anthropology; business scholars tend to embrace outside theories that are currently fashionable within the substantive disciplines from which they are borrowed. Once Hall's perspectives lost ground on their own turf, they became less attractive to business researchers. As a result, Hall is seldom discussed today, except in an historical context or when discussing the evolution of business thought.

Hall's work, nonetheless, provides a useful means of avoiding the pitfalls of miscommunication when interacting internationally. In addition, Hall's suggestions and advice provide useful clues on how to apply the culture at a distance method within qualitative marketing/consumer research. Indeed, on at least one level (that of mastering a culture at an ad hoc level), Hall provides techniques that are of profound potential value to qualitative marketing/consumer researchers. It stands as a useful set of techniques ready and willing to serve qualitative marketing/consumer researchers.

Thus, although the configuration model lost ground after World War II, variants of this basic approach survive. The work of Edward T. Hall is one example. Focusing on Hall is doubly useful because he is connected with the configuration method on the one hand and has made significant contribution to business thought on the other. Hopefully, largely ignored models (such as those of Hall) will return to useful service in the near future.

MORE FOCUSED ALTERNATIVES

As argued above, the cultural configuration approach (beginning with
Boas, expanded by Benedict and Mead, and further developed by Hall)
has significant value when marketing/consumer researchers seek to distill similarities and parallels that unite all (or most) members of a particular culture. This kind of analysis has an obvious value, especially in
situations where the researcher seeks to explore mass marketing strategies that respond to the culture as an overarching entity.

Other situations exist, however, in which the focus of interest is not
the similarities shared by all (or most) members of a culture but, instead,
centers upon the differences between various segments of society. Many
cultures (although they may have a collective ethos) are also composed
of subgroups, enclaves, and subcultures that are distinctive and, perhaps,
at odds (to a greater or lesser extent) with the overarching culture or the
national character. Thus, a firm may seek to market a product in different
ways to different segments of society; when employing this strategy,
centering upon parallels between all people is not particularly useful. On
these occasions, marketing/consumer researchers are primarily interested in the distinctiveness of certain market segments. Marketing/con-
sumer research has largely centered on these issues of difference.

These approaches can largely be identified with the existential philosophy that emerged in France after World War II. Although existentialism
and its offshoot is a complicated and multifaceted phenomena, in the
final analysis it tends to focus upon the individual/circumscribed sub-
group (or the distinctive enclave), not the collective society or the homogeneous national character. Existentialism also focuses upon the fact
that society often assigns identities and roles to people that are arbitrary
and, perhaps, inappropriate or exploitative. These are issues that center
around the plight of the individual and/or groups that are distinctive
from the national culture; and the beliefs and emotional lives of specific
groups may not reflect the overarching patterns of the society (if, indeed,
a homogeneous core of behavior and belief actually exists at all).

Such individualistic orientations have value to those who are concerned with target marketing because they emphasize the uniqueness of
specific groups. Thus, these techniques have been explored by researchers such as Barbara Stern, Elizabeth Hirschman, and Morris Holbrook.
Because these methods will be specifically dealt with in later chapters,
they will not be considered at length here.

CONCLUSION

The methods of the social sciences and the humanities offer a wide
range of tools that can usefully deal with diverse issues that face mar-

keting/consumer researchers. These methods, furthermore, do not merely deal with ad hoc goals that people harbor; they delve deeper into the ingrained patterns of behavior, goals, and beliefs that are embraced by people as members of their culture.

This chapter has provided an introduction to the "culture at a distance" method and how it has been refined by later researchers, such as Edward T. Hall, in ways that are relevant to qualitative marketing/consumer researchers. These pioneers innovated ways to extrapolate the essence of a culture using various artifacts as surrogate evidence, even when formal fieldwork could not be conducted. The goal of this research was to understand the national character of a people—the recurring and prevailing social structures and belief patterns that characterize a culture.

Although interest in this kind of analysis has declined, the recent interest in marketing ethnography potentially opens the door for a rebirth of interest in such research strategies. The method can also be used to extrapolate how the character of specific groups differ from the norm of the national culture and how these differences can impact behavior, including consumer response. These methods are capable of providing profoundly important insights to marketing/consumer research; updated and adjusted to the realities of the 21st century, they should be returned to useful service.

NOTE

1. Although published as a popular book in 1946, Benedict conducted her research during the war and provided advice to decision makers.

REFERENCES

Benedict, Ruth. (1934a). "Anthropology and the Abnormal." *Journal of General Psychology* 10: 59–79.
Benedict, Ruth. (1934b). *Patterns of Culture*. Reprint, Boston: Houghton Mifflin, 1959.
Benedict, Ruth. (1946). *The Chrysanthemum and the Sword*. Boston: Houghlin Mifflin.
Boas, Franz. (1940). *Race, Language and Culture*. New York: Free Press.
Hall, Edward T. (1959). *The Silent Language*. Garden City, NY: Doubleday.
Hall, Edward T. (1966). *The Hidden Dimension*. Garden City, NY: Doubleday.
Hall, Edward T. (1976). *Beyond Culture*. Garden City, NY: Anchor Press.
Lederer, William J. and Burdick, Eugene. (1958). *The Ugly American*. New York: Norton.
Marks, Barry. (1963). "A Concept of Myth in Virgin Land." *American Quarterly* 15: 15–17.
Marx, Leo. (1964). *The Machine in the Garden*. New York: Oxford University Press.
Mead, Margaret. (1935). *Sex and Temperament in Three Primitive Societies*. New York: Morrow.

Mead, Margaret. (1942). *And Keep Your Powder Dry: A New Expanded Edition of the Classic Work of the American Character.* Reprint, New York: Morrow, 1965.

Sapir, Edward. (1949). *Selected Writings in Language, Culture and Personality,* ed. David G. Mandelbaum. Berkeley: University of California Press.

Slotkin, Richard. (1986). "Myth and the Production of History." In *Ideology and Classic American Literature,* ed. Sacvan Bercovitsch and Myra Jehlen. New York: Cambridge University Press, pp. 70–90.

Smith, Henry Nash. (1950). *Virgin Land: The American Land As Myth and Symbol.* Cambridge, MA: Harvard University Press.

Smith, Henry Nash. (1957). "Can American Studies Develop a Method?" *American Quarterly* 9: 197–208.

Trachtenberg, Alan. (1977). "Myth, History, and American Literature in *Virgin Land.*" *Prospects* 3: 127–29.

Walle, Alf H. (1998). "Evolving Structures and Consumer Response: Dynamics Transformations of *The Fugitive* and *Mission Impossible.*" *Management Decision* 30(3): 185–96.

Walle, Alf H. (2000). *The Cowboy Hero and Its Audience: Popular Culture as Market Derived Art.* Bowling Green, OH: The Popular Press.

CHAPTER 9

Social Structures and the Consumption of Art: The Myth and Symbol Method

The foregoing chapters have focused on how the social structural (or *volksgeist*) model underlies important paradigms of the social sciences. In this chapter, the use of these models within the humanistic tradition is discussed. Specifically, the myth and symbol method of humanistic analysis is spotlighted. My goal is to both demonstrate the strengths of the myth and symbol method and to show how it employs structural principles to explain why many members of a particular culture tend to consume artistic products in similar or parallel manners.

In order to accomplish this task, this chapter analyzes how large segments of the American public responded to the cowboy story in parallel ways from the 1820s until about 1970 as a result of impacts connected with our society's evolution. Before doing so, it is useful to discuss the intellectual and cultural milieu of literary criticism as it evolved in the 20th century.

FORMAL VS. SOCIAL CRITICISM

Since World War II, literary criticism and cultural analysis has seen the rise of a series of rival models, each of which has dominated in its own time and place. A particularly powerful methodology that held the stage from the late 1930s until the early 1960s was the New Criticism. During the early part of the 20th century (before the vogue of the New Criticism), a wide array of intellectuals (in and out of the university establishment) wrote literary analyses that are best described as social criticism. Many of these scholars sought to deal with issues of culture and social structure via an analysis of literary art. All too often, however, specific critics had partisan axes to grind; as a result, self-serving rhetoric was often disguised as objective research.

As a result of an outpouring of biased and partisan rhetoric that masqueraded as objective criticism, many professional literary scholars became dismayed by what they believed was shallow, unrigorous propaganda clothed in the grab of respectable scholarship. As is often the case, "one action creates an equal and opposite reaction." In this case, the "action" was social criticism that focused on a subjective analysis of the culture and its literature, while the "reaction" was a rising vogue of formal analysis that was pursued in nonsubjective ways, coupled with a general indifference to the actual content (plotline, characterizations, etc.) of the sample of literature that was analyzed. The goal increasingly became focusing clearly upon the essence of fine writing in a rational and "impartial" manner.

First appearing in the late 1930s, this movement ultimately came to be known as the New Criticism, a name suggested in a 1941 essay written by John Crowe Ransom, one of the movement's leaders. The New Criticism emphasized the close and careful analysis of literary texts and focused on how specific examples of literary art were written and structured. As a result of this emphasis, the New Criticism tended to downplay the social and/or biographical context of literary art. Leaders of the New Criticism include Cleanth Brooks, Kenneth Burke, John Crowe Ransom, Allen Tate, and Robert Penn Warren. Immediately after World War II, the New Criticism gained a strangehold over university-based literary criticism; this situation continued until approximately 1960.

The classic modus operandi of the New Criticism is to focus entirely upon the form of literary art and to disregard both the context and the content (the primary phenomena of interest to social critics). The goal of this kind of analysis is to distill and analyze the essence of excellent and effective writing. The New Critics were very influential, and properly so; because they focused attention upon the writer's craft, and since they resisted the temptation to let other, extraneous phenomena distract them from their mission, the New Critics provided significant insights regarding the nature of high-quality writing.

Nonetheless, by concentrating purely on literary methods, tactics, and strategies, the New Critics inevitably overlooked other important aspects of literary art and popular culture. As indicated above, the New Critics ignored or underplayed the actual cultural content of literature and popular culture in order to concentrate upon the essence of the writer's craft. Although doing so is a legitimate strategic choice in many situations, it is also a trade-off in which one series of questions is pursued by turning a blind eye to other considerations which are, thereby, strategically ignored. As a result of their intellectual choices, the New Critics strategically ignored the impact of the culture and the social structure upon literature and its consumption.

Some observers have suggested that the dominance of the New Criticism in the early 1950s may also be a response to the threat of ultra-conservative forces of the era, such as Joe McCarthy. Many of the social critics who preceded the New Criticism embraced leftist political ideas; as a result, the university-based literary critics of the McCarthy era often felt an urge to strategically distance themselves from that tradition. In addition, the themes and plotlines of much fine literature were anti-establishment; during the anti-communist witch-hunt of the 1950s, many critics sought to insulate themselves from these threats. The research agendas of the New Criticism provided a strategy and a methodology for doing so; by concentrating on the principles of excellent writing and ignoring content, literary critics were able to pursue their career in a way that sidestepped political controversy. Pursuing critical analysis in ways that investigated the form of literature in isolation and did not actively consider its content in any significant and sustained manner was, therefore, a safe professional strategy, and it was facilitated by the New Criticism.

By the late 1950s and early 1960s, however, the pendulum had begun to swing back, and content-oriented criticism (which centered upon the meaning of literature, its social content, and its place within a specific social/economic milieu) returned to respectability and dominance. The popularity of this type of social criticism was further encouraged by the counterculture of the later 1960s and the ethic of social activism that went hand in hand with it. During this era, much exciting, content-oriented social criticism was written and the New Criticism became somewhat unfashionable. Although the formal New Critics had lost ground when social/content-oriented criticism gained the upper hand in the 1960s, they and their formal leanings did not die and, ultimately, these scholars (and their intellectual tradition) began to search for a new way to reestablish themselves. Their means of doing so lay in embracing aspects of the poststructural movement, as articulated by French philosopher and critic Jacques Derrida. As a result of linking themselves with poststructuralism and deconstructionism, the formal critics were able to reestablish themselves within the critical world.

This, in a nutshell, is a social history of literary criticism from the late 1930s until the present. After a period of flowering early in the 20th century, social criticism became stigmatized both methodologically and politically. Ultimately, however, it returned to favor in the 1960s. Today, however, it has become somewhat unfashionable due to the inroads made by poststructural models and an interest in the phenomena that these non-structural models are designed to examine. Nonetheless, social criticism continues to be a legitimate (although slightly unfashionable) method of literary analysis; as such, it has a legitimate role to play in marketing/consumer research that embraces the techniques of humanistic analysis. Social criticism is especially useful in situations where the researcher is interested in mass marketing that is designed to influence large segments of a particular society in parallel ways. It is less valuable in situations involving target marketing that seek to resonate from differences in the patterns of consumption that characterize specific groups.

LESLIE FIEDLER: A REPRESENTATIVE SOCIAL CRITIC

Humanists, such as literary critics, American studies researchers, and popular culture scholars, have long been concerned with the public's response to artistic and cultural products. Why a particular plotline proves to be popular (marketable) at a specific point in time is of obvious interest to these humanistic scholars, as well as to marketing/consumer researchers. Examining changes in the popularity of specific plotlines and/or heroic types, furthermore, has long constituted an important analytic strategy. The basic technique of this approach can be traced back to the critical methods of the ancient world. Aristotle, for example, based his theories of literature upon empirical evidence (i.e., literature with a track record of being either effective or ineffective). As a result, Aristotle was very concerned with what was popular in the "marketplace" and he interpreted literature accordingly. Due to this emphasis upon what, empirically, had been effective or ineffective, Aristotle (in his *Poetics*) clearly anticipates the techniques of later literary critics who concern themselves with why certain examples of literature are accepted by the public while others are overlooked or rejected. Hardly a historic footnote, Aristotle continues to be highly regarded and his work has greatly influenced 20th-century American literary critics such as Irving Babbitt, T. S. Eliot, and W. H. Auden. Thus, a market-related critical method existed thousands of years before the establishment of marketing and consumer research as distinct disciplines.

As we have seen, however, the focus of critical analysis immediately after World War II concentrated primarily upon the techniques of excellent writing, not the social or cultural context of literature. In the 1960s, however, culturally oriented criticism returned to favor. Although a broad and multifaceted research stream evolved, I will explore this trend with reference to a particularly important critic, Leslie Fiedler. Due to his long intellectual evolution and his far-ranging impact, Fiedler is a perfect mirror of this trend in cultural analysis and popular culture scholarship.[1]

The foundation of Fiedler's intellectual paradigm was originally nested around a reworking of what is best described as "myth criticism": the premise that certain myths and symbols that appear and reappear in a canon of literature can be usefully analyzed by the critic in order to discern social patterns. Employing this approach, Fiedler reads American literature in order to abstract certain mythic themes that, he suggests, dominate the literary heritage of our culture; by doing so, he merges social and literary criticism with popular culture scholarship and American studies.

Fiedler has likened this technique to the anthropological method, and he has even described his work as a sort of intuitive anthropological analysis.[2] Having isolated the mythic content of a canon of literature, Fiedler goes on to interpret society and literature according to his anthropologically inspired model. Most representative of this phase of his career are his seminal *Love and Death in the American Novel* (1960) and the shorter, but more focused, *Waiting for the End* (1964) and *The Return of the Vanishing American* (1968).

By the 1960s, when Fiedler hit his stride and became an internationally recognized critic, the impact of television was profoundly influencing American culture, art, and public response. Fiedler responded by increasingly focusing upon popular culture, not the highbrow literature that catered to the elite. Particularly revealing in this regard in his *What Was Literature? Class Culture and Mass Society* (1982). The goal of that monograph is to analyze why specific works of art possess an ability to please or satisfy an audience. Building upon and refining his mythic techniques and relating them to prevailing social structures, Fiedler suggested that certain cultural products respond to unconscious desires/needs that are inculcated by the culture. Although these feelings may be unarticulated, they nonetheless profoundly influence its members. Fiedler goes on to suggest that a particular literary work may possess a potential for popularity, even if it is simultaneously riddled with profound "flaws" that repel New Critics, who concentrate primarily upon the craft of writing, not its functioning within the social or cultural milieu.

In order to demonstrate these thematic perspectives, the second section of *What Was Literature* consists of a number of case studies involving profoundly influential works of literature which, if evaluated according to standard critical criteria, emerge as profoundly flawed. Nonetheless, Fiedler demonstrates their value and significance as well as the legitimacy of seriously studying them. Thus, *What Was Literature?* can be read as a tour de force of popular culture scholarship that attempts to unravel the underlying structures of society through an analysis of its art and how people respond to specific examples of it.

Fiedler, without mentioning the term, possesses an obvious interest in "consumer behavior" and he affirms that analyzing consumer response, not merely embracing the evaluative criteria of "fine writing" (as enumerated by the New Critics) to specific works of literature, is a crucial aspect of the critic's obligations. Furthermore, by transcending elite and "ivory tower" criteria of formal evaluation, Fiedler perfectly merges lit-

erary criticism with related disciplines such as popular culture scholarship and American studies. And because popular culture scholars are
concerned with the culture's impact upon consumption, Fiedler's interests and strategies parallel marketing/consumer research.

By embracing the tools of social criticism as represented by Fiedler,
marketing/consumer researchers can better come to grips with the cultural triggers underlying consumption. By embracing this critical
tradition, marketing/consumer researchers gain a finely developed
method of analysis that is well-equipped to examine consumption patterns related to a particular type of product (literary art/popular culture)
and to link this behavior to the culture and the social structure.

FROM FIEDLER TO MARKETING/CONSUMER
RESEARCH

As indicated above, the style of critical analysis represented by Leslie
Fiedler demonstrates how the work of socially focused literary criticism
and marketing/consumer research can be closely intertwined. Fiedler
and his colleagues, however, wrote without an awareness of the theories
and methods of marketing/consumer research. As a result, social criticism has not made the tight connections between the two fields, just as
marketing/consumer researchers (working within another intellectual
tradition) have not fully employed critical theory and practice.

Today, however, these connections are being made by various mar-
keting/consumer researchers who both study the consumption of art/
literature and embrace various critical techniques when doing so. A classic demonstration of how marketing/consumer research can be merged
with critical analysis is Holbrook and Grayson's "The Semiology of Cinematic Consumption: Symbolic Consumer Behavior in *Out of Africa*"
(1986). While most marketing/consumer researchers study popular culture (such as film and TV) in order to gain insights about the nature of
consumption, Holbrook and Grayson observe: "The present approach
differs from these [previous] efforts in focusing not on the issue of what
artworks tell us about consumer behavior or how art is consumed, but
on the question of what consumption can tell us about works of art"
(375).

Having completed their analysis, Holbrook and Grayson reaffirm that
it is possible and legitimate to use consumer research to understand popular culture as well as exploring consumer response through an analysis
of popular culture. While it is possible to accomplish either goal, the
decision on which tact to take depends on the goals of the specific research project. As a result, it becomes difficult to state where either criticism or marketing/consumer research begins or ends; they may be too
intertwined to be easily unraveled.

More recently, I (Walle 1996), writing in the popular culture literature, drew a parallel between consumer research and popular culture scholarship. I observed:

The discipline of popular culture has not significantly embraced the field of marketing and consumer research. . . . Because the creation of popular art is largely a market related activity, cross-disciplinary research would benefit both disciplines . . . the fields of marketing/consumer behavior and popular culture are converging. These disciplines came from different roots, but increasingly they focus on the same phenomena. (Walle 1996: 194–95)

My work, as Holbrook's and Grayson's, points to profound parallels between marketing/consumer research and humanistic research; it also affirms that both can benefit from working in tandem with each other.

For many years, both cultural critics and humanistic marketing/consumer researchers have been using ad hoc and independently invented models for analyzing audience and consumer response. As a result, neither has fully benefitted from what the other had to offer. The techniques of social criticism, however, provide an array of useful techniques and orientations from the humanities that can be merged with marketing/consumer research in powerful analytic ways. By creating linkages between these two intellectual traditions, marketing/consumer researchers will be able to integrate the tools of social criticism into their work.

As demonstrated by Holbrook and Grayson (1986) and myself (Walle 1996), marketing/consumer researchers recognize that the tools and techniques of social criticism have a significant potential of value to those who analyze the consumption process. By embracing relevant aspects of social criticism, these two disciplines can be usefully merged in mutually beneficial ways.

THE CASE FOR STRUCTURAL ANALYSIS

In many circumstances, scholars (both in the humanities and in marketing/consumer research) are concerned with investigating how people, as members of their specific culture or society, respond in parallel or analogous ways to the phenomena they face. Even the most casual analysis of human behavior will demonstrate that this type of response often occurs. In the last chapter, for example, we saw how the cultural configuration anthropologists made use of this perspective. Research agendas that are based on the overarching influence of culture have a long and illustrious history (even if they need to be employed with caution).

Thus, social analysis is a valuable activity and it is intellectually respectable. This observation does not deny the importance of other paradigms (such as formal analysis that focuses upon the processes of the writer's craft); I am merely observing that in many situations of interest to marketing/consumer researchers, some kind of social structural analysis best fulfills the needs of the research agenda.

A key means of pursuing collective cultural/social analysis is to consider a set of shared beliefs, behavior patterns, tastes, and preferences. Having identified patterns that exist within the culture or society, it becomes possible to analyze these similarities in systematic, social structural ways. By doing so, the scholar can gain a better understanding of the culture and the social milieu in which consumption takes place. Changes over time, furthermore, can provide clues regarding cultural evolution and how changes in the culture may alter consumption patterns.

Although members of a larger culture may simultaneously be part of one or more smaller circumscribed groups, they are also a part of the larger society/culture and, on many occasions, they respond as such. I, for example, acknowledge that a particular person may simultaneously be a part of the larger society and a member of a circumscribed group(s). Much of my research, for example, stems from the discipline of folklore (which concentrates upon the distinctiveness of various cultural and social enclaves). Folklorists, of course, clearly recognize that a specific person may simultaneously be a part of a "folk culture" and the mainstream society.

The key issue being advanced here is that in many circumstances, people react and behave as members of a larger social entity, even though they may also be members of smaller circumscribed groups and/or act as individuals. By studying their behavior, it becomes possible to explore responses that stem from the culture at large. Many situations exist in both literary analysis and in marketing/consumer research, where an analysis of the impact of the larger culture is useful and productive. Where this is true, collective analysis aimed at understanding the underlying social structure and its impact upon behavior is the most appropriate analytic tool.

The collective/social structural paradigm is not universally appropriate for all analytic analysis; this is true in both criticism and marketing/consumer research. Nonetheless, social structural analysis has a vital role to play, and the toolkit of marketing/consumer research is incomplete without it.

THE MYTH AND SYMBOL METHOD

The myth and symbol method is a specific social structural model that has proved to be very useful within literary criticism, American studies, and popular culture scholarship. It will be reviewed here as a useful method that embraces the essential techniques used by Fiedler and the social critics. It will also be argued that this method is capable of serving the needs of marketing/consumer researchers.

Humanists often seek to understand the nature of North American civilization in general. In doing so, they typically investigate this phenomena through an examination of its artistic products and the public's response to them. As with other areas of scholarship, the techniques used and the paradigms embraced by the myth and symbol method have been impacted by broad trends within the intellectual community. These scholarly traditions provide a focused and well-established research stream that explores society, culture, and behavior patterns that stem from both.

The myth and symbol method is a classic means of pursuing this type of research. The approach is based on the belief that an overarching entity (usually envisioned as "national character") exists and that it predisposes many, if not most, people in a society to respond in roughly parallel ways to certain examples of art, literature, and popular culture. This methodology clearly parallels Herder/Hegel's concept of the *volksgeist*; the analyst assumes that a culture/social structure exists, asserts that this culture/social structure creates a specific national character, and affirms that the response to art is an artifact of the social/cultural milieu. Thus, the national character creates a propensity to respond to specific works of art because of the themes of "effective" art resonate from the ethos of the culture/social structure. By understanding the culture, it becomes possible to predict what works of art will be embraced by its members and, vice versa, by extrapolating the patterns that exist in art, the culture can be better understood.

A favorite technique of the myth and symbol method is to suggest that American literature and popular culture embody distinctively American themes (myths and symbols) and that a large number of Americans respond to these artifacts in almost identical ways. Those seeking an overview of the myth and symbol method are referred to Sklar (1975), Slotkin (1986), and Smith (1957).

Two classic examples of the myth and symbol school that focus on the American frontier experience are Henry Nash Smith's *Virgin Land* (1960) and Leo Marx's *The Machine in the Garden* (1964). Since Smith's work can be easily connected with later and more sophisticated versions of the myth and symbol school (i.e., the work of Richard Slotkin 1973, 1985, 1992), the present analysis focuses upon him. As the title suggests, *Virgin Land* is primarily concerned with the image of the frontier and its impact upon American self-identity. Smith forcefully argues that the image of the 19th-century West has profoundly impacted American culture and the worldview that Americans embraced.

Essentially, Smith argued that the image of the West provides a number of myths and symbols that have been worked and reworked for generations. By examining these symbols (in artifacts such as literature), Smith argues that the essence of American society can be better understood. Thus, literature is a secondary variable that is impacted and influenced by a primary variable consisting of American national character. By examining the secondary variable, the primary variable (that is reflected therein) can be usefully analyzed.

Being fundamentally concerned with his substantive subject, not with methodological hair-splitting, Smith has been attacked on the grounds that he lacked a systematic theory and a coherent methodology. Other scholars, however, have come to Smith's defense and extrapolated the methodology which is implicit in his work (Marks 1963; Trachtenberg 1977).

For a number of reasons, the myth and symbol method, like other methods of social criticism, has fallen from fashion in recent years. This fate, however, does not indicate a fatal flaw in the method; it is merely an artifact of changing research tastes. As mentioned above, many contemporary scholars are concerned with the unique vision, worldview, and preferences of individuals or specific groups. These scholars tend to concentrate upon distinctive subgroups (as defined by race, sex, social class, and sexual orientation) and how the members of these groups view the world in their own unique way. Given these research interests, the myth and symbol method is not the most fruitful methodology for these scholars to employ. As a result, these scholars favor more individualist models, such as poststructuralism and deconstructionism. The decision not to use the myth and symbol method in such circumstances, however, is basically strategic in nature.

COLLECTIVE ANALYSIS AND THE COWBOY STORY

As indicated above, the myth and symbol method examines literature, film, and popular culture in order to document and analyze culture and society. This discussion will continue by demonstrating the value of this approach to a specific investigation: the case study of the evolution of the American cowboy story from the 1820s until approximately 1970.

There is a long tradition of analyzing the cowboy story within the humanities and critical disciplines. Various mainstream critics have included popular Western or cowboy stories[3] within the sample of works they analyze; by doing so, critics gain a greater flexibility than if they had concentrated solely upon so-called "serious literature." Other critics have specialized in analyzing the cowboy story as a specific genre. This brief analysis will examine the cowboy story as a distinct genre from the time of James Fenimore Cooper to approximately 1970 and use it as a test case that demonstrates the value of the social structural/myth and symbol method to marketing/consumer research. The reason for the cut-off date is purely practical; using a 150-year time frame, I am able to show how social trends impacted the propensity to consume certain plot-lines within a genre of popular literature. If the analysis were continued to the present, furthermore, the argument would have become overly complex because in recent years the cowboy story has become inter-twined with issues involving diverse themes, including the plight of the American Indian, feminism, and ecology. As a result, the clean and crisp argument would have become blurred and nothing would be gained in the process.

While a number of general, mainstream critics examine the Western along with other genres of literature, film, and popular culture, other critics focus primarily upon the Western or cowboy story (see, for example, French 1973; Kites 1969; McDonald 1987; Parks 1982; Wright 1975). Over the years, a vast critical tradition regarding the Western has developed. Typically, the Western is investigated and various aspects of American culture are explored either by a close analysis of a few, care-fully chosen, examples or via a broad investigation of a large canon of work that examines the Western alongside other genres. This scholarly tradition often attempts to provide generalized theories about cultural trends, belief structures, and/or the national character of the United States.

Since the amount of critical materials on the Western is vast, even a superficial review of this scholarly tradition is impossible. It becomes necessary, therefore, to cull the discussion down to one representative and particularly illustrious critic, Richard Slotkin (whose work also served as an example of the contemporary application of the myth and symbol method). Having pointed to Slotkin's excellent work as a rep-resentative touchstone, the specific model to be employed will be pre-sented.

Like many other critics and cultural observers who examine the cow-boy story, Richard Slotkin is a native of the East, and for him the West is primarily a symbolic place, not a home. Over the last 25 years, Slotkin has written an impressive multivolume review of Western American lit-erature and popular culture (which he calls "mythology"). Slotkin's strat-egies and terminology make it rather easy to connect the myth and symbol method (which his work represents) with tactics that have long existed within consumer research. Noted marketing theorist Sidney Levy (1981), for example, explicitly employs concepts associated with mythol-ogy in order to make more effective use of qualitative consumer research. In that article, Levy is primarily interested in using the techniques of mythology in order to understand micro social units, such as the family. In this regard he observes:

The broad brush strokes indicated above may encourage further studies on how families develop the particular little myths [which impact consumer behavior]: how consumer myths change over time; how facts of behavior are modified in the telling; what the facts or the modified tellings are being used to say. . . . (Levy 1981: 60)

Consequently, although Levy is concerned with the micro/family sphere while Slotkin and the research stream that he represents focus upon societal wide issues and trends, the essential techniques and goals are somewhat parallel: studying a popular "mythology" in order to understand broader belief structures and/or behavior patterns. Thus, a clear precedent[4] for employing techniques in ways analogous to Slotkin's use of the myth and symbol method has long existed within marketing/ consumer research.

To a large extent, Slotkin's vision of the Western is a reaction against that of Henry Nash Smith, whose *Virgin Land: The American West as Myth and Symbol* (1950) was long acknowledged as the definitive treatment of the subject. As discussed above, Smith forcefully argues that the image of the 19th-century West profoundly impacted American culture and the worldview that Americans embraced. Smith went on to argue that much of this symbolism was positive: a garden of Eden; heroic, larger-than-life heroes; the adventure of empire building; bountiful opportunities; and so on. An eloquent writer, Smith's largely upbeat treatment of his subject (and the implications it had for interpreting American national character) was convincing to a generation of critics.

The 1960s and the era of social activism and protest that coincided with it, however, gave rise to a new generation of scholars who possessed a different vantage point. Slotkin represents this later tradition and, over the years, has authored a multivolume tour de force on the subject and become a major spokesman for the position that he represents. In the early 1970s, Slotkin's doctoral dissertation was reworked and published under the title *Regeneration Through Violence: The Mythology of the American Frontier, 1600–1800* (1973). Slotkin systematically undercut Nash's (then-conventional) views; he agreed with Nash that the key to American history and national character lay in the West. Slotkin, however, focused upon traits such as violence and racism, and the negative potential of the Western movement. Slotkin, incidentally, was overtly influenced by phenomena such as the Vietnam War and a string of abuses that he suggested our country had committed, both domestically and internationally, over the years.

The second volume in the series, *The Fatal Environment: The Myth of the Frontier in the Age of Industrialization, 1800–1900* (1985), focuses upon the ruthless aspects of the settling of the West and how both the native peoples and immigrants who settled there were negatively impacted by this process. As in *Regeneration Through Violence, The Fatal Environment* transcends the more positive perspectives of earlier scholars (such as Nash) and concentrates upon the negative alter ego of the West. The last volume of the trilogy, *Gunfighter Nation: The Myth of the Frontier in Twentieth-Century America* (1992), draws parallels between the classic "cowboy and Indian" movies and American foreign policy after World War II.

In *Gunfighter Nation*, Slotkin focuses upon the image of the Western gunfighter who has the power to dispense justice in a hostile world, and he suggests that it is a mythic archetype that became transformed into an ideology that justified America's post–World War II role as "watchdog to the world." In accordance with the myth and symbol method, Slotkin interprets American culture through a content analysis of a particular genre of literature.

Slotkin is an excellent writer, and the general strategies that he embraces are representative of the myth and symbol method. At the beginning of *Regeneration Through Violence*, for example, Slotkin observes: "The mythology of a nation is an intelligible mask . . . of national character" (1973: 3). Having made this statement, he studies this "mythology" of the West and the frontier in order to understand American culture. Thus, Slotkin finds mythology to be a secondary variable that is impacted by national character, the primary variable. By examining and exploring this secondary variable, therefore, key aspects of the primary variable (the subject of interest to the scholar) can be better understood.

By looking at this technique, so well demonstrated by Slotkin's work, it becomes possible to quickly grasp the methodology to be used in this chapter:

1. It seeks a greater knowledge of the American national character and/or the belief structure typically held by Americans.

2. It is assumed that the propensity to consume examples of popular culture that embrace specific myths and symbols is, to some degree, influenced by the prevailing belief structure and national character.

3. Since it is possible to examine the popular culture of earlier generations and how the public of those eras responded to it, popular culture scholars and consumer researchers can chart how changes in national character and/or belief structures have impacted changes in the consumption of certain types of popular culture.

A discussion of the modus operandi of the technique lays the methodological foundation that is embraced in this analysis. In order to simplify the analysis that follows, key aspects of the argument to be presented can be outlined as:[5]

1. The personality of the cowboy hero has typically been held constant by writers.
2. The fate of the hero has emerged as a variable.
3. As the belief structures of large segments of the American population hae shifted, the popularity of specific plot formulas have evolved accordingly.
4. By studying these variations though time and by considering them with reference to the evolving culture and worldview of society, popular culture scholars or consumer researchers can perceive how consumer demands for certain kinds of literary products evolve in concert with transformations in the national character and worldview.

The theory that the personality of the hero remains constant while the fate of the hero changes in tandem, which changes in society, is a distinctive theme of my analysis. These tendencies can be usefully analyzed by merging the myth and symbol method with marketing/consumer research. Using this overview as a touchstone, I will analyze a number of noted Western American authors/novels and an array of important cowboy movies.[6]

JAMES FENIMORE COOPER: THE INTRODUCTION STAGE

James Fenimore Cooper, the first major American novelist, created an immortal heroic figure who possesses an uncompromising morality but is profoundly vulnerable to the amoral forces of society. In a nutshell, Cooper's frontier fiction concentrated upon the plight of strong-willed and moral individuals who live in a collective and immoral world. Cooper believed that the noble and self-reliant hero would ultimately be displaced by a society that he depicted as amoral at best. Such sentiments can be seen as a partial reworking in America of Jean-Jacques Rousseau's concept of the noble savage as merged with Cooper's vision of morality and the perspectives of social change that were influential in Cooper's time.

Cooper's most profound achievement was to create a distinctive frontier protagonist who was ultimately recast as the cowboy hero (Walle 1974). Cooper, like later writers, nested the fate of the hero into what can be viewed as the flow of history. So doing, the "Leatherstocking Tales" (Cooper's five-volume frontier saga featuring Natty Bumppo, the frontiersman hero) and especially *The Pioneers* and *The Prairie* (two volumes in the series), emerge as a symbolic/mythic epic that caught the imagination of Cooper's contemporaries. The consuming public accepted the flow of Cooper's plotlines and his work emerged as the popular literature of his era.

In *The Pioneers*, Natty Bumppo, the noble hero, has long helped the residents of Templeton (presented as a symbolic microcosm of the emerging sedentary culture) to establish themselves in the wilds of up-state New York. Bumppo represents the frontier personality who has the misfortune of being displaced by the coming of civilization. Throughout *The Pioneers*, Natty evaluates people, statuses, rights, and privileges using his own standards; as a result of his personal style, he must eventually go West, where society has not entrenched itself and where he can act according to his beliefs. The climax of *The Pioneers* is a case in point: Judge Temple is the leader of the society that is entrenching itself in upstate New York. He is the owner of the land, the maker of the laws, and the self-styled judge of other people. Natty, using frontier logic, kills a deer in violation of Judge Temple's arbitrary laws and, in the eyes of the established legal system, he becomes an outlaw. As a last straw, Natty disrupts the decorum of established law and is banished to the wilds, where his character is not at odds with the prevailing regime. He and his dog are last seen retreating into the untamed forest, where society has not yet entrenched itself. This plotline connects the idea of the noble savage with views of society that were held by the social elite of early-19th-century America.

Many noted critics view Cooper as a true visionary. In this regard, Francis Parkman, the acclaimed historian of the American West and author of the ever popular *The Oregon Trail*, observes:

Of all American writers, Cooper is the most original, the most throughly national; His genius . . . [sprang] from the soil where God planted it, and rose to a vigorous growth . . . [although Cooper had faults as a writer.] A rough diamond, and he is one of the roughest, is worth more than a jewel of paste, though its facets may not shine so clearly. (1852: 147)

Here, in line with the needs and priorities of marketing/consumer research, this orientation will be followed. Cooper's fiction resonates from the spirit of the times and it symbolically depicts the prevailing worldview held by the elites of early-19th-century America. The consuming public embraced Cooper's work because it symbolically portrayed (even as it helped to define) their belief structure.

In *The Prairie* (sequel to *The Pioneers*, where Natty Bumppo had earlier been banished to the wilds), he finds a permanent home in "the Great American Desert," where organized society cannot usurp him. In accordance with the worldview of the times, Cooper depicted the prairie as a desert where sedentary, "civilized" life cannot establish itself. Cooper, accepting the conventional wisdoms of his times, falsely depicted the Midwest as an uninhabitable desert which, in reality, was not the case (Flaganan 1941). Finding a haven in the barren prairie, Cooper's strong-willed and highly moral Bumppo is able to live out his days without being dispossessed by the encroachment of an effete and amoral society.

Cooper's literary innovation, represented by the combined plotlines of *The Pioneers* and *The Prairie*, therefore, has three basic components:

1. The hero is a moral person whose very morality makes him the antithesis of established culture. He is somewhat (but not totally) related to the concept of the noble savage.
2. Due to conflict between the individualist hero and a culture based on conformity and compromise, society rejects the noble hero.
3. The hero retreats to where society cannot usurp him.

This plotline flows in accordance with the prevailing worldview held by the elites of Cooper's era.

Beyond doubt, Cooper's work well satisfied his market. Both *The Pioneers* and *The Prairie* were best-selling novels of their day and they established Cooper's reputation as a major literary talent and taste maker. Years later, primarily because of public demand coupled with Cooper's financial needs, he wrote three additional Natty Bumppo novels that deal with his hero's younger years. As with the sequels of many authors, however, these latter works are not of the same quality as the originals, and I do not feel that they advance Cooper's vision as much as the earlier volumes.[7]

As is often the case when new, innovative products are first being marketed, Cooper's original customers (his readers) were educated, affluent, and of relatively high social class; they emerge as "innovators" according to the diffusion of innovations model. And, as is also typical of the adoption curve, as time went on, the product was embraced by other groups ranging from "early adopters" to the "late majority." A product variant aimed at the late majority is the so-called "dime novels" of the late 19th century. These cheap, uninspired versions of Cooper's original plotline were marketed to poor, uneducated people of low social class. A good discussion of this phenomena is Daryl Jones' *The Dime Western Novel* (1973), where the popularity of specific plot formulas is analyzed.

Thus, although the typical customers for this product changed over the years, its basic structure was retained; quality, however, sank lower and lower. And, in line with the diffusion of innovations model, those who consumed this product ceased to be the elite as the product became embraced by those on the lower rungs of society. As is usually the case under such circumstances, the product became tailored to the demands of the late majority as quality fell.

Cooper, therefore, created a major innovation by portraying the frontier hero as a noble, but overspecialized, product of the wilds, destined for eventual oblivion and banishment as society asserted itself. As is usually the case with new products, Cooper's original customers can be viewed as the innovator class, and Cooper went to great lengths to cater to this group. Various other groups embraced the product as it was simultaneously abandoned by the elite. For 70 years after its introduction, Cooper's plot formula remained current although, in accordance with the theories of marketing/consumer theory, the people buying the product evolved from social elites to the lower classes. By the turn of the 20th century, the product survived primarily in low-quality magazines and cheap novels aimed at the masses.

A RESTART OF THE PRODUCT LIFE CYCLE

As indicated above, by the late 19th century, the product of the cowboy story (as represented by Cooper's original plot formula) was in the later stages of the product life cycle. And, in accordance with the diffusion of innovations model, the product was primarily embraced by individuals who were members of what consumer researchers call "the late majority": lower-class individuals, the last to adopt a product. Thus, Cooper's innovation exhibited all the earmarks of a product in serious decline. By and large, the literary elites had gone on to other things, such as the psychological novel (as developed by elite writers such as Henry James). Although Cooper's variant of the frontier or cowboy story survived in cheap fare marketed to the lower classes, the future for the product looked bleak. A plotline that suggested that the frontier personality cannot make the transition to the modern world had become passe. In addition, the symbolic displacement of the distinctive American hero undercut the attempt of the North American elite to assert that North American civilization existed on a par with (if not actually superior to) older European society. Since Cooper believed that civilization and the frontier were incompatible, furthermore, his plot formula seemed to depict European-derived civilization as superior to that of the new world; as a result, Cooper's plotlines came to contradict the vision of the late 19th-century American elite (who increasingly viewed the frontier heritage as the catalyst that gave Americans a distinctive superiority). The 1890s was the era that codified the "frontier thesis" of American history, which argued that Americans had evolved a unique and superior civilization due to the impact of the frontier experience. According to historian Frederick Jackson Turner (1893), the existence of a rugged frontier and 400 years of Americans being in contact with it had created a new breed of person and a new type of culture. The ancestry of most Americans came from the old world where, Turner suggested, individual strength had become submerged beneath the dictates and priorities of a complex culture and an overbearing society. Nonetheless, Turner continued, the challenge of a raw frontier helped such civilized weaklings to regain a degree of self-reliance and personal strength that had atrophied in a more sedentary Europe.[8]

The frontier, Turner continued, had closed about 1890 and although occasional pockets of wilderness survived, they were increasingly surrounded by civilization and are being relentlessly and inevitably annexed by it. Nonetheless, Turner insisted, the heritage of the frontier experience would continue to impact American culture and society for many years to come, since it had given rise to a strong and virile personality type and created a national character that led to both personal and national greatness.

Originally formulated in 1893, the frontier thesis was quickly embraced by the American elite. For many years, Americans had been made to feel like second-class intellectuals by Europeans who suggested that American achievements were but pale reflections of more sophisticated European prototypes. The frontier thesis, in contrast, reversed the tables by asserting that on the wild frontier Americans had honed their skills to an edge far sharper than that of their European counterparts and, in the process, they had created a distinctiveness all their own. Clearly, this new vision needed to be portrayed in a symbolic way. Published in 1902, Owen Wister's *The Virginian* phrased this emerging worldview in fictional form to create what many critics believe is the seminal or archetypical cowboy story.

Significantly, Wister borrowed some aspects of the Cooper formula while discarding and adjusting others. The personalities of Cooper's Natty Bumppo and Wister's Virginian, for example, are identical; both are strong men who are willing to use their own personal morality as a guide, even if doing so results in transcending the norms of mainstream society. While Cooper's and Wister's heroes are largely interchangeable, their fates are profoundly different. Cooper's Natty Bumppo is cast out of society and forced to survive in a hinterland where society is unable to establish itself. Wister's Virginian, in contrast, learns the practical and moral lessons of individualism while living on a wild frontier; after this apprenticeship, he is able to rejoin society and emerge as superior to it.

The Virginian was quickly embraced by the elites of society because it updated Cooper's formula using perspectives that are provided by the frontier thesis. As often happens in marketing, an innovation in an existing product restarts its product life cycle; as a result, the product is again successful and influential. While keeping the personality of the frontier hero constant, Wister transformed his protagonist from a vestigial remain banished to the hinterland to an all-powerful superman who, having learned the lessons of the frontier, returns to civilization vital and triumphant. At the end of *The Virginian*, for example, Wister observes: "[The Virginian] was an important man with a strong grip on many various enterprises" (1902; 506). While Cooper's Natty Bumppo had to hide out in the desert, the Virginian returned East and became a pillar of society. Not only is the Virginian a strong moral influence, he is able to forcefully achieve pragmatic goals in his dealings with society.

Becoming established around the turn of the 20th century, this updating of the cowboy story originally appealed to social elites who sought an apology for capitalism as well as a means of portraying American civilization on a par with (if not altogether superior to) older European cultures. In view of the fact that European intellectuals often asserted their superiority and depicted the New World as provincial, the American elites needed a means of blunting Old World claims of supremacy. The frontier thesis provided an intellectual rationale for doing so, and *The Virginian* emerged as a symbolic articulation of these beliefs.

Wister, himself, was a "blueblood," socially connected, and he had many elite tastemakers as personal or family friends. Revealingly, *The Virginian* was dedicated to Wister's personal friend, Theodore Roosevelt, who was president of the United States when the novel was published and whose flamboyant life demonstrated how a strong dose of the frontier could lead to both personal success and profound achievement. Equally significant is the fact that Roosevelt personally took a hand in fine-tuning this emerging American "myth"; speaking directly to Roosevelt in his dedication, Wister observes: "Some of these pages you have seen, some you have praised, *one stands new-written because you blamed it*" (1902: iv; emphasis added). Owen Wister's cowboy hero, via his social Darwinistic portrayal of the frontier thesis, provided the American elite with the intellectual justification its members needed to portray themselves as superior to their rivals from the Old World. It also intellectually justified the economic system that was beginning to dominate in early 20th-century America. The social elite was concerned with both issues and it found a symbolic working out of these tensions in the cowboy story. Thus, according to Moody Boatwright, Wister had a publishing contract with publishers who were dedicated to advancing the worldview of the elite:

Horace Lorimer, who took over the editorship of the *Saturday Evening Post* in 1898 and, frankly, made it the voice of American business, assembled a stable of Western writers, including Wister, and through them kept before his readers *the cowboy as a symbol of the rugged individuals that had made America great*. (1951: 151; emphasis added)

As time went on, popular writers and various forms of mass communication (movies, radio, and TV programs) brought Wister's innovation to a wider audience. As in the case of the later variants of Cooper's plotline, furthermore, Wister's heroic figure came to be embraced by people who lay further down the rungs of the diffusion of innovations ladder. In addition, the Wistersque hero became involved in a long series of morality plays directed primarily at children. Thus, although a few examples of "the thinking man's Western" may have survived, Wister's innovation increasingly become niched as a genre for people of low social class and for children. This situation remained until the 1960s, when the formula again changed.

ABORTED INNOVATIONS

As is widely acknowledged within marketing/consumer research, creating a significant innovation does not insure success in the marketplace. Besides providing a new option, innovations must be made available at a time when the public is willing to embrace them; they must mesh with the national character or *volksgeist* of the people. Otherwise consumers will not accept the product even if it is "superior" according to criteria which the producer or its apologists hold dear. If the timing is wrong, innovations cannot be successfully marketed.

In the history of the 20th-century cowboy novel, there are at least two classic examples of high-quality innovations that failed because the public rejected them. They are represented by Zane Grey's *The Vanishing American* (1925) and Walter Van Tilburg Clark's *The Ox-Bow Incident* (1940). Both novels significantly transcended Wister's social Darwinistic/ frontier thesis plotline by updating its message to new realities, and both are excellent examples of fiction created by acknowledged writers. Neither, however, was able to impact the evolution of the cowboy story in any meaningful way. From a marketing/consumer research point of view, both were unsuccessful innovations because they were presented to a public that was not ready to accept them. From a humanistic point of view they did not mesh with the national character or *volksgeist* of the era and they were rejected accordingly.

Zane Grey, of course, was a wildly successful author of cowboy novels that were targeted toward the general public (majority, late majority). For many years, Grey provided his readership with tales in which the hero, after overcoming great obstacles, emerges victorious. On one occasion, however, Grey experimented with an innovative plotline in which the noble hero fails and dies. Grey published this notable innovation in *The Vanishing American* (1925); eventually, however, Grey reverted back to upbeat plotlines (that were reflective of the prevailing *volksgeist*) in order to please his paying customers.

In *The Vanishing American*, the hero, a Navajo, finds himself pitted against government agents who administer the reservation. Many immoral actions of the debased Eastern bureaucrats are chronicled, as are the hero's attempts to correct them. At book's end, the strong, noble individualist totally embraces his indigenous (i.e., frontier) culture and in a traditional rite of passage, he performs a ceremony that involves exposing himself to the elements. However, as a result of this ritualistic ordeal, which indicates his maturity and a positive embrace of his heritage, he catches influenza—a disease brought by the Whites—and dies. Symbolically, the novel asserts that those who are noble and true to themselves will be destroyed by an inferior, but dominant culture, metaphorically depicted by the lowly bacteria that had been brought by the White man. In recent years, the plight of the American Indian has been increasingly recognized and discussed in both fiction and non-fiction. The reader is encouraged to consult Berkhofer (1978) for a relevant background. Although these themes regarding Native Americans have only recently been forcefully articulated in fiction and non-fiction, they were anticipated by Grey, who strategically abandoned them when they proved to be unpopular with the reading public of his era.

The whole message of *The Vanishing American* is that even a strong, noble, and superior individualist is no match for the impersonal forces of society. Just like Cooper's Natty Bumppo, the cards are stacked against Grey's hero and he cannot win; both are fatalistic heroes who, although glowing with individualism and "self-actualization" (to use Abraham Maslow's term), are ultimately defeated. Death comes to Grey's hero as a direct result of a positive asserting of one's true self. Viewed objectively in terms of writing quality and plot development, *The Vanishing American* is a highpoint in Grey's career (Walle 1976). Such plotlines, however, were not demanded by the reading public of Grey's era and he adjusted himself accordingly; he never replicated this pessimistic plotline and he reverted to upbeat stories which were popular with his audience and provided consumers with what they wanted to experience. In the marketplace, consumers responded according to their national character, not with regard to the inherent "quality" of art.

While Grey's aborted innovation depicted the noble hero who remains true to himself and dies as a result, Walter Van Tilburg Clark created amoral potential heroes who are forced to capitulate in order to live. Clark's *The Ox-Bow Incident* (1940) was one of the most celebrated Westerns of the 20th century. Made into a highly successful movie, the antiheroic message reached a wide audience. Today, it is highly regarded by literary and film critics.

In *The Ox-Bow Incident*, three innocent men who are suspected of murder and cattle rustling are hanged at a lynching. In large part, the story is an analysis of the interworkings of mob rule. The plot, however, is much more complex than that; more central to the concern of my analysis is the fact that the posse includes two members who doubt that the suspects are guilty. They alone can save the doomed prisoners from the irrational mob. Why don't they? Precisely because they are strangers in the area and, therefore, they are the only other possible suspects. By not interfering with the posse, these capitulaters allow the mob's vengeance to be dissipated in a way that does not threaten them. In an article I wrote a few years ago, I observe: "*The Ox-Bow Incident* is about the eclipse of morality by personal interest . . . [the main characters] allow a lynching to take place because they have a vested interest in transferring suspicion from themselves to someone else. . . . As a result of their inaction, three innocent men are hanged" (Walle 1995: 60–61). Thus, while the hero of *The Vanishing American* confronts evil and dies, the antiheroes of *The Ox-Bow Incident* abandon their code of virtue in order to insure their own partisan interests.

Although *The Ox-Bow Incident* was a best-selling novel and although it is still highly regarded by literary and film critics, it did not undercut the dominance of the Wisteresque cowboy story, which depicted the hero as a moralistic superman whose prowess was wrought on the frontier. Instead, critics viewed the novel as "serious fiction," that merely used the conventions of the Western as a literary device. Some critics even dreamed up the far-fetched notion that the novel was a symbolic tale about Nazi Germany set in the Old West. In a similar way, Leslie Fiedler suggests that the plotline metaphorically depicts race relations in the American South and the posse is analogous to the Ku Klux Klan. Fiedler argues that the lynching, authorized by a former Confederate officer, replicates oppression and genocide directed at Black Americans (1968: 142).

Clark rode the waves of *The Ox-Bow Incident*'s success to an impressive literary career, but he made a professional transition from writing cowboy stories to writing "serious fiction" and other, more highbrow literary forms that catered to the elite. As in the case with Grey's *The Vanishing American*, Clark's *The Ox-Bow Incident* came and went without influencing the genre of the cowboy story or the tastes of the general public.

Marketing/consumer researchers are aware of many examples of seemingly superior innovations that ultimately proved to be unsuccessful among consumers because the public was not ready for them. In such cases, a product might be ranked as "superior" based on many criteria, but still be unsuccessful in the marketplace. It is a truism of marketing/consumer research that a great number of new products and product types fail in the marketplace. In many cases, a product, although "superior" according to yardsticks of evaluation held by those who produce them, might not win sales and loyalty. Clever marketers often develop specific techniques for overcoming resistance; thus, Microsoft's Windows 95 was a superior product when released, but its developers realized that the market might resist it since parts of the product were "new" and "strange." Microsoft's solution was to allow the user to adjust the interface in order to make the new innovative product "look like" the old, familiar Windows 3.1. *The Vanishing American* and *The Ox-Bow In-*

cident, in contrast, reflect the potential failure of products that cannot be adjusted to mesh with the expectations of consumers and their demands. Both were excellent works of fiction and each, in its own way, advanced the formula of the cowboy novel by adjusting it to an evolving world. Both, however, were rejected by the public because the timing was off; the content did not mesh with the tastes and expectations of the audience. As a result, neither innovation was able to transform the cowboy story and restart it on a new product life cycle.

In the 1930s and 1940s, the frontier thesis, which argued that the frontier had honed American national character to a new level of greatness, was still a strong and widely cherished belief that reflected the prevailing national character or *volksgeist*. *The Vanishing American* and *The Ox-Bow Incident* undercut these popular visions by suggesting that the strong moral force wrought on the rugged frontier faces two unenviable alternatives: remaining true to itself and dying and/or capitulating to the immoral forces of society in order to survive. Because Grey's and Clark's innovative products contradicted the popular worldview of the times, they did not emerge as prototypes, even though literary critics have praised them.

A FINAL RESTART OF THE COWBOY STORY PRODUCT LINE

Marketing/consumer researchers agree that innovations (even if superior and skillfully wrought) will not impact a product or influence potential consumers if they are offered at the wrong time or in an inappropriate context. As has been argued, in the 1920s through the 1950s the fatalistic and antiheroic Western plotlines were innovations that were out of sync with popular belief, the national character, and the *volksgeist* of the United States. As a result, these products were rejected by the consuming public and they failed to exert a lasting impact upon the product line of the cowboy story.

Ultimately, there was nothing "wrong" with these innovations; the timing was merely off. As American culture evolved, however, these plot formulas came to symbolically portray a worldview that became increasingly popular with a sizable segment of society. When this occurred, the fatalistic and antiheroic product variants were able to restart the product life cycle of the cowboy story once again.

In post–World War II America, an evolving worldview began to undercut the viability of the frontier thesis that asserted that the rugged individualist was an all-conquering hero. A number of notable monographs analyzing American culture, including William Whyte's *The Organization Man* (1956), David Reisman's *The Lonely Crowd* (1950), and Phillip Slater's *The Pursuit of Loneliness* (1970), pointed to the fact that many Americans were hurtfully cut off from others and unable to successfully function in isolation. Here, *The Organization Man*[9] will be dealt with as a representative of this tradition of cultural self-reflection. *The Organization Man* written in the 1950s, reflects the changing temper of the times; its basic premise is that although Americans hold rugged individualism as an ideal, in the modern world of bureaucracies it becomes increasingly difficult to successfully live by such a code. According to Whyte, post–World War II Americans found themselves in the untenable position of having to either abandon their individualistic ideals in order to survive/succeed in the modern world or live an individualistic life and become a dysfunctional failure as a result. Note how these two orientations parallel the plotlines of Grey and Clark.

If *The Organization Man* is used as a barometer with which to chart a major adjustment in the American worldview and transitions in the prevailing national character or *volksgeist*, a turning away from the Turner thesis by a significant segment of the market can be seen. This emerging worldview/national character acknowledges that individualism does not inevitably lead to success and that it can ultimately prove to be counterproductive in interactions within society. In some ways, Whyte's orientations are a reembrace of James Fenimore Cooper's belief that the strong-willed individualist could not function effectively in a collective, social world.

In the 1960s, as this worldview became popular among Americans, the fatalistic and antiheroic innovations of the cowboy story, unacceptable from the 1920s to the 1950s, emerged as viable products. The fatalistic Western used the cowboy to symbolize a vestigial remain that might be noble and heroic but is ill-equipped to function in the modern world. Perhaps the classic and most popular example of the genre is Paul Newman and Robert Redford's *Butch Cassidy and the Sundance Kid*.[10] In this highly regarded blockbuster film, the lives of two rough-and-tumble, devil-may-care Western individualists face an encroaching civilization. Increasingly unable to compete in the modern world that is emerging, the heroes (like Natty Bumppo) retire to vestigial hinterland retreats. Mass civilization, however, relentlessly pursues them and they are finally unceremoniously gunned down by an army of lackluster automatons. Although individually Butch and Sundance are portrayed as superior to the "organization men" who destroy them, their death is depicted as the inevitable result of their refusal to adjust to changing times.

While the fatalistic Western chronicles the displacement and/or death of the noble, individualistic product of the frontier, the antiheroic Western demonstrates how people can survive if they abandon heroic virtue. Clint Eastwood's early Westerns are classic examples of this genre (Walle 1976). In these films, Eastwood portrays a Westerner who has abandoned the last vestiges of heroic virtue associated with the "white-hatted" cowboy hero. Although (and possibly because) they rejected a noble life, Eastwood's characters survive. Eastwood's characters capitulate and/or compromise themselves; as a result, they don't have to die like Butch and Sundance.

Although these fatalistic and antiheroic Westerns closely parallel the earlier prototypes of Grey and Clark, they were not influenced by them. Instead, they sprang from the minds of writers, directors, and actors who were influenced by changing times, not by literary history. By the 1960s, American worldview had changed to such an extent that scenarios dealing with the non-viability of the individualist hero were popular with the public and made sense to it. When applied to the cowboy story, these plotlines emerged as viable innovations that restarted the product life of the cowboy story once again.

Both of these subgenres, furthermore, were embraced by what can best be viewed as "innovators" or "early adopters," elites who embrace a product before it reaches a mainstream audience. In this case, innovation is also associated with youth. In the post–World War II era, the ability of individuals to profoundly influence the world was declining and, therefore, the Western plot formula associated with Owen Wister and Fredrick Jackson Turner was increasingly inappropriate. The adult population, however, tended to prefer the older plot formulas. Such preferences reflect the findings of consumer researchers such as Holbrook and Schindler (1989, 1994) who find that "tastes for popular culture" are formed at "sensitive periods," typically during the early 20s. According to Holbrook and Schindler, such orientations are useful in predicting consumer demand for products. The segment of the population that reached adulthood prior to the 1950s were introduced to the Wisteresque version of the cowboy story at a "sensitive period" in their lives and, as a result, they developed a preference to it.

Those who came of age at a later date, in contrast, were more likely to be influenced by other worldviews, which militated against the symbolic view of American history presented by Turner and Wister. By the 1950s the white-hatted cowboy hero, who was noble and invincible, had emerged as a stickman that was marketed primarily to children and not embraced, at face value, by adults. It became all too easy for the baby boom generation to view the Wister-type cowboy story as juvenile and to discard it as maturity arose.

I can personally remember various conversations during the 1960s in which some people objected to antiheroic and fatalistic westerns because of a belief that the cowboy should maintain his virtue and should succeed. The logic of such observations hinged around a perceived need to preserve the noble image of the cowboy so that it could be mimed by children. Even in "adult Westerns," however, the Wister formula fought against pessimistic revisions. John Wayne and Howard Hawks, for example, explicitly made *Rio Bravo*, a conventional Western where virtue prevails, in order to rebut *High Noon*, a proto-fatalistic Western in which the hero, abandoned by the town he loves, develops a contempt for civilization because he was "thrown to the wolves" when his friends found it expedient to do so (Walle 1992). As is often the case in the heat of creation, some people do not realize when a restart of the product life cycle is taking place. Wayne seemingly viewed *High Noon* as a random event, not as a prelude to the evolution of the genre.

Others foresaw the transformation for what it was: the emerging fatalistic plotline represents a restart of the cowboy story on a new product life cycle. In the case of *Lonely Are the Brave*, for example, Kirk Douglas clearly realized his fatalistic film, scripted by Dalton Trumbo, marked a departure from earlier Westerns. In this low-budget but influential film, the hero (a symbol of the rugged individualism associated with the Old West) comes in conflict with society and he faces minor legal proceedings triggered by his disrespect for authority. When he escapes from jail, however, this insignificant trouble escalates and he becomes a wanted man being hunted down by a highly organized and well-financed posse. Nonetheless, the individualist hero is able to thwart all attempts by "organization men" to defeat him. When he attempts to cross a highway, his last hurdle to freedom, however, he is struck and killed by a truck full of toilet bowls. The truck and its cargo (flush toilets are symbolically used to depict civilization) demonstrate that although the hero is superior to the specific "organization men" whom he faces, the onslaught of modern civilization is unstoppable and individualistic people who stand in its way will be destroyed.

Douglas, aware that the film was a significant transformation, wanted to initially cater to innovators. He states:

I disagreed with their [the studio's] releasing pattern. . . . I pleaded with them to put it in one little theater in New York and just wait and see what happened. Instead, they released it to a large number of theaters like an old-fashioned Western which, of course, it wasn't. (Douglas 1976)

In an ill-conceived marketing blunder by the film distributors, *Lonely Are the Brave* was not released to innovators as Douglas had hoped, but dumped at a mainstream, late majority audience that was not ready for it. As a result, the film was not particularly successful financially when it was initially released, although it is now recognized as a masterpiece of the fatalistic subgenre.

Within a few years of the release of *Lonely Are the Brave*, the new plotlines had proceeded through the diffusion of innovation cycles and the fatalistic *Butch Cassidy and the Sundance Kid* emerged as a blockbuster at the box office. Thus, between 1820 and 1970 the cowboy story has gone through various permutations that reflect both the product life cycle and the diffusion of innovations model. This transformation is best understood by using a social interpretation that links the myth and symbol method with models of marketing/consumer research.

VOLKSGEIST, NATIONAL CHARACTER, AND CONSUMER RESPONSE

The basic purpose of this chapter is to demonstrate how marketing/consumer research can benefit from employing the myth and symbol method as a means of social structural analysis. The essence of this method, of course, goes back to Herder and Hegel and their embrace of the *volksgeist* method. Herder especially sought to interpret creative art in terms of the essence of a culture, and he was very successful in doing so (especially in his cross-cultural comparisons of folk songs).

The myth and symbol method, although largely evolving in America and, seemingly, influenced by the culture at a distance method, clearly accomplishes goals that are similar to those of the *volksgeist* scholars. Artistic achievement is used as empirical evidence by which the essence of the culture can be better understood. By examining specific works of art and why they were embraced by a people, their patterns of consumption can be better understood. The relevance of this research strategy to marketing/consumer researchers is obvious.

Using a specific empirical example (the evolution of the cowboy story from 1820 until 1970 and how it was marketed to the public), a clear-cut case study that has an obvious relevance to marketing/consumer research is presented. By exploring the consumption process in terms of overarching social structures, it becomes easier to understand how and why people consumer the products they do.

NOTES

1. I admit that I am partisan here. I have known Fiedler and considered him a friend for almost 30 years, I am deeply influenced by his method, and he was a member of my dissertation committee.

2. Personal communication.

3. This chapter tends to equate the terms "cowboy story," "Western," or "frontier fiction" and use them interchangeably. Some readers may object and legitimately point to important distinctions. This chapter equates the terms because it views the cowboy story as a specific component or subset of the Western genre. The strategy in this chapter is to focus upon change and stability within a specific genre; the terminology chosen advances this research goal. The author, furthermore, had done so in refereed scholarly journals (1974). Thus, professional critics acknowledge the method as legitimate.

4. Although the present author applauds Levy's insights regarding the value

of literary theories, such as those which derive from mythology, the current chapter does not make explicit use of Levy's model (which derives from the mental structural work of anthropologist Claude Levi-Strauss). On other occasions, however, the present author has employed a Levi-Strauss type of analysis (Walle 1996). Although this chapter does not build upon Levy's model because he is concerned with mental, not social structures, I do follow Levy's precedent of using mythological theory in marketing/consumer research.

5. For readability, the narrative of the presentation will contain minimal citations. Readers who seek a more fully developed presentation of the ideas contained herein are referred to the author's research, which presents this basic chain of thought (Walle 1974, 1976). Of these works, Walle (1974) presents a quick and useful overview as related to the folklore literature and is recommended.

6. Although not specifically discussed here, I find the work of Warshow (1954) and Schein (1955) to be two readable and insightful overviews of the Western as a genre. They, in particular, are recommended to the reader who has an interest in the subject.

7. Some may disagree with this assessment.

8. Of course, Americans derive from many places besides Europe. I am merely presenting Turner's chain of thought.

9. A useful updating of such ideas can be found in Lipsky and Abrams (1994).

10. The seminal films of this type are Samuel Peckinpah's *Ride the High Country* (1961) and Kirk Douglas and Dalton Trumbo's *Lonely Are the Brave* (1962).

REFERENCES

Berkhofer, Robert. (1978). *The White Man's Indian: Images of the American Indian, from Columbus to the Present*. New York: Vintage.

Boatwright, Moody. (1951). "The American Myth Rides the Range: Owen Wister's Man on Horseback." *Southwestern Review* 36: 157–63.

Clark, Walter Van Tilburg. (1940). *The Ox-Bow Incident*. New York: Random House.

Cooper, James Fenimore. (1823). *The Pioneers*. Reprint, New York: Appleton, 1892.

Cooper, James Fenimore. (1827). *The Prairie*. Reprint, New York: Airmont, 1964.

deMan, Paul. (1979). *Allegories of Reading: Figurative Language in Rousseau, Rilke, and Proust*. New Haven, CT: Yale University Press.

Douglas, Kirk. (1976). Personal communication.

Fiedler, Leslie. (1960). *Love and Death in the American Novel*. New York: Stein and Day.

Fiedler, Leslie. (1964). *Waiting for the End*. New York: Stein and Day.

Fiedler, Leslie. (1969). *The Return of the Vanishing American*. New York: Stein and Day.

Fiedler, Leslie. (1982). *What Was Literature? Class Culture and Mass Society*. New York: Simon and Schuster.

Flanagan, John T. (1941). "The Authenticity of Cooper's *The Prairie*." *Modern Language Quarterly*.

French, Philip. (1973). *Westerns: Aspects of a Movie Genre*. New York: Viking.

Grey, Zane. (1925). *The Vanishing American*. New York: Harper & Brothers.

Holbrook, Morris and Grayson, Mark. (1986). "The Semiology of Cinematic Consumption: Symbolic Consumer Behavior in *Out of Africa*." *Journal of Consumer Research* 13(3): 374–82.

Holbrook, Morris and Schindler, R. M. (1989). "Some Exploratory Findings on the Development of Musical Tastes." *Journal of Consumer Research* 16 (June): 119–24.

Holbrook, Morris B. and Schindler, R. M. (1994). "Market Segmentation Based on Age and Attitude Toward the Past as Predictors of Consumers' Aesthetic Tastes for Cultural Products." *Journal of Marketing Research* 31 (August): 412–22.

Jameson, Fredrick. (1976). "The Ideology of the Text." *Salamagundi* 31(2): 204–26.

Jones, Darryl. (1973). *The Dime Western Novel*. Bowling Green, OH: Popular Press.

Kites, Jim. (1969). *Horizons West*. Bloomington: Indiana University Press.

Leniricchia, Frank. (1980). *After the New Criticism*. Chicago: University of Chicago Press.

Levy, Sidney. (1981). "Interpreting Consumer Mythology: A Structural Approach to Consumer Behavior." *Journal of Marketing* 45(3): 49–61.

Lipsky, David and Abrams, Alexander. (1994). *Late Bloomers: Coming of Age in Today's America: The Right Place at the Wrong Time*. New York: Times Books.

Marks, Barry. (1963). "A Concept of Myth in *Virgin Land*." *American Quarterly* 15: 71–76.

Marx, Leo. (1964). *The Machine in the Garden*. New York: Oxford University Press.

McDonald, Archie. (1987). *Shooting Stars: Heroes and Heroines of the Western Films*. Bloomington: Indiana University Press.

Parkman, Francis. (1852). "The Works of James Fenimore Cooper." *North American Review* 74 (January): 147–61.

Parks, Rita. (1982). *The Western Hero in Film and Television: Mass Media Mythology*. Ann Arbor: University of Michigan Press.

Reisman, David. (1950). *The Lonely Crowd: A Study of the Changing American Character*. New Haven, CT: Yale University Press.

Schein, Harry. (1955). "The Olympian Cowboy." *American Scholar* 24: 209–20.

Sklar, Robert. (1975). "The Problem of American Studies 'Philosophy': A Bibliography of New Directions." *American Quarterly* 27: 245–62.

Slater, Philip. (1970). *The Pursuit of Loneliness: American Culture at the Breaking Point*. Boston: Beacon Press.

Slotkin, Richard. (1973). *Regeneration Through Violence: The Mythology of the American Frontier, 1600–1800*. Middletown, CT: Wesleyan University Press.

Slotkin, Richard. (1985). *The Fatal Environment: The Myth of the Frontier in the Age of Industrialization, 1600–1800*. New York: Atheneum.

Slotkin, Richard. (1986). "Myth and the Production of History." In *Ideology and Classic American Literature*, ed. Sacvan Bercovitch and Myra Jehlen. New York: Cambridge University Press, pp. 70–90.

Slotkin, Richard. (1992). *Gunfighter Nation: The Myth of the Frontier in Twentieth-Century America*. New York: Atheneum.

Smith, Henry Nash. (1950). *Virgin Land: The American Land as Myth and Symbol*. Cambridge, MA: Harvard University Press.

Smith, Henry Nash. (1957). "Can American Studies Develop a Method?" *American Quarterly* 9: 197–208.

Trachtenberg, Alan. (1977). "Myth, History, and Literature in *Virgin Land*." *Prospects* 3: 127–29.

Turner, Frederick Jackson. (1893). "The Significance of the Frontier in American History." In *Annual Report of the American Historical Society*. New York: American Historical Society.

Walle, Alf. (1974). "The Frontier Hero: A Static Figure in an Evolving World." *Keystone Folklore* 19: 207–24.

Walle, Alf. (1976). "The Cowboy Hero: A Static Figure in an Evolving World." Doctoral dissertation, University at Buffalo.

Walle, Alf. (1996). "Hack Writing vs. Belle Letters: The Strategic Implications of Literary Achievement." *Journal of Popular Culture* 30(3): 185–96.

Warshow, Robert. (1954). "The Westerner." *Partisan Review* 21(2): 190–203.

White, William. (1956). *The Organization Man*. Garden City, NY: Doubleday.

Wister, Owen. (1902). *The Virginian*. New York: Macmillian.

Wood, Michael. (1977). "Deconstructing Derrida." *New York Review of Books* 3 (March): 27–30.

Wright, Will. (1975). *Six Guns and Society*. Berkeley: University of California Press.

CHAPTER 10

Social Structures and Strategic Behavior: The Face to Face Method

SOCIAL STRUCTURES AND STRATEGIC BEHAVIOR

On many occasions, marketing/consumer researchers assume that behavior is purposeful and that people are consciously aware of why they act in the way they do. Certainly, some research strategies recognize that various patterns of response are triggered by influences that lie below the level of consciousness (such as in Freudian and other depth psychological analyses), but other models recognize that people are overtly aware of their motives and the strategic options available to them and, with this knowledge in mind, goal-oriented decisions are consciously made.

Much consumer behavior is the result of conscious choice and tactical response. The concept of the "fashion statement," for example, implies that people often make consumption decisions (wearing certain clothes) in order to strategically convey some sort of "statement" or message to other people. Doing so constitutes rational and purposeful behavior. Although different scholars may be in disagreement regarding whether a specific action is conscious and strategic or not, few observers would disagree with the premise that some consumer response falls into the category of conscious, rational, and strategic action.

Due to the fact that some consumer behavior is obviously rational and strategic, addressing that reality is a worthwhile and legitimate activity of marketing/consumer research. In this chapter, the potential of analyzing rational and strategic consumer behavior is demonstrated via the analysis of the methodology of Erving Goffman. A major social thoerist, Goffman is clearly identified with the "face to face" school of social analysis and he developed ways to apply an intuitive game theoretic analysis to a range of everyday social interactions. Due to the specific subject matter that Goffman investigated, he and his approach are especially appropriate for a wide range of marketing/consumer research initiatives. In addition, Goffman's research and his analytic style are reflective of much of the current work in marketing ethnography that has been conducted by researchers such as Russell Belk, John Sherry, and Melanie Wallendorf. As a result, this chapter begins with a brief review of this important research agenda within our profession.

THE ETHNOGRAPHIC METHOD IN MARKETING AND ITS IMPLICATIONS

During the last 15 years, marketing/consumer researchers have embraced a variety of qualitative research techniques. Scholars who have done so note that quantitative analysis and the scientific method are unable to adequately examine a wide array of consumer response and, as a result, alternative methodologies are employed. In general, the goal of this research stream is to place consumer response within a specific social context; in order to do so, qualitative methods are employed.

The scholars who advance this research agenda refer to their research technique as "naturalistic" in order to indicate that investigation takes place "in situ" and is not conducted within an artificial/contrived circumstance, laboratory, or environment. These scholars acknowledge that, in order to understand how people behave, it is may be necessary to observe a random "slice of their lives" in order to determine why people act in the way they do in a particular circumstance. On occasion, these researchers may even need to personally participate in the phenomena being studied and do so in a spontaneous and unstructured way.

This research stream is closely linked to the consumer behavior "Odyssey" and the key researchers associated with it including Belk, Sherry, and Wallendorf. The goal of this research has been to demonstrate the value of qualitative research strategies that view the consumption process within an actual cultural milieu. The role of participant observation has also been showcased.

The successes of the marketing ethnography movement have been many; in general, by analyzing the conscious feelings, goals, and opinions of the individuals being investigated (and viewing the information gathered about them on its own terms), valuable insights can be gained.

The investigator needs to be aware of the costs and benefits that typify a specific research tactic; nonetheless, naturalistic or ethnographic research in consumer research has a significant role to play, and it has proven to be a valuable addition to the toolkit of marketing/consumer researchers.

Now that the value and legitimacy of naturalistic or ethnographic consumer research has been generally recognized, grafting more specialized methodological options onto this research agenda becomes important. Here, I will do so by employing the "face to face" method associated with Goffman in order to show how this specific research tactic can serve the marketing ethnography movement in useful and illuminating ways.

THE FACE TO FACE METHOD: AN OVERVIEW

There is a general acknowledgment among social psychologists and social scientists that although a culture provides people with specific orientations, patterns of response, venues, and overarching goals, individuals are not merely automatons responding to circumstance. Thus, even Marxist scholars (who tend to embrace a fairly strict version of socioeconomic determinism) have labored to reintroduce a recognition of the uniqueness of specific people and their individual goals into the equation of behavior. The Frankfurt School (Arato and Gebhart 1978; Jameson 1971), for example, consciously broadens Marxist analysis in order to expand beyond Marx's overly determinist and mechanical model; it does so by acknowledging and analyzing individualistic aspects of behavior.

Anthropology and sociology typically nest individual behavior within a cultural milieu. As a result, human response is assumed to be structured by the culture and it is viewed as existing within a specific social and cultural milieu and is profoundly influenced by it. Thus, the structure of the society, the goals of the individuals, and the resulting patterns of behavior are all considered; their mutual influences are also recognized. An important subdiscipline of social anthropology, for example, is "culture and personality" which, while examining social behavior, acknowledges the impact of the unique individual upon actual behavior. Culture and personality specialists recognize that certain behaviors and relationships (while existing within society and responding to prevailing norms, social relationships, and protocols) do not totally define a social situation. The unique motivations of the individuals who are involved must also be taken into account. Nonetheless, this individualist phenomena can also be examined with reference to the social structure.

Thus, anthropologist Fredrik Barth observes in an influential essay: "Once one admits that what we empirically observe is not "customs" but "cases" of human behavior, it seems to me that we cannot escape the concept of [individual] choice" (1996: 1). Although people may be somewhat "locked into" their culture and social structure, they also make individual decisions in order to achieve their own personal goals.

In the case of much social intercourse and consumer behavior, individuals work within the norms of a culture while simultaneously following their own partisan motives. Doing so constitutes individual choice, even though behavior takes place in accordance with established social conventions.

One of the seminal thinkers who promoted such a point of view is Erving Goffman, whose paradigm of analysis is akin to that of the University of Chicago and the work of George Herbert Mead. Goffman was a strong advocate of the symbolic interaction perspective of social interaction. In a wide array of writings, Goffman centered upon the face to face relationships of the people he studied, and his work draws attention to the ways in which people consciously manipulate the social situation. Goffman labels such goal-oriented behavior as "impression management," which includes "all the activities of a given participant in a given occasion which serves to influence in any way the other participants" (1959: 15). Another key concept from Goffman is the idea of a "front," which he defines as the "part of the individual's performance [in face to face encounters] which regularly functions in a general and fixed fashion to define the situation for those who observe the performance" (1959: 22). Goffman's approach is valuable in many contexts when people choose to consume specific products in order to create an image or to advance some conscious goal; in essence, patterns of consumption are often a part of a person's "front." Because the concept of impression management provides a useful means of analyzing the consumption strategies that people employ in order to control the social situation and/ or to influence the behavior of other people, it has a valuable role to play in marketing/consumer research.

Goffman's method is commonly known as dramaturgical analysis. The basic strategy of this technique is to draw an analogy between face to face relationships and the theater: "The perspective employed . . . is that of the theatrical performance, the principles are dramaturgical ones . . . the part one plays is tailored to the parts played by the others present, and yet these others constitute the audience" (1959: ix). Such performances are significant and important because "information about the individual [part player] helps to define the situation enabling others to know in advance what he [the part player] will expect of them and what they may expect of him" (1959: 1). Therefore, Goffman's special interest is "the study of impression management, of the contingencies which arise in fostering an impression and of the techniques for meeting contingencies" (1959: 80). This impression management is carried out via the performance consisting of "all the activity of a given participant on a given occasion which serves to influence in any way the other participants" (1959: 15). Goffman divides relevant persons in an interaction into two groups, "a team of performers who cooperate to present to an audience a given definition of the situation" (1959: 238). The composition of the team units can vary considerably; Goffman, for example, treats the situation of two people meeting as a "two team interaction in which each team contains only one member. . . . logically speaking, one could even say that an audience which was duly impressed by a particular social setting would be an audience witnessing a team performance in which the team was one of no members" (1959: 80).

For many years, sociologists tended to view Goffman as a rather insignificant (although engaging) "micro-sociologist" because he focused upon some rather mundane patterns of social life. Today, however, he has come to be regarded as a major social theorist who used commonplace patterns of behavior as his empirical evidence. In any event, many of the examples that Goffman uses and the techniques that he employs are directly relevant to qualitative marketing/consumer researchers.

In short, Goffman deals with face to face research; his work is of value to marketing/consumer researchers because of the methodological options it provides. In many situations involving consumption, people consciously manipulate the situation in order to give a specific impression that is designed to achieve a conscious goal. Dealing with another person in this way can be viewed as a "two team interaction in which each team contains only one member" (1959: 80). The face to face method is a well-established and appropriate means of conceptualizing the situation and its strategic dynamics; it, therefore, has a significant (if not central) contribution to make within marketing/consumer research.

Another reason for embracing Goffman's perspective is that there exists a long tradition of employing theories and methods that parallel the face to face school of sociology in marketing/consumer research. An example of an earlier prototype of this basic approach is the work of German philosopher and sociologist Georg Simmel (1858–1918). A classic explanation of fashion, known as "trickledown theory," for example, was initially formulated by Simmel at the turn of the 20th century. Simmel states that the social elites, being proud and jealous of their position, are interested in distinguishing themselves from those who are lower on the social scale. In order to do so, Simmel theorized that these elites consume products in ways that demonstrate and reinforce their dominant position. Ever-changing clothing styles and constantly evolving fashions are examples and artifacts of this tendency.

Those who are lower on the social scale, Simmel continues, emulate the elite by adopting the styles currently being flaunted by the rich and famous. As a result, these high fashions eventually become passe because, once they are embraced by the mainstream, styles cease to be symbols of wealth, status, and privilege. In order to maintain their distance and social superiority, Simmel concludes, the elite are ultimately forced to move on to new fashions, which are once again able to depict their social superiority. In essence, Simmel depicts an endless cycle of distinctive fashions which, because they are emulated by social inferiors, eventually lose their luster.

More recently, Simmel's trickledown model has been updated by Grant McCracken, who points to specific phenomena, such as an increased number of women in the workplace, and concludes: "Simmel's theory . . . requires revision for modern day application. Theoretical revisions of the trickledown theory that must be made to accommodate the clothing of professional women [for example]" (McCracken 1985: 45). Expanding beyond ad hoc issues, McCracken then goes on to discuss general theoretical issues such as those involving the symbolic roles of products and how an understanding of symbolism is crucial to the rehabilitation of trickledown theory. McCracken observes in a later article: "[the elite] are distinct opinion leaders: individuals who by virtue of birth, beauty, or accomplishment are held in high esteem" (1986: 76).

McCracken proposes adjustments which he believes are needed to rehabilitate the classic trickledown theory and suggests they

1. must expand beyond social class to consider variables such as sex, age, and ethnicity; and
2. the symbolic nature of consumption must be adequately addressed and factored into the analysis.

Crucial to the trickledown theory, which has a long and useful history within marketing/consumer research, is the fact that people are assumed to consciously "play a part" and develop a "front" in order to affirm and/or enhance their social status. This, ultimately, is conscious and goal-related behavior that is centered around both face to face behavior and strategic interaction that stems from it. The importance of this basic model of symbolic interaction has long been noted by social theorists as well as marketing/consumer researchers who have embraced this theory and method. In essence, Simmel in the early 20th century used a primitive version of the face to face method, and this model has been embraced by marketing/consumer researchers.

While the Simmel example is a good one, Goffman's theoretical position is more sophisticated and embraces a more robust methodology. As a result, Goffman's dramaturgical techniques of analysis can be embraced as a theoretical and methodological framework; specific theories such as Simmel/McCracken's trickledown theory can, as a result, be viewed as a variant of Goffman's dramaturgical theoretical orientation. Actually Simmel wrote long before Goffman and, therefore, Goffman's model is more advanced. Viewed in this way, a wide array of purposeful consumer responses can be more effectively evaluated, compared, and researched using Goffman's well-developed and highly appropriate research strategy.

CRITIQUES OF GOFFMAN

As might be anticipated, various scholars have questioned the rigorousness, applicability, and value of Goffman's research tactics. Indeed, Goffman has been severely criticized on a number of grounds, including the following:

1. Goffman uses an intuitive game theoretic model, but game theory is inappropriate for projects involving face to face interaction such as Goffman's.
2. Goffman and those who employ his basic approach make dubious assumptions about the nature of mankind and human behavior.
3. Goffman's model is basically descriptive and theoretical. His work offers little explanation beyond the specific examples being analyzed and he offers little explicit evidence that can be used to verify his general statements.

These critiques will be addressed on a point-by-point basis.

A key objection to Goffman and his method centers on his use (and some might suggest misuse) of game theoretic models.[1] Goffman's intellectual debt to game theory goes back to at least 1959. Although he doesn't use an explicit game theoretical model in his breakthrough monograph *The Presentation of Self in Everyday Life* (1959: 16), the seeds are certainly there. Goffman overtly directs the reader to John von Neumann and Oskar Morgenstern's *Theory of Games and Economic Behavior* (1944) and he adopts the terminology of von Neumann, a major game theorist. By 1969, Goffman's concern with ongoing chains of behavior had further developed and he explicitly adopted a game theoretic orientation. The importance of the game theoretic paradigm is underscored in his paper "Strategic Interaction," in which he provides an intuitive view of game theory. He states:

Whenever students of the human scene have considered the dealings individuals have with one another, the issue of calculation has arisen. . . . In recent years this traditional concern about calculation has been taken up and refined by students of game theory. . . . This paper attempts to isolate the analytical framework implied by the game perspective and show its relationship to other perspectives in analyzing interpersonal dealings. . . . My ultimate interest is to develop the study of face-to-face interaction as a naturally bounded, analytically coherent field. (1969: ix, 85)

Goffman's model is a pioneering example of combining a game theoretic orientation to the interpretation of social relationships. As such, he is often viewed as an important theorist and as a methodological pioneer, even if others quarrel with him and the research strategies he represents.

Although Goffman's models have been praised in some quarters, he has also been strongly criticized elsewhere. It may be observed, for example, that face to face behavior is too complex for the methodology of game theory as it is usually employed. In a classic overview of game theory, Luce and Raiffa (1957) insist that game theory is not equipped to deal with complex episodes of social interaction involving multiple variables and numerous individuals. It is important to note that Luce and Raiffa's *Games and Decisions: Introduction and Critical Survey* (1957) is one of the seminal books in the field and it was a basic text used in graduate courses in disciplines such as political science (Riker 1996: 14–15) and anthropology until the 1980s. (The author was introduced to this book and to game theory during his graduate student days in social anthropology in the 1960s.)

Social scientists are not the only group that questions the assumptions of game theoretic models. In a tongue-in-cheek example of organizational double-talk, McDonald observes: "In fact, whether practical military problems can by solved by the theory of games is itself a military secret" (1950: 124). Although developments in game theory have been made since McDonald wrote his amusing observation, he does portray the game theoretic model as ill equipped to deal with a wide range of complicated problems.

Game theory, of course, is a valuable tool. As Richard Salisbury observes, game theory is able "to demonstrate how most rationally to maximize specific magnitudes under various conditions of risk, where differing time spans exist or one decision is contingent on other people's decisions" (1968: 478). In short, game theoretic analysis is a deductive exercise that assumes that people are going to attempt to maximize their opportunities in a rational and calculated way. As research projects deal with more and more variables, unfortunately, the model becomes increasingly complex, unwieldy, and unreliable. This, seemingly, undercuts the value of Goffman's game theoretic paradigm.

In order for specific instances of face to face behavior to be amenable to game theoretic inquiry, they must meet the criteria set up by the simpler game types (i.e., the two-person zero-sum game). International negotiations may be amenable to this simple model and they have been successfully examined using game theory. In such negotiations, however, there are often two distinct "players" or "opponents" (even if each of the two entities are themselves comprised of allied factions) that seek benefits at the expense of a block of opponents. In addition, the goals of both groups are, more or less, clearly defined. Such phenomena are especially amenable to game theoretic analysis. Although many of the citations cited above are old, they are not dated. Thus, Gates and Humes observed in 1997:

Game theoretic modeling constitutes one type of rational choice theory. When we speak of rationality, we refer to some form of goal directed behavior. . . . Game theory as a way to model strategic interaction relies on . . . assumptions of rational [action]. . . . Game theoretic models also typically assume that players of a game possess common knowledge. By this we assume that everybody in a game knows something, everybody knows that everybody knows something . . . and so on ad infinitum. (1997: 9)

When investigating more informal aspects of face to face relations, however, the crisp, clear-cut variables found in the classic game theoretic situation are lacking. First of all, people typically do not act in a purely "rational way" and, according to the premises of depth psychology, they may actually be unaware of their true motives. Although international negotiations may be relatively rational even if emotions run high, other behaviors (such as those involving consumption decisions) do not necessarily meet this criterion. In addition, the more complicated a decision (for example, attempting to choose products a person likes on the one hand while pleasing/influencing others and getting a good value for one's money on the other), the more complex and unwieldy the analysis becomes. Game theoretic models can become unworkable when applied to such complicated situations.

Goffman, himself, admits that the more complex game theoretic models are needed to explain actual behavior. He observes: "The idea of all out "zero-sum" opposition and of a pure and tight game, does not cover all that is to be considered" (1969: 113). Thus, Goffman concedes that the situations he studies require complicated mathematical techniques that are more complex than the intuitive style of analysis that he (and those who embrace his approach) are able to provide.

Even if the problems of game theory were resolved, however, the appropriateness of employing game theory in situations involving face to face behavior would still be in doubt. This is because game theory deals with "how people would behave (1) if they were guided entirely by unambiguous interests . . . (2) if they were able to utilize all the information available to them . . . and (3) if the rules governing the range of permissible acts were explicit and fixed" (Rapoport 1960: 369). The researcher must satisfy these criteria in order to rigorously employ game theory. To the extent that these criteria are not satisfied, the value of a game theoretic approach is compromised. In the study of complex face to face interactions (such as people actively attempting to define a social situation), none of these criteria can usually be satisfied.

Goffman, in addition, relates human behavior to the achievement of some future goal (such as impressing others) and he does not conceptualize face to face interaction as an end in itself. There is ample evidence, however, that much behavior may be carried on for its own sake. (Perhaps some people enjoy wearing stylish clothes as an end in itself, for example.) While few researchers would doubt that some behavior is amenable to the Goffman method, it is ascientific to assume at the onset of a research project that behavior is the result of a game theoretic-maximization-dramaturgical process. This tendency must be demonstrated empirically, not assumed, without adequate analysis and evidence.

If these critiques were not damning enough, Goffman's ethnographic method lacks rigor. He (1) presents only the evidence that fits his case, (2) provides no systematic context, and (3) rarely rises above anecdotal examples. In a somewhat generous light Deutsch and Krass state: "Both by training and personal inclination, Goffman tends to concern himself more with wide-ranging social perspectives than with matters of precision and scientific rigor. . . . Goffman does not hesitate to draw from fiction, autobiography and memoirs, newspaper and magazine reports, and gleaned information from personal conversations" (1965: 203).

A. R. Louch, not so generous, drives to the heart of the matter:

Having elevated his piecemeal descriptions to a general theory he is led to see all sorts of behavior as dramaturgical where it is no longer clear that such a device has explanatory value. For example (pp. 194 ff), the sexual act becomes a "reciprocal ritual performed to confirm symbolically an exclusive social relationship" and (p. 230) housewives who enter each others' kitchens without knocking are showing that they have nothing to hide. One can imagine that the sexual act performed by two individuals might have this significance, or two housewives might very well wish to show to a third neighbor how friendly they are. But the [value] of such observations is restricted to those special cases where the particular circumstances warrant such an analysis. (Louch 1966: 214)

Goffman, although a noted social scientist who has much to contribute to marketing/consumer research, is vulnerable to serious theoretical and methodological attack. Those using his methods need to be aware of the damning critiques many opponents have lodged against his work.

GOFFMAN DEFENDED

Although these damning assessments cannot be denied, it is also possible to evaluate Goffman's work with reference to the significant contributions that he and his work have made and the recognition he has received from his fellow sociologists. Discussing hurtful methodological biases that have long existed in the social sciences, for example, Alvan Gouldner (1970) complains that the dominance of one paradigm of sociology (functionalism) was proving to be counterproductive and that its unyielding supremacy could potentially undercut the field. Gouldner, however, looked with hope toward a new day that would be typified by what he called theoretical polycentrism: a situation in which various paradigms, models, and methods could exist simultaneously in mutually reinforcing ways. Goffman's work represents one component of this polycentrism, and this chapter is dedicated to demonstrating the value of such a polycentric analysis in general and within marketing/consumer research in particular. Goffman's methods are embraced here for that reason.

Goffman has, on occasion, been dismissed as a weak theorist and as a flawed methodologist; many of these criticisms have a legitimate cast to them. Even as a defender of Goffman and as a scholar who has long used methods inspired by him, I must concede that developing and employing rigorous and scientific methodologies are not Goffman's strengths. Goffman, however, made a significant contribution because he developed ways to use an ethnographically inspired analysis in order to isolate some of the intimate workings of social life. Goffman's shortcomings notwithstanding, his model (even with its obvious limitations) has proved to be useful and for that reason it is championed here.

In view of the fact that Goffman and his work have been subject to attack and that his methods and theories are somewhat dubious, it is important to justify the decision to employ his method and to affirm what it has to contribute to marketing/consumer researchers. It is possible to forcefully do so; indeed, although Goffman has long been dead (he died in 1982), his ideas and methods live on. Although he was controversial in life and still has his detractors, he has made a permanent mark on fields such as sociology and social anthropology. Thus, at least two monographs on Goffman were published in the 1990s (Burns 1992; Manning 1992) and a special "focus section" on the work of Goffman appeared in *Sociological Perspectives* (Fall 1996). The reader is referred to these publications if they seek a more detailed analysis of Goffman, his perspectives, and why they are prized by today's social theorists.

Although Goffman was once written off as merely an eccentric fieldworker who concentrated on often-ignored details of social life, today he is emerging as a significant social theorist. Speaking of the general significance of Goffman's work, Manning observes "An understanding of Goffman's ideas and those of allied schools of thought will deepen our understanding of how the social world is experienced and reproduced" (Manning 1992: 27).

Burns (1992) provides a more expanded assessment of Goffman and his work and he argues that Goffman, himself, seems to have been unaware of the broad implications of his theoretical positions. As a result, Goffman may have hesitated to present his theories outside of a fairly circumscribed universe. Burns goes on to suggest that Goffman made important contributions to social theory; today's scholars are employing Goffman's models in ways that are broader than he envisioned. Thus, in addition to whatever limitations may exist in dramaturgical analysis, Goffman's own inability to see the full implications of his work may have prevented it from being fully recognized during his lifetime. Nonetheless, today it has become obvious that Goffman's face to face dramaturgical analysis has withstood the test of time and it actually shows indications of emerging as stronger and more valuable as the years go by. As a result, employing a version of Goffman's perspectives within marketing/consumer research is a legitimate methodological decision. A strategically oriented face to face analysis can help marketing/consumer researchers to chart the goals, choices, and influences that underlie observed behavior and help to explain why people consume products in the way they do.

A METHODOLOGICAL CONCLUSION

Over the years, marketing/consumer researchers have employed variants of the face to face method of social analysis. The existing literature, however, has tended to embrace specific and dated models (such as Simmel's trickledown theory) and manipulate them in relative isolation. As a result of this research strategy, a general theory and methodology aimed at analyzing the face to face behavior of consumption (as suggested by Goffman) has not been embraced by our field. Marketing/consumer researchers can profitably unite the techniques that Goffman represents into a more organized and uniform conception of consumer response; doing so has positive implications for our profession.

In many situations, marketing/consumer researchers can benefit from the type of face to face analysis that Goffman represents, as well as his strategies of analysis. Much consumer response is a strategic means of controlling a situation. Where this is true, Goffman's example provides suggestive clues of immense value. Much consumer behavior is purposeful, and on many occasions social actors consume products in order to consciously control or influence a social situation; these are clearly in the realm of face to face anlaysis.

Face to face research can be viewed as "social structural" in nature because it acknowledges the existence of established social patterns, structures, and relationships within society and it suggests that people, so influenced, seek to manipulate themselves in order to achieve a specific goal. The approach is able to graft an investigation of individual choice onto a structural model. In doing so, rational and purposeful behavior is investigated with reference to the options, goals, and constraints provided by the culture or society. This kind of approach has much to contribute to marketing/consumer research.

Although Goffman and his approach can be critiqued on methodological grounds, his approach, nonetheless, provides a useful means of analyzing and comparing diverse patterns of consumer behavior, and for this reason it has a valuable role in explaining why people respond in the ways they do within marketplace and consumption situations. As a result, Goffman's method provides invaluable techniques that are poised to serve marketing/consumer researchers. Indeed, the essence of face to face techniques has enjoyed a long tradition with marketing/consumer research (Simmel/McCracken's trickledown theory) and it has served well in the past. Goffman's more robust and operationalized research design can make this research stream even more powerful and attractive.

NOTE

1. A full review of the history of game theory will not be presented due to issues of space. The reader, however, is referred to Aumann (1981).

REFERENCES

Arato, Andrew and Gebhardt, Eike, eds. (1978). *The Essential Frankfurt School Reader*. New York: Urizen Books.

Argyle, Michael. (1988). *Bodily Communication*. New York: Methuen.

Aumann, Robert. (1981). *Essays in Game Theory and Mathematical Economics in Honor of Oskar Morgenstern*. Mannheim: Bibliographisches Institut.

Barth, Fredrik. (1966). *Models of Social Organization*. London: Royal Anthropological Institute.

Burns, Tom. (1992). *Erving Goffman*. London: Routledge.

Gates, Scott and Humes, Brian. (1997). *Games, Information and Politics*. Ann Arbor: University of Michigan Press.

Goffman, Erving. (1959). *The Presentation of Self in Everyday Life*. Garden City, NY: Doubleday Anchor Books.

Goffman, Erving. (1969). "Strategic Interaction." In *Strategic Interaction*. Philadelphia: University of Pennsylvania Press.

Gouldner, Alvin. (1970). *The Coming Crisis of Western Sociology*. New York: Basic Books.

Jameson, Fredrik. (1971). *Marxism and Form*. Princeton, NJ: Princeton University Press.

Jordon, David K. and Swartz, Marc J. (1990). *Personality and the Cultural Construction of Society: Papers in Honor of Melford E. Spiro*. Tuscaloosa: University of Alabama Press.

Louch, A. R. (1966). *Explanation and Human Behavior*. Berkeley: University of California Press.

Luce, Duncan and Raiffa, Howard. (1957). *Games and Decisions: Introduction and Critical Survey*. New York: Wiley.

Manning, Philip. (1992). *Erving Goffman and Modern Sociology*. Cambridge: Cambridge University Press.

McCracken, Grant. (1985). "Rehabilitating the Trickledown Theory." In *The Psychology of Fashion*, ed. Michael R. Solomon. Lexington, MA: Lexington Books.

McDonald, John. (1950). *Strategy in Poker, Business and War*. New York: Norton.

Rapoport, Anatol. (1960). *Fights, Games, and Debates*. Ann Arbor: University of Michigan Press.

Riker, William H. (1996). "Political Science and Rational Choice." In *Perspectives on Positive Political Economy*, ed. James E. Alt and Kenneth A. Shepsle. Cambridge: Cambridge University Press.

Salisbury, Richard. (1968). "Anthropology and Economics." In *Economic Anthropology: Readings in Theory and Analysis*, ed. Edward E. LeClair and Harold K. Schneider. New York: Holt, Rinehart & Winston.

Sociological Perspectives. (1996). Special Issue on Erving Goffman (Fall).

Von Neumann, John and Morgenstern, Oskar. (1944). *Theory of Games and Economic Behavior*. Princeton, NJ: Princeton University Press.

CHAPTER 11

The Structural Perspective: A Synthesis

Structures are a fact of life. Although various intellectual traditions employ obscure philosophical musings in order to deny the existence, power, significance, reality, and/or impact of structures, they certainly do exist and they exert profound influences upon human life and thought. This fact is self-evident. Although I make this assertion in a rather unguarded way here, I have presented the case for this position in earlier discussions. And a prestigious array of intellectual traditions backs me up, detractors notwithstanding.

In Chapters 6 through 10, a variety of structural perspectives were discussed and their relevance to marketing/consumer research was documented. Each of those discussions, however, was fairly self-contained. In the present synthesis (which concludes the structural section of this book), I seek to discuss these different, although interrelated, perspectives in terms of one another. It is hoped that this overarching discussion will help me to share my vision of the power and relevance of structural analysis with the reader.

I began by drawing attention to what I refer to as the "mental structural vs. social structural" dichotomy. This was followed by a more in-depth analysis of various social structural options that have developed and how they mesh with, expand upon, and reinforce each other. Throughout these discussions, my analysis of structural analysis is clearly intertwined with the needs, goals, and priorities of marketing/consumer research.

THE MENTAL STRUCTURAL MODEL

Most commonly, intellectuals have come to think of structuralism with reference to poststructuralism. Structuralism, as a distinct and high-profile view of human nature, emerged in the post–World War II era as a means of understanding how people think. The basic strategy of the mental structural method is to draw attention to the existence of some kind of inherent structure of the human mind. Since World War II this perspective has become intimately associated with French anthropologist Claude Levi-Strauss, who argues that the human mind functions in a highly structured manner and that various artifacts of social life (including mythology, literature, and art) reflect these innate and universal patterns of human thought.

Eventually, a criticism of structuralism (closely associated with French philosopher Jean Jacques Derrida) resulted which suggested that structuralism, as a viable method of analysis, is dead; the basis of this critique hinges around some rather belabored (albeit self-evident) arguments that suggest that different people think in different ways and, therefore, that the structural model was inadequate in this, that, or the other way. The high profile of Derrida's rejection of Levi-Strauss' structural perspectives has come to dominate the attention of the intellectual world to such an extent that a more far-reaching vision of mental structural analysis has significantly atrophied.

Viewed from a broader perspective, however, various mental structural models can be seen to exist. In some fashion, all of these perspectives seem to be (overtly or covertly) akin to the perspectives advanced by Immanuel Kant (as discussed in Chapter 2), who emphasized that the human race, as a species, possesses certain inherent and innate ways of thinking and that dealing with this reality is essential for scholars who truly seek to understand human nature and thought. In order to deal with the implications of this perspective, three different models (those of Claude Levi-Strauss, Karl Gustav Jung, and Sigmund Freud) were briefly analyzed as a non-exhaustive sample of the mental structural approach. By reviewing these approaches, it becomes possible to expand mental structural methods beyond the narrow confines that led to their rejection by detractors, such as Derrida. In doing so, the validity and value of the mental structural approach is clearly reaffirmed.

THE SOCIAL STRUCTURAL MODEL

While mental structuralism focuses on the universal nature of the human mind, social structuralism accepts human nature as a "given" and it concentrates upon structures that are inherent in society and social life. Although more humanistic thinkers seem to have embraced mental structuralism, social structural models have been more popular and useful within the mainstream of the social sciences. Because of the wealth of social structural theories, coupled with the fact that mental structural discussions have already exerted a powerful influence within marketing/consumer research, this book focuses largely upon social structural models.

An overview of social structuralism was presented in Chapter 7. This was followed by a discussion of a number of social structural refinements that offer marketing/consumer research useful options. As with the chapter on mental structuralism, the specific social structural methods that are discussed are not envisioned as an exhaustive list, and they are merely presented as illustrative of the variation that exists within the social structural tradition. Specific chapters discussed the "culture at a distance" approach, the "myth and symbol method," and Erving Goffman's "dramaturgical analysis." The choice of methods analyzed portrays a wide variety of approaches that can be nested under social structural analysis and the fact that these methods expand beyond sociology to anthropology, literary criticism, American studies, and social psychology. It is useful to briefly discuss what each method accomplishes and why it was chosen as representative of the social structural method.

The Culture at a Distance Method

The culture at a distance method is a practitioner-oriented expansion of the "historical particularist" method of American anthropology which suggested that cultures need to be evaluated on their own terms. The reason for such a focused analytic strategy stems from the fact that since cultures evolved in the face of unique pressures, they must be interpreted accordingly. Somewhat transcending what is usually viewed as classic social structural analysis, it nonetheless clearly assumes that social structures exist and that these structures profoundly impact social life.

The culture at a distance method, incidentally, can be easily linked with practitioner-oriented anthropologists such as Ruth Benedict, Margaret Mead, and Edward T. Hall. In view of the fact that many social structural theorists tend to be ivory tower intellectuals, the practitioner orientation of the culture at a distance method demonstrates the practical applications of social structural models.

The Myth and Symbol Method

The myth and symbol method assumes that specific cultures and societies possess what can be viewed as a "national character" or an overarching structure that influences all or most members of society in parallel ways. Although the national character model must be used with care, it has served well over the years and continues to have relevance within business research. To whatever extent we believe that the Japanese, Germans, or Americans have distinctive personality types and/or are prone to respond in predictable ways that resonate from their cultural traditions, we are using some version of the national character approach. Although national character models may be vulnerable to misuse, they are inherently useful.

The myth and symbol method is notable because it embraces the notion of national character from social structural theories (which can be traced back to Herder's and Hegel's *volksgeist* model) and applies it to American studies and literary criticism. The model does this by assuming that national character exists and that it influences both people and their actions. The myth and symbol method examines consumer response (to various cultural works, such as literature, art, and film) and asserts that these responses are reflective of national character. Thus, consumer choices can be viewed as artifacts of national character; this assumed relationship between national character and patterns of consumption provides the myth and symbol method with a significant role to play within marketing/consumer research. This ability to contribute to marketing/consumer research, furthermore, stems from the social structural perspective that it embraces.

Dramaturgical Analysis

Erving Goffman appears, at first glance, to be an eclectic scholar whose work cannot be easily discussed in terms of the social structural approach. Nonetheless, Goffman links the strategic behavior of individual social actors with a structured social context. Goffman's method, more than the other structural models discussed, focuses upon rational and purposeful behavior. Goffman also believes that many consumption decisions are made in order to strategically manipulate a social situation to advantage. Due to this focus, Goffman's structural model is of significant value wherever marketing/consumer researchers seek to explore how people rationally and consciously make consumption decision for strategic reasons. Thus, Goffman offers a well-conceived method of transcending models of "depth psychology" that merely deal with people's unconscious motivations.

These models, as indicated above, are not an exhaustive listing of the full range of social structural options available to marketing consumer research. It is hoped, however, that by discussing a diverse array of approaches, a taste for the power and diversity of social structural analysis has been presented. The reader is encouraged to mine the social scientific literature for other relevant methods and theories.

CONCLUDING STATEMENT

The structural model is compelling, powerful, and diverse. Due to the rejection of structuralism by poststructuralism in recent years, not only have many people come to feel that structuralism is "dead"; in addition, they came to view the approach from an inappropriately narrow context. By expanding our perspectives with a recognition of the full range of mental and social structural options that are available, a more even-handed vision results. And objectively viewed, structuralism emerges as a powerful method, even if, at times, it must be used with care.

Being divided into mental structuralism and social structuralism with relevant subcategories of each, the structural method offers a varied and fruitful set of paradigms, approaches, and research strategies. Mental structuralism deals with the inherent structure of the human mind and, therefore, it deals with human universals. Social structuralism, in contrast, considers the products and influences of specific cultures which, while being unique, are also based, in part, upon universal aspects of human thought.

Due to the high profile of Levi-Strauss' mental structural model coupled with Derrida's compelling rejection of it, the intellectual world has come to view structuralism in rather circumscribed ways. This is unfortunate. By keeping in mind the wide variation of approaches that are nested under structural analysis, however, a diverse and highly useful toolkit presents itself.

PART III

Individualistic and Poststructural Perspectives

The basic goal of Part II was to build upon the self-evident observation that human life is structured and that this patterned foundation stems both from the structure of the human mind and the structure of mankind's cultural and social life. In dealing with various structural perspectives, we saw that a wide array of paradigms exist and that there is wide variation in the theories that can be nested under the umbrella of structural analysis. Although they are diverse, structural theories all emphasize that patterns (whatever they are) exist and that these patterns exert a profound impact upon social life, cultural artifacts, and the intercourse that takes place when people and groups function internally and interact with one another.

In recent years, in contrast to the structural method, various intellectuals have come to emphasize the position that the nature and the impact of these structures do not adequately explain the way in which people think, respond, and perceive the world. Modern poststructural philosophy and the paradigms of thought that stem from them often seek to deny (or least go beyond) structural analysis. The beginnings of this general vision stem from 19th-century pioneers who reacted against structural analysis (such as Søren Kierkegaard and Friedrich Nietzsche, and their focus upon more individualistic patterns of thought and response). After World War I and especially after World War II, the existential movement and its individualistic posture rose to prominence.

In more recent years, the existential movement has matured into visions represented by deconstructionism and poststructuralism. These philosophic positions and the research agendas suggested by them provide ways of getting beyond the structures that are forced upon people, either by their cultures or their innate nature; by doing so, the unique choices made by individuals and circumscribed groups are analyzed. Today, this focus upon more idiosyncratic behaviors and thought dominates the work of many intellectuals and researchers, both in the humanities and in more "applied disciplines" such as marketing/consumer research.

I begin by providing a discussion of the evolution and analytic strategies of existentialism. Tracing this individualistic philosophy back to its roots (which were conscious repudiations of Herder and Hegel), it will be shown how the method came to full flower in the post–World War II era; this popularity was, in large part, a response to the horrific events of that era.

For a number of reasons, in the 1960s existentialism no longer "spoke" to large segments of the intellectual world with the same power as it had in the 1940s and 1950s. The individualist perspective, however, remained strong. In that era, furthermore, the mental-structural perspectives of Claude Levi-Strauss arose as a significant rival to more individualistic views of mankind. In such an intellectual milieu, poststructuralism (1) rejected mental structuralism, (2) reaffirmed the individual, and (3) provided a mechanism to deal with the key issues of the era, such as those concerned with civil rights and affirming the differences between different people and groups.

In order to deal with these developments, Chapter 12, on the existential tradition, is followed by a review of the major leaders of the poststructual movement, which gives the reader a "taste" of various poststructural positions and, thereby, portrays the movement as a complex and varied set of analytic tools and intellectual positions.

Although the benefits of existentialism and poststructuralism have been many, classic social structural analysis can often provide the same services. Although severely attacked during the 1960s and although somewhat unfashionable today, the social structural model did not die. Instead it has reworked itself in appropriate ways and transformed its methods and perpectives accordingly. One example of the evolving traditions of social structuralism is conflict theory, a specialized structural model that deals with many of the same problems addressed by poststructualism (although perceived via a structural perspective).

Thus, Part III deals with the issues of individual action and the distinctiveness of circumscribed groups on the one hand while affirming that these phenomena can be analyzed using either poststructural or structural models on the other.

CHAPTER 12

Alternatives to Structural Analysis: The Existential Initiative

A BROAD HUMANISTIC PERSPECTIVE

The next two chapters deal with existentialism and poststructuralism, two schools of philosophical thought which, rising to prominence in France in the post–World War II era, have emerged as general cultural and intellectual movements. I initially want to acknowledge that I deal with these movements in a general way, as a humanist, and not as a professional philosopher. As a result, I am concerned with the broad implications of these movements, not with narrow technical issues of concern to those who specialize in the subtle aspects of philosophic analysis.

Although I am a structurally oriented scholar, I do not seek to dismiss or debunk existentialism and poststructuralism. Thus, I view existentialism and poststructuralism as means of usefully tempering structural thought. Although I don't embrace these methods in my own work, I recognize it is legitimate for others to do do; existentialism and poststructuralism are strong and rich intellectual traditions. I hope that my comments will prove to be useful to the reader in particular and to marketing/consumer research in general.

Since World War II, alternatives to structural analysis have arisen; they are represented by the emergence (and by the vogue) of both existentialism and poststructuralism. Existentialism emerged as a major intellectual movement immediately after World War II; poststructuralism flowered from existential roots in the 1960s as a means of countering mental structural analysis. One strategy for doing so is to depict structures as an illusion; thus, a key aspect of poststructuralism is to undercut the belief in mental structuralism that was discussed in Chapter 6. The individualistic tradition represented by existentialism and poststructuralism continues to flourish and it has made numerous contributions to the humanities, the social sciences, and to practitioner disciplines such as marketing/consumer research. This chapter deals with existentialism and its vogue from the end of World War II until the 1960s.

Existential/poststructural analysis is very different from structuralism since the focus is upon the dilemmas of the individual in a confusing, alienating, and absurd world. Although often depicted as transcending structural analysis, existential/poststructural methods are not intrinsically superior; instead they are specialized tools that are useful in a number of specific circumstances; that is certainly the perspective from which this book considers the existential/poststructural method.

In this discussion, we will deal with existentialism from a historical perspective and focus upon what it can and cannot accomplish; in this regard, its strengths and weaknesses are discussed through a comparison with structural analysis. The next chapter will deal with the poststructural movement.

THE PEDIGREE

As has been emphasized in earlier chapters, it is often useful to focus upon society as an overarching and structured entity and to downplay the roles, thoughts, and feelings of specific individuals. As we have seen in Chapters 6 through 10, such perspectives have a vital contribution to make to marketing/consumer research.

There is a long tradition of such perspectives. The ancient Greeks (and the sophisticated philosophy that they developed) initially centered upon the collective city-state as an overarching and structured entity, and they discounted individuals accordingly. Eventually, however, Alexander the Great's conquests established a process of political and economic centralization that ultimately undermined the city-state (and its self-contained, collective orientation); as a result, a largely homogeneous region (the circum-Mediterranean basin and beyond) emerged where individuals could range far and wide and function largely unfettered as freestanding individuals. This new, more fluid environment nurtured individuals, not collective groups (such as city-states), and gave rise to the vogue of new philosophies, such as stoicism, which (like existentialism) emphasized the individual, not the larger cultural entity.

After the fall of the Roman Empire in the West, however, the Christian church grew in power and, increasingly, it demanded collective obedience and adherence to its dogmas (even though Christian doctrine incorporated a wide variety of stoic principles). During this era (often labeled the Dark Ages), a new era of collectiveness arose and worldviews that were appropriate for this kind of highly structured social organization emerged. By the time of the Renaissance, however, the pendulum swung back once more and the vogue of the individual was again on the rise. These emerging conditions again led to individualistic worldviews, most notably in the work of René Descartes, the dominant philosopher of the era.

From a marketing and consumer behavior point of view, these developments demonstrate how intellectual products (such as philosophical systems that profoundly impact people's behavior) tend to evolve over time and do so in tandem with the evolution of the culture and its political/economic underpinnings. Ultimately, this tendency of product preference is another example of structural principles in action since they show how the structure of the culture leads to particular responses by its members. Ironically, however, some of these structured principles encouraged individualistic sentiments that actually militated against the prevailing social structure. Nonetheless, Descartes (1596–1660) emerged on the scene during an upswing of the individualistic perspective and his philosophy bears the imprint of that era; it was widely embraced for that reason. Marketing/consumer research can view this response by the intellectual community as an example of the impact of culture and cultural evolution upon the transformation of patterns of consumption; the temper of the times is clearly linked to the popularity of Descartes' work.

Descartes is a towering figure in the history of philosophy and in the development of mathematics and scientific research methods. When Descartes received his education, however, traditional Scholastic thought still dominated philosophy. Scholasticism was collective in nature because it emphasized comparing and contrasting the views of the recognized authorities of the past and forging new knowledge by deductively building upon and/or interpreting the collective efforts of earlier scholars. In complete opposition to the traditions of the Scholastic method, Descartes began his philosophy with an individualistic inward orientation and he built his philosophical edifice from that point.

The slogan or catchphrase that depicts Descartes' work, of course, is "I think, therefore, I am." Beginning from that individualistic point of departure, Descartes rejects the academic accomplishments of the collectively oriented Scholastics and he forges his own individualistic philosophy that is centered around the experiences of the individual. Descartes (living in an age that increasingly emphasized the thoughts and dilemmas of specific people) gave the world a philosophical undergirding that clearly responded to the needs of this intellectual, cultural, and economic environment. The positive reception that Descartes and his work received can be viewed as another example of how the shifting belief structures of a people and the cultural/economic milieu in which they exist can influence the attractiveness of specific products (in this case, intellectual products).

The era of the Enlightenment, which followed on Descartes' coattails, was also individualistic in nature. As discussed above, the term "Enlightenment" refers to the intellectual movement of 18th-century Europe that culminated in the French Revolution. The movement's advocates often referred to their work as "enlightened" in order to assert how it transcended centuries of ignorance and did so through the application of human thought and reason.

Apologists for the Enlightenment also tended to emphasize the rights of the individual over the power and needs of the culture. Furthermore, they tended to believe that if individuals received an appropriate education, they would behave in humane and enlightened ways. Largely identifying their movement with the individualistic stoic philosophy of the Roman Empire, advocates of the Enlightenment urged people to use their individual powers of reason and not to blindly accept the pronouncements embraced by the collective society, such as those deriving from the Bible or St. Thomas Aquinas.

During the Enlightenment, people were urged to focus on the lives they were living and not to be preoccupied with the hereafter. Thus, the individual's immediate needs and cares were emphasized, not the salvation promised by the collectively oriented Church. Indeed, the leaders of the Enlightenment were untiring in their criticism of the church, its wealth, political power, and the way in which the church suppressed individual reason.

The ways in which the Enlightenment was championed by its advocates provides significant and useful examples to those who are interested in marketing, promotion, and consumer response. While most philosophical movements are dominated by professional scholars, the cause of the Enlightenment was advanced by a group of popularizers who tended to be skilled and informed communicators, not formally trained or scholars. Thus, they are known collectively as the "philosophes," not as philosophers. These philosophes wrote largely for the general, informed reading public of their era and they typically did not use the formal academic treatise as their chosen means of communication, opting instead for the partisan pamphlet and forms of creative writing such as plays, essays, and novels as their primary means of expression. This promotional strategy was highly successful. Interestingly enough, 20th-century French intellectuals who advanced existentialism (and other individualistic worldviews stemming from existentialism) follow a similar strategy; indeed, much existential thought was born in the coffee houses of Paris, not in the university seminar room. In my opinion, it was this "extra-university" promotional strategy that helped existentialism to rapidly reach a wide audience immediately after World War II. The temper of the times, of course, added to its popularity.

As we saw in Chapters 3 and 4, however, there was an eventual re-action against the individualistic positions represented by the Enlight-enment. Instead of focusing upon individual people and their powers of reason, for example, key aspects of the romantic era of the 19th century centered upon collective forces of thought and action. A culmination of this perspective is the concept of the *volksgeist*, which has been a key underpinning of the structural theories that were examined in the cluster of chapters presented above.

To a large extent, this collective orientation was a reaction to the power of the industrial revolution that was beginning to exert a profound im-pact upon the Western world. As we have seen, the leaders of the En-lightenment foresaw a future utopia that was based on reason and universal solutions to the moral problems in ways that mirror the con-temporary focus upon postindustrial society. As a result, the leaders of the Enlightenment celebrated human thought as a means of achieving the best of all possible worlds. The Enlightenment also focused attention upon the individual; as a result, individual rights were championed and celebrated as more important and basic than the needs and perspectives of the collective culture.

The experiences of the industrial revolution, however, presented a dif-ferent picture. Although some theorists (such as Adam Smith) argued that individual thought and initiative would be directed by an "invisible hand" that served the needs of the general public, the industrial revo-lution gave every indication of debasing mankind, culture, and life; so viewed, "progress" was not seen to be providing any great advance for mankind. As a result, many thinkers began to focus upon the structure of social life, its importance, its impact, and how it could be adjusted in more appropriate ways.

As discussed in Chapter 4, Karl Marx provided an important collective perspective. Building upon the dialectical cultural perspective provided by Friedrich Hegel, Marx argued that cultures inevitably evolve collec-tively and that they are primarily influenced by economic considerations. Marx's argument emphasizes that people are merely pawns in an his-torical unfolding that is bigger and more powerful than the individual and that the flow of history is a collective process over which specific personalities have no control.

Thus, there have been two streams in Western thought; one focuses on the culture, the other centers upon the individual. In Chapters 6 through 10 we focused on the culture and its power; starting with this chapter, our attention will be directed toward individuals and how they can be envisioned as a powerful force that must be integrated into the equations of life, culture, history, and consumption.

THE RISE OF 19TH-CENTURY INDIVIDUALISM

As indicated above, the emphasis upon the collective nature of life (represented, for example, by Hegel and Marx) came to dominate in the 19th century and to supplant the more individualistic thought of the Enlightenment. As we shall see, however, a number of intellectuals (most notably Søren Kierkegaard and Friedrich Nietzsche) continued to focus upon the individual and they argued that even in a world largely driven by the relentless flow of society, economics, and culture, the demands, feelings, and power of the individual still needed to be considered.

This alternative paradigm emphasized that even in a collective and industrial world, individual differences continue to survive. While the 19th century was impacted by the industrial revolution (a collective influence), certain aspects of the Romantic movement (such as the cult of the romantic hero, for example) celebrated the individual. While collective orientations (as represented by Marx) clearly advocated models of economic determinism that overshadowed the accomplishments of specific people, other intellectuals (such as Kierkegaard and Nietzsche) celebrated and championed the individual.

Although all four were influenced by the same forces of the industrial revolution, Hegel and Marx responded with a collective paradigm while Kierkegaard and Nietzsche followed a different, more individualistic path; thus Hegel and Marx centered on society while Kierkegaard and Nietzsche focused on the plight and dilemma of distinct human beings. Although Kierkegaard and Nietzsche exhibit profound differences (Kierkegaard, for example, embraced religion while Nietzsche repudiated it), both rejected collective, structural models (such as those represented by Hegel and Marx) because their intellectual opponents did not adequately deal with the individual.

A seminal thinker living and writing before his time, Kierkegaard insisted that individual people should embrace what they believe and what is right for them. This position is very different from that of Hegel (who focused upon the *volksgeist* of a people) and Marxist orientations that argue that culture (as impacted by economics) moves with the inevitable flow of history that individual people are incapable of resisting.

As an example of Kierkegaard's tendency toward the individual, it is useful to look in passing at his "The Present Age" (1846). Paralleling today's individualistic thinkers, Kierkegaard complains about the influence of the mass media and he goes on to observe: "The man who has no opinion of an event at the actual moment accepts the opinion of the majority or, if he is quarrelsome, of the minority" (1846: 265). Thus, Kierkegaard argues that individual people are apt to embrace the will or worldview of the collective society (or reject it) without adequate reflection. While Hegel and Marx consider such a response to be inevitable, Kierkegaard urges people to fight against the tendency.

Carried to its logical extreme, Kierkegaard objects: "The [current] generation has rid itself of the individual and of everything organic and concrete and put in its place "humanity" and the numerical equality of man and man ... [nevertheless] every individual must work for himself, each for himself" (1846: 269). Significantly, in this quotation, Kierkegaard overtly juxtaposes his individualistic position with Hegel's organic model of society. Kierkegaard, it should be mentioned, was vehemently opposed to Hegel and his collective view of mankind.

It is useful to briefly consider the collective perspectives (found in Hegel's *Phenomonology of Mind*) because Kierkegaard rebelled against them. Hegel perceived the emotional development of people to start with an individualistic/hedonistic phase, proceed to a romantic phase, and mature or culminate in the development of a sense of duty. Thus, personal development went from focusing on the needs and feelings of the individual to the demands of the greater, collective society. Kierkegaard clearly felt that Hegel went too far by disregarding or downplaying the individual, and much of his work can be viewed as his attempt to correct or augment Hegel's collective views by adding an individualistic component.

Kierkegaard affirms that it is important for people to look into themselves and to make decisions based on their own genuine feelings, not merely with reference to some sort of external set of guidelines. This perspective is clearly present in his religious writings, especially his *Fear and Trembling* (1954), which deals with the story of Abraham and Isaac that appears in the Old Testament. As the reader may recall, while Abraham and Isaac were traveling, God, for no apparent reason, commanded Abraham to kill his beloved Isaac. This command appears to be without merit if viewed according to the dictates and perspectives of society and mankind. Nonetheless, a grief-stricken Abraham demonstrates his willingness to abide by God's will, but at the last possible moment, God rescinds the order and a ram is sacrificed in Isaac's place.

According to Kierkegaard, the message of *Fear and Trembling* is that rational thought (such as that provided by the culture and society) is not appropriate for making key decisions about life. Instead, Kierkegaard insists, we (like Abraham) should respond to deeply held beliefs and convictions, such as obeying God, even if doing so seems illogical. Thus, while Hegel views mankind as overcoming individualistic tendencies in order to act according to the dictates of the larger world and culture, Kierkegaard affirms the value of individualistic thought, even if it conflicts with the dictates of the culture or the logic provided by society.

This basic view of Kierkegaard (expanded beyond religion and secularized) is one of the basic underpinnings of existential thought and other contemporary individualistic philosophies.

Moving from Kierkegaard to Nietzsche, a further emphasis upon the individual is advocated. Somewhat influenced by the theory of evolution and the concept of the survival of the fittest, Nietzsche combined Arthur Schopenhauer's focus upon the will with Charles Darwin's theory of evolution. Nietzsche assumed that all individuals possess an innate desire to gain power. Given this inherent need and propensity, Nietzsche celebrated the hero as a "superior" individual who is able to achieve his goals through vision, personal power, and resolve. This individualistic perspective is profoundly different from collective paradigms such as those held by Hegel and Marx, which suggest that social and cultural circumstances, not the will or personal strength of the individual, lead to heroic action, status, and/or cultural advances.

Indeed, Nietzsche criticizes social institutions (such as religion) because he complains that they deemphasize the individual. Suggesting that no moral system (*volksgeist* and/or *volksgeist* theory of law) is universally appropriate in all circumstances and that variation can and should exist, Nietzsche does not view collective obedience (to the dictates of an effete culture) to be the handmaiden of achievement; instead, he focuses on the will of strong heroic leaders. These are individualistic perspectives that repudiate the social structural position.

Since I was trained as a literary critic and anthropologist, I tend to view Nietzsche in terms of his work as a cultural observer. As a result, his *The Birth of Tragedy* (1956) is a good place to begin a discussion of his perspectives. According to Nietzsche, ancient Greek culture was profoundly impacted by a tension which, he asserts, can be discussed in terms of a dichotomy between two Greek gods, Apollo and Dionysus (Bacchus).

According to Nietzsche, Apollo represents the defined order that is affirmed and demanded by the culture. Nietzsche suggests that there is a tendency for socialized people to ignore the inconsistencies and horrors of the world by embracing the illusion that is provided by the culture. This is what he depicts as an Apollonian way of thinking.

The alter ego of this accommodating perspective is to discard the Apollonian "rose-colored glasses" and accept reality as it exists. According to Nietzsche, this kind of realistic vision typically takes place when people are in an altered state of consciousness; thus Dionysus (Bacchus) is the god of wine.

As demonstrated by *The Birth of Tragedy*, Nietzsche had a significant interest in religion, although he went on to be become its fierce opponent. The most important (and most widely remembered) phrase of Nietzsche, of course, is his pronouncement "God is dead" which appears in *Thus Spake Zarathustra*.

Being an atheist, Nietzsche did not believe God was dead because what has never lived cannot die. The point he was making, however, is that the belief in God was being discarded. Nietzsche argues that for centuries people have followed a moral code because they believed that God gave it to them. He then asserts that as the belief in God declines, moral codes based on religion are destined to fall like a house of cards once their foundation is shaken.

From this point, Nietzsche (in his *Beyond Good and Evil*) (1973) presents a conjectural history of mankind. Originally, he theorizes, strong warriors ruled and they adopted a code that emphasized strength and power as inherently good while depicting weakness as appalling. This is what Nietzsche calls the "master mentality." Eventually, however, the lowly masses began to reverse this worldview by insinuating that weakness and humility are good while strength, domination, and aggression are evil and perverted. Nietzsche finds the resulting "slave mentality" to be reprehensible, self-serving propaganda that had been dreamed up by the weak and incompetent in order to control the powerful who, he asserts, are the legitimate leaders of society. Having made this point, he went on to attack the Judeo-Christian tradition as a bastion of the slave mentality.

Nietzsche's conjecture, incidentally, can be viewed as the opposite of the trickledown theory that has emerged as a staple of modern marketing/consumer research. The trickledown theory postulates that styles of thinking and consumption are originally innovated by the powerful. Eventually these ideas are emulated by the lower classes who have less power, prestige, and money. Thus, this theory argues that ideas tend to trickle down from the elite to the masses. The slave mentality position, in contrast, argues that ideas start within the lower, weaker classes and are then adopted and embraced by rich and affluent. This tendency for weak individuals to innovate is commonplace in many kinds of products (such as music and clothing styles), but trickledown theory does not adequately deal with it.

Ultimately, Nietzsche's thinking culminated in his idea of the "superman," the strong-willed and passionate visionary whose demands ultimately lead to progress and cultural fulfillment. Significantly, the superman thinks for himself and he employs his own personal morality (and is not, therefore, inhibited by the dictates of a feeble and inept society). Essentially, Nietzsche firmly advances the individualistic perspective and he undercuts more collective orientations such as those arising from Hegel, Marx, and the social sciences.

Exerting an influence during their own era, Kierkegaard and Nietzsche have had their greatest impact in the post–World War II era because they significantly influenced existential philosophy and its offshoots. Studying the social milieu of Europe in the post–World War I era, a significant transformation away from an optimistic belief in cultural "progress" provided by the collective society can be clearly discerned. It became painfully obvious to those living in that era that the industrial revolution had not eliminated human misery. Indeed, the mechanization of war had made suffering all the more horrible. And while the industrial revolution sometimes led to economic prosperity, it also made society vulnerable to economic collapse (such as the international economic depression of the 1930s). Facing these impacts, many intellectuals sought a more individualistic alternative to paradigms that centered around society, technology, and the modern collective world. Because Kierkegaard and Nietzsche advocated a clearly individualistic perspective, they provided a key for dealing with these issues and they exerted a profound influence upon the development of existentialism and upon poststructural methods that build upon the existential model.

Thus, Kierkegaard and Nietzsche can be viewed as antecedents of the modern focus upon individualism in philosophy and cultural analysis.

A TIDE OF INDIVIDUALIST THOUGHT

While Kierkegaard and Nietzsche provided the first glimmerings of a neo-individualism that transcended the social structural paradigm, other intellectual forces were eventually marshaled in this direction. In America, the frontier thesis of American history and pragmatism (a philosophical movement) emphasized and celebrated the individual. In Europe, philosophers Edmund Husserl and Martin Heidegger came to emphasize the conscious thought of specific people. A brief overview of these contributions (and their influence) will help to present the post–World War I intellectual climate in which existentialism initially flowered.

Although the canon of modern individualistic thought stems from Kierkegaard and Nietzsche as reworked by Husserl and Heidegger, and culminates in the legacy of Jean-Paul Sartre and Jacques Derrida, the forces of individualism were active in other places. In America, they are represented by American historian Friedrich Jackson Turner and his frontier thesis of American history, as well as by the rise of pragmatism as a philosophic vision that is also distinctly American.

Turner viewed the history of North America, since its colonization by pioneers of European stock, in terms of a reawakening of the spirit of individualism that, he asserted, had been allowed to atrophy in the Old World. Turner suggested that the Old World was totally civilized and had been so for thousands of years; in this milieu, he reasoned, the collective culture, not the individual personality, had come to dominate.

In the New World, Turner continued, civilization was weak and the rigors of an untamed frontier demanded personal strength. In this environment, people were forced to reassert their individuality without the power of the culture backing them up; as a result, Turner affirmed that Americans had regained the personal vigor that had declined in a sedentary Europe.

Acknowledging that the North American frontier was closed (or tamed) by 1890, Turner affirmed that the first phase of American history was at an end; nonetheless, he theorized, the individualistic lessons that Americans had learned during this struggle in a wild and untamed land would continue to provide our civilization with a strength and a distinctiveness that would continue to set them apart from their more civilized and effete European cousins.

Turner's thesis, hinged as it was around individualism, went on to become a major underpinning of the philosophy of American history, and his thinking has long been used to explain the uniqueness of the American personality type.

The influence of an overt "American-ness" has also been observed in the work of the pragmatic movement in philosophy that is a distinctively American innovation. The initial catalyst for the movement was the thinking of American philosopher Charles Sanders Pierce, who stated that belief was something that could motivate people to act in a particular way. Eventually, these ideas were rephrased by psychologist William James, who asserted that the meaning of a specific idea was determined by the specific impact it had upon a person's behavior. Note how James' thinking was becoming increasingly individualistic.

The idea of pragmatism was further refined by John Dewey, who leaned heavily upon the ideas of Charles Darwin. Calling his method "instrumentalism," Dewey emphasized the goals of specific people and he developed his model from that point. Ultimately, pragmatism exerted a profound impact upon American life and thought and it has been dubbed the most representative American philosophy. Like Turner's frontier thesis of American history, pragmatism is optimistic, action oriented, and centers upon the individual.

In spite of these New World developments, the emphasis upon individualism took another route of development in Europe. In this regard, it is useful to consider the work of Husserl and Heidegger because they exerted a profound impact upon Jean-Paul Sartre (the leading figure of existential thought).

During the first third of the 20th century, depth psychology as advanced by its advocates (such as Sigmund Freud and Carl Gustav Jung) exerted a profound impact upon both scientific and lay views of the world. Depth psychology focuses upon what goes on below the level of consciousness; there is no reason to doubt the power and importance of this productive and fruitful research agenda.

Nonetheless, by focusing upon unconscious thought, the interactions of the conscious and rational mind were underemphasized or ignored. During the same time that depth psychology was establishing an intellectual beachhead, German philosopher Edmund Husserl was directing his attention toward conscious, rational thought. Husserl (who owed an intellectual debt to James) viewed thought and action as intentional; his work led to the establishment of phenomenology as a basic philosophical position that centers upon the conscious experience of phenomena by individual people. Husserl's strategy was to deal with conscious thought and, therefore, he provided a useful way of envisioning individualistic experiences and thought.

These ideas were reworked and expanded by Heidegger, a student of Husserl. Heidegger's work is preoccupied with human existence and, following from Husserl, he largely concentrated upon conscious thought and its interlinkings with existence. Heidegger also drew attention toward Nietzsche. Thus, Heidegger, by building upon Husserl and Nietzsche, prepared an environment where existentialism, as we know it, could develop as a mass movement. The intellectual stage had been set for the emergence of Sartre.

No discussion of the rise of existentialism and the individualistic vision it entails, however, would be complete without a discussion of the impact of World War I. As was indicated above, the ethos of the Enlightenment (while individualistic) was one of optimism; rational thought was celebrated as providing a vision that would remake the world in a kinder frame. This belief followed from the assumption that if people became informed and enlightened, their true goodness would come to the surface. Education, it was thought, would channel society (and the people who exist within it) to act in good and noble ways. Ultimately, the Enlightenment cast a long shadow; throughout the 19th and even into the early 20th century, its vision of progress and the inherent goodness of mankind continued to sway pubic opinion. Thus, while Nietzsche pointed to evolutionary theory as evidence of the brutishness of mankind, social Darwinists used the same evolutionary theory to argue that society was inevitably evolving upward and onward for the greater good of all.

World War I and its aftermath, however, dispelled these pipe dreams. While the 19th century (after the fall of Napoleon) had been an era of material progress and relative peace, the horrific role of technology in World War I proved that "progress" was a mixed blessing at best. The economic panics following the war (culminating in a worldwide depression) underscored, even more sharply, the fact that technological progress and complex schemes of social and industrial organization do not inevitably lead to a better life.

Among American writers, the post–World War I era gave rise to what Gertrude Stein called the "lost generation"; members of this group of writers and intellectuals (such as Ernest Hemingway) wrote about the horrors of life and the wasteland wrought by the modern world. Even more than his war novels, Hemingway's Nick Adams stories (concerning a character from Michigan who lives in a world despoiled by the greed of the lumber barons) depict a world where the last vestige of the Enlightenment has gone extinct. The characters in his war novels, furthermore, portray (in his crisp and unpretentious style) the lives and thoughts of men and women who, due to circumstance, were deprived of purpose and moral values. The work of writers, such as Hemingway in the 1920s, underscores a shift in thought and sentiment that was to culminate in what has come to be called existentialism and postmodernism.

SARTRE AND THE RISE OF EXISTENTIALISM

The leading proponent of existentialism as a social movement (and not merely as an obscure branch of academic philosophy) is Jean-Paul Sartre. In order to understand this profoundly important social crusade, it is necessary to evaluate the vision that Sartre brought to his thinking and writing, and not merely consider the earlier thinkers who influenced him. Nonetheless, it is useful to briefly review the intellectual milieu in which his ideas were forged.

As indicated above, Descartes, the philosopher of the Renaissance, emphasized the individual in his subjectively oriented slogan "I think, therefore, I am." Most generally, Sartre embraced Descartes' individualistic thrust as a jumping-off point. This focus upon individual conscious thought was given a more modern flavor through Sartre's studies of Husserl and Heidegger while a student in Berlin in the 1930s. Although Sartre eventually acknowledged a debt to Karl Marx, his connections to the individualistic perspective provided by Husserl and Heidegger are vital and prominent.

Focusing upon this intellectual lineage in isolation, however, would distort reality because Sartre brought his own vision and agenda to his work; he was overtly hostile to society and to the social structure in which he was raised. Consider, for example, the bitterness that runs through his autobiography *The Words* (1964b), the story of his life until 1917 when he was 12 years old. Sartre presents an unyielding frontal attack on both his mother and his grandparents; in the process, he provides a scathing indictment of the middle-class world in which he was raised.

Sartre's father died when he was but 15 months old and, as a result, he and his mother had to retreat back to the roof of her parents in order to forestall poverty and privation. His family, incidentally, was made up of well-connected intellectuals; his mother's uncle, for example, was the acclaimed theologian and missionary Albert Schweitzer. Her father (Sartre's grandfather) was also a noted writer who specialized in textbooks.

Instead of welcoming Sartre and his mother in their time of need and grief, the grandparents accepted Sartre and his mother, but there were significant strings attached to their generosity. As is often the case when parents and their adult children are in close contact, there was a tendency for Sartre's mother to be treated as a child and for her parents to reassert the dominant parental role.

These tendencies were bolstered by the economic vulnerability faced by mother and child. Sartre recalls: "She was not refused pocket money; they simply forgot to give her any. When her former friends, most of them married, invited her to dinner, she had to seek permission well in advance, and promise that she would be back before ten. . . . Invitations became less frequent" (1964b: 18).

Although Sartre received an excellent education through the help of his grandfather, the most powerful passages in *The Words* concern the old man's patriarchial nature and how he used economic leverage to lord over his daughter and to control her in hurtful, unreasonable, and self-serving ways. Thus, from his early boyhood on, Sartre viewed himself as an individual downtrodden (although not totally overwhelmed) by a pretentious and overbearing social system represented by his grandfather.

This hostility toward culture did not fade once Sartre reached adulthood. Consider, for example, Sartre's acclaimed play *No Exit* (1958). Presented on a sparsely equipped (though brightly lit) stage, the play's three characters each sit on their own small sofas. The audience quickly learns that they are all dead and condemned to Hell. Surprisingly, however, no hellfires burn and there is no overt punishment of any kind. The punch line of the play is the oft-quoted observation that "hell is other people." Ultimately, being forced to endure others is punishment enough. I hardly need to underscore the anti-social nature of such a plotline.

No Exit, incidentally, was the first play produced in Paris after the retreat of the German occupation forces in 1944. The horrors of that conflict, no doubt, created an environment where the theme of the play probably rung true for most of the audience. Expanding this observation, it may be possible to get a feeling for the experiences of the era and how the temper of the times gave existentialism an irresistible attractiveness.

In any event, existentialism quickly emerged as a dominant philosophical position among a wide range of intellectuals and other informed people. It quickly transcended the university and the ranks of professional philosophers and it emerged as a major social movement. This course of events has significant implications for marketing/consumer research. Fads and mass movements are commonplace in consumer goods;

these tendencies however, also have their parallels in major cultural and intellectual movements. Due to the external pressures caused by World War II, large sections of the public were rethinking their relationship with their culture and seeking a means of relying upon their own personal morality or judgement in a confusing world. While these ideas predate World War II (Sartre's *Nausea*, for example, was originally published in 1938), after years of German occupation, the French people were ready to enthusiastically embrace such perspectives. And in a world largely despoiled and exhausted by the war; existentialism quickly went on to become an international movement.

In many ways, existentialism can be viewed as a reaction against Hegel's cultural orientations, coupled with the realization that the search for truth is elusive. Hegel, as the reader may recall, emphasized culture as the handiwork of a great mind yearning and striving for fulfillment. In a spirit similar to evolutionary theory, Hegel foresaw a world that was becoming even more perfect; the legacy of the "great mind" that created it. Evolutionists also saw a universal force perfecting itself, although they did not depict it an as a conscious and rational anthropomorphic god. Even in the 19th century, however, there had been some intellectuals who reacted against such a depiction; besides the writings of Kierkegaard and Nietzsche, Dostoyevsky's *Notes from the Underground* (1960) is a good example of this tendency; there the hero raves against the truisms of a humanistic, rational worldview. As I have argued elsewhere (Walle 2000), it is not unusual for a wide variety of ideas to be available within a culture at a particular time. Some of these ideas, however, may be presented before they can be accepted by most members of a culture as a mass movement. As a result, they will have an insignificant impact upon the marketplace when originally articulated, although at a later period they may be embraced because they fit the temper of the times. Dostoyevsky appears to be such a writer; by the mid 20th century his ideas fit into the intellectual scene and he was celebrated as a pioneering existentialist (or at least as a proto-existentialist). When published, however, his work, although well-crafted and respected, could not fuel or be a part of a mass movement.

After World War I and the economic crises that followed in its wake, however, people increasingly began to lose faith in a great and good "world force" that helped people to perfect themselves. The atrocities and carnage wrought by World War II, quickly following on the heels of the first great conflict, exerted a profound impact. These two great conflicts and their impacts, operating in tandem, undermined (and largely drove into extinction) the optimistic visions that tended to prevail in the 19th century.

Coupled with the loss of faith in a better world was the belief that, in the final analysis, there is no true source of knowledge and no correct formula for making the hard decisions in one's life. Thus, people must make decisions, but they have no objective means of doing so and no universal ethical standard upon which to draw. Like Nietzsche's superman, they must fall back upon their own individual judgement.

Sartre discusses this dilemma in his famous speech of October 1945 (published under the title "Existentialism Is a Humanism"). In a world where World War II was a fresh memory, he provided an example to which many in his audience could, no doubt, relate. It concerns a young man who came to Sartre asking for advice on what to do. His older brother had been killed in the war and now he lived with his mother who had no one but him in her life. He wanted to provide for her and be her companion. On the other hand, he wanted to escape to England, join the free French military contingent, and fight the Germans. The young man asked for advice on what to do. Sartre observed: "Who could help him choose? Certainly not Christian doctrine, since both choices satisfy the criteria of a Christian choice. . . . I had only one answer to give, "You're free, choose. . . . No general ethic can show you what is to be done" (1977: 36).

Ultimately, this dilemma presents another of the key issues that preoccupied Sartre's work: the notion that people are, in the final analysis, "condemned to be free." In his 1947 novel *The Age of Reason*, Sartre again deals with the emotional trauma wrought by World War II; in this case the hero is fighting the German army. Sartre observes: "He was free . . . to act like an animal or like a machine. He could do what he wanted to do . . . free and alone, without an excuse; condemned to decide without an excuse . . . condemned forever to be free" (1947). As has been emphasized, existential thought is a means of acknowledging that even though people may be products of the culture, they still must make decisions; once made, furthermore, they must embrace these actions and their consequences.

This set of affairs led French existentialism to emphasize the absurdity of life. Various authors such as playwright Samuel Becket contributed to this vision. The classic statement by Becket is his *Waiting for Godot* (1956), where Becket focused upon the absurdity of life and the need for individuals to cope with this reality. During the era when existentialism was a dominant buzzword, the concept of absurdity called attention to the fact that reality defies a rational explanation and, yet, people must somehow learn to cope with this irrational world. Those who are firmly entrenched within a social system, in contrast, do not raise these questions and, by and large, they accept the status quo without questioning its absurdity. By focusing on absurdity, however, a hornet's nest of doubt that structuralists tend to ignore rises in a swarm.

CONCLUSION

This chapter has dealt with the "flip-flop" of the vogue of "individualist" vs. "collective" worldviews and it dealt with them in terms of the pressures faced by people during different periods of history. The ultimate focus has been upon the existential thought of the post–World War II era. As emphasized throughout the text, the rising and falling vogue of various belief systems can be viewed as an example of consumer response; so envisioned, it is useful to our profession as an example of how and why people act in the way they do.

During the Renaissance, Descartes' individualism was embraced because it fit into the temper of his time. The same is true of the individualism of the Enlightenment. The horror of the French Revolution and the inequities of the industrial revolution, however, led to a transcendence of the individualistic vision by philosophers and social activists such as Hegel and Marx; their visions are distinctly social and not individualistic.

After World War II, in turn, existentialism, a new form of individualism, rose to prominence. Its popularity largely resulted from a disenchantment with the collective, social vision and the need for people to find personal ways to make moral judgments in a confusing and conflicting world.

These visions provide a classic example of the process by which patterns of consumption evolve; it does so by connecting the ever-changing pressures of life with shifts in public belief and sentiment. As such, the rise and fall of ideologies and the concomitant impact upon the products people choose to consume can be more effectively explored. In passing, I have provided brief asides that have dealt with these tendencies; I hope they were useful and informative.

By the 1960s, however, Sartre, the leader of the existential movement, increasingly redirected his attention and effort toward ad hoc political issues, not general philosophical or theoretical issues. As he became more of a political activist, furthermore, the existential method became attacked by the mental structural position of Levi-Strauss.

Due to the void created by the change of focus in Sartre's work, others who stem from the existential tradition arose and provided a response to mental structuralism. This movement, of course, is poststructuralism.

We are currently in an era that is impacted by a poststructural view of the world. As a result, much marketing/consumer research is hinged around this worldview. In order to understand the poststructural vision, it is necessary to perceive the pressures and influences that gave rise to it. The chapter above can be read as a foundation that is useful for understanding poststructuralism and its impact upon marketing/consumer research. We are now ready to examine the poststructural movement and how it impacts how people think and consume products.

REFERENCES

Becket, Samuel. (1956). *Waiting for Godot*. London: Faber and Faber.

Dostoyevsky, Fyodor. (1960). *Notes from the Underground*, trans. Ralph E. Matlaw. New York: Dutton.

Hegel, Friedrich. (1949). *The Phenomonology of Mind*, 2nd ed. London: Allen and Unwin.

Kierkegaard, Søren. (1846). *"The Present Age" and Two Minor Ethico-Religious Treatises*, trans. Alexander Dru and Walter Lowrie. Oxford: Oxford University Press, 1940.

Kierkegaard, Søren. (1954). *Fear and Trembling, and The Sickness unto Death*, trans. Walter Lowrie. Garden City, NY: Doubleday.

Nietzsche, Friedrich Wilhelm. (1905). *Thus Spake Zarathustra*, trans. Thomas Common. New York: Modern Library.

Nietzsche, Friedrich Wilhelm. (1956). *The Birth of Tragedy and The Genealogy of Morals*, trans. Francis Goffing. Garden City, NY: Doubleday.

Nietzsche, Friedrich Wilhelm. (1973). *Beyond Good and Evil: Prelude to a Philosophy of the Future*, trans. R. J. Hollingdale. Harmondsworth, UK: Penguin.

Sartre, Jean-Paul. (1947). *The Age of Reason*, trans. Eric Sutton. New York: Vintage.

Sartre, Jean-Paul. (1958). *No Exit: A Play in One Act*, adapted by Paul Bowels. New York: French.

Sartre, Jean-Paul. (1964a). *Nausea*, trans. Lloyd Alexander. Norfolk, CT: New Directions.

Sartre, Jean Paul. (1964b). *The Words*, trans. Bernard Frechtman. New York: G. Braziller.

Sartre, Jean-Paul. (1977). *Existentialism and Humanism*, trans. Philip Mairet. London: Eyre Metheon.

Walle, Alf H. (2000). *The Cowboy Hero and Its Audience: Popular Culture as Market Derived Art*. Bowling Green, OH: The Popular Press.

CHAPTER 13

Poststructural Leaders and Marketing/Consumer Research

POSTSTRUCTURALISM: AN OPENING STATEMENT

As stated in the last chapter, poststructuralism provides an updating of the individualist thrust of mental structuralism. Furthermore, it is currently being embraced by marketing/consumer research. When scholars borrow ideas they make every effort to provide a review of the intellectual foundations of their work; nonetheless, journal space is in short supply and, as a result, these discussions are often culled to a minimum. Due to this situation, the distinctiveness of the various pioneering thinkers who originally forged the poststructural movement can easily be clouded and obscured. My goal here is to provide a general and evenhanded background of these seminal thinkers in a way that goes beyond the truncated discussions so commonly provided in journal articles.

In order to present this overview, the major figures of the poststructuralist movement are presented as distinct personalities. As a group of close-knit French scholars, the term poststructuralism usually refers to Jacques Derrida, Michel Foucault, Jacques Lacan, Roland Barthes, and Julia Kristeva[1]. The major theoretical positions of these scholars were formulated in the 1960s and 1970s. At approximately the same time, their ideas began to influence literary criticism (in the United States and elsewhere). In recent years, marketing/consumer research has been introduced to poststructuralism; the work of Barbara Stern, Firat Fuat, and John Sherry immediately come to mind in this regard. In Stern's case, the methods of Jacques Derrida, as adapted by the "Yale school" of literary criticism, have exerted a strong impact upon her work.

To provide an indication of the range of poststructuralism, I will initially nest poststructuralism within its intellectual frameworks; this will be followed by a sketch of each of the founding members (as enumerated above). A conclusion will discuss the value of the method to marketing/consumer researchers.

AN OVERVIEW OF THE POSTSTRUCTURAL MOVEMENT

As has been argued above, the social structural model of culture and human behavior has a long and illustrious history; up to and including the end of World War II, it (in its various permutations) dominated the social sciences. Eventually, however, a number of influential intellectuals (largely spearheaded by Claude Levi-Strauss) began to concentrate upon the inherent structure of the human mind, not the unique social structures of specific cultures. This led to what has been described (in an earlier chapter) as a form of "mental structuralism." Initially developed in anthropology, this mental structural approach eventually came to exert a strong influence upon humanities disciplines such as mythology, folklore, and literary criticism.

During the same basic period in which mental structuralism was exerting its impact, other intellectuals became increasingly preoccupied with the plight of the individual, not the collective society or universal patterns of human response. The first forceful articulating of these concerns was the pre–World War II development of existentialism; after the war, existentialism and the individualist perspective it championed became the vogue in many intellectual circles.

Rather quickly, existentialism emerged as a mass intellectual movement with Jean-Paul Sartre as the leading theoretician and spokesperson. Over time, however, Sartre became increasingly involved with partisan and ad hoc issues such as his rather belabored merging of existentialism and Marxism. As a result, when Levi-Strauss and his mental structuralism challenged existentialism, Sartre was preoccupied with other concerns centered around partisan politics. The poststructuralists are the individualistic-oriented scholars who, having existential roots, filled the gap left by Sartre's inability to respond to the threat of mental structuralism.

Thus, over time, two very different paradigms developed. The mental structuralists focused upon the universal workings of the human mind, while the existential/poststructural movement centered upon the unique mental activities of individuals, not uniform patterns of thought. Ultimately, this dichotomy was articulated by Jacques Derrida, who asserted that structuralism was dead. Derrida's approach (which can be viewed as a expansion and revision of the individualistic themes of existentialism) came to be called deconstructionism.

For a variety of reasons, the deconstructionist method quickly caught hold among many literary critics in the United States. The reason for its embrace, however, had much to do with the intellectual infighting among rival literary critics, especially formal critics who had lost ground due to the vogue of social criticism. In reduced circumstances, the formal critics were thrashing around for a new means of rehabilitating themselves.

Derrida provided two basic tools of significant value to the formal critics. First, because Derrida argued that structures do not really exist, the formal critics could use this premise to "pull the rug out from under" critics who embraced both mental and social structural models. Secondly, since Derrida employed very close textual analysis, the formal critics were provided with a role model with which to rehabilitate formal analysis.

Although the history of poststructuralism is, obviously, more complex than this, the connection between the formal traditions of literary criticism and poststructural theory is quite strong. Another key attraction of poststructuralism is that it provides a means of social analysis and even social activism. "Old guard" formal criticism, in contrast, was ill prepared to serve in this capacity. Poststructural models (stemming from existentialism), however, provided formal methods with orientations and methods that could be mated with a social consciousness. As a result of this dual focus, the method grew in popularity. This trend is important because it allowed formal criticism to deal with a range of ad hoc, topical, and partisan issues that had long been the bastion of social criticism.

THE POSTSTRUCTURAL PIONEERS IN REVIEW

As indicated above, the term poststructural tends to refer to the collective work of a cluster of French intellectuals who made their definitive statements of theory and method in the 1960s and 1970s. As is the case with almost all intellectual leaders, each of these pioneers is distinct and unique; although poststructuralism is often viewed as a monolith, in reality there is significant variation within it. Here, I will briefly discuss (in ways that are relevant to marketing/consumer researchers) the pioneers of poststructuralism on (what I feel are) their own terms.

I do so with no axe to grind, except to provide an objective overview presented in a way that is tailored to the needs of marketing/consumer researchers. In order to maintain the objective nature of this chapter, I, at times, indicate my own methodological and personal biases.

Jacques Derrida

Jacques Derrida is a major 20th-century philosopher who has contributed specialized work in the field of metaphysics; the branch of philosophy that searches for the ultimate foundations of truth and knowledge. Although widely known within the literary world for his impact upon the deconstructionist techniques of literary criticism, some observers speculate that Derrida's specialized work in metaphysics, not his impact upon literary criticism, "will give Derrida a place in the history of philosophy" (Rotry 1978–1979: 160).

As a result of his metaphysical research, Derrida began to think about language in general and about written language in particular. His early works were detailed analyses of philosopher Edmund Husserl (1859–1938), a major influence upon existentialism's Jean-Paul Sartre. As is the case with many fledgling intellectuals, Derrida's early publications were offshoots of his doctoral dissertation. Derrida's specialized work on Husserl, however, was followed by his more general *Writing and Difference* (1967b) and *Of Grammatology* (1967a), which present definitive statements of his approach and have gained the status of classic/seminal texts.

A central theme of *Of Grammatology* is that Western philosophy depicts the written word as a handicapped and limited substitute for spoken speech. In order to demonstrate his approach, Derrida engages in a number of very close readings of various texts and he uses these examples as exercises or case studies that display the points he presents regarding metaphysics. It was this technique of close textual analysis that ultimately attracted literary critics to Derrida. This emphasis upon close textual analysis firmly places Derrida within the poststructural camp because Derrida suggests that there exists no universal or uniform way in which language communicates.

One way in which Derrida and his advocates present their argument is to suggest that the "binary system" that is typical of the Western languages and societies is not a human or linguistic universal. The alternative example of the Oriental languages, for example, can be used to portray the atypical nature of the Western tradition.

An unrelated example of this kind of approach that stems from American social anthropology is the Sapir-Whorf hypothesis, which suggests that different languages create different mental patterns that cause speakers to perceive the world in distinct and non-analogous ways. Thus, alternative methods are available to deal with the issues that deconstructionism raises and, therefore, it is not necessary to adopt that method when dealing with them. Indeed, a more substantive approach is possible and it was well worked out by Edward Sapir (1956) and Benjamin Lee Whorf (1956) years before poststructuralism was developed.

Nonetheless, the method that Derrida inspired has become known as deconstructionism, a term that Derrida traces back to philosopher Martin Heidegger (1889–1976), an existentialist pioneer, a student of Husserl, and another influence upon Sartre. Thus, Derrida connects his critical method to certain narrow and circumscribed issues within contemporary philosophy that center around conscious thought, not the more substantive perspective of anthropological linguists, such as Whorf and Sapir.

Part of the assessment that Derrida has received from the community of literary criticism hinges upon the fact that he is first and foremost a philosopher and a specialist in metaphysics. In such a vein, Gasche (1986) observes that Derrida's key contributions deal with philosophical speculation and are not actively concerned with literary texts. As a result, Gasche maintains that deconstructionism, as a specific school of literary criticism, is an independent phenomena and is only indirectly connected to Derrida himself.

According to such a view, Derrida, although exerting a strong influence, is a specialized scholar dedicated to contemporary philosophy and he has made only indirect contributions to literary criticism and, by extension, to marketing/consumer research that builds upon deconstructionist criticism. To whatever extent deconstructionism is independent of Derrida (even if somewhat inspired by him), marketing/consumer researchers can get more relevant counsel by going straight to the deconstructionist methods of literary analysis as they have been developed (largely by the Yale school) and bypass Derrida himself. Personally, I accept Gasche's position; this orientation and strategy, furthermore, seems to be the path by which marketing researchers, such as Stern (1996), have embraced deconstructionism.

Those who consider using Derrida should be forewarned that his work is highly controversial. Marketing/consumer researchers must decide upon the degree to which they wish to base their work on such controversial theories. Derrida's rallying cry, for example, is "There is nothing outside the text." This is a polemical premise, however, that clearly contradicts Leslie Fiedler's earlier observation: "Text [the actual literary work] is merely one of the contexts of a piece of literature, its lexical or verbal one, no more or less important than the sociological, psychological, historical, anthropological, or generic" (1960).[2]

Fiedler is an internationally acclaimed social critic; his contradiction of Derrida's rallying cry demonstrates the controversial nature of deconstuctionist analysis. Being involved in controversy, while providing excitement, may also place one's intellectual and methodological foundations on the shifting sands of intellectual fads; marketing/consumer researchers need to consider the risk of doing so before embracing such methods. Strategically, I seek an intellectual nesting within the more traditional structural methods and models of social anthropology and social criticism, even though these methods are not particularly fashionable today. Therefore, I consciously seek to avoid controversial (and some would argue "flash in the pan") theories such as those raised by Derrida. In addition, even though I have a working knowledge of poststructuralism that goes back to my graduate student days in the early

1970s, I realize the complexity of deconstructionist analysis and the danger of applying it (or rather, misapplying it) within the context of either literary criticism or marketing/consumer research.

In any event, Derrida is a metaphysician who has examined the inability of certain kinds of language to effectively communicate. His efforts have encouraged a branch of literary criticism known as deconstructionism. Although the degree to which this critical method actually stems from Derrida himself is a matter of debate, it is recommended that marketing/consumer researchers first read literary critics who have refined deconstructionism as a method of literary criticism (such as Paul de Man) and only deal with the actual writings of Derrida when specifically required.

Derrida (or rather literary critical methods based on his work) have already exerted a strong influence on marketing/consumer research. Barbara Stern, in particular, has made use of this research strategy and it has been well received and fruitful. In her work, Stern attempts to show how specific phenomena (such as advertisements) can be interpreted in different ways by different people. As such, the thinking of Derrida is exerting an influence upon copywriting and marketing communications.

Roland Barthes

While Derrida is primarily a philosopher and his true relationship to literary criticism is tentative,[3] Roland Barthes was connected to the literary/critical establishment and its evolution from the end of World War II to 1980 (the year of his death). Initially nesting himself within the traditions of 19th-century Marxist writings and the existentialism of France in the late 1940s and 1950s, Barthes originally emerged as a structural critic.

Particularly impressive is his *Mythologies* (1957), which consist of an array of short essays concerning a number of phenomena including the strip tease, professional wrestling, and tour guides. Marketing researchers will be especially interested in his analysis of laundry detergent. Barthes' goal is to use disparate empirical evidence in order to demonstrate how the bourgeois worldview is communicated to society. This type of work, of course, can be viewed as structural since it argues that the structure of society is reflected in a parallel structure manifesting itself in literature and popular culture.

This interest in structuralism led to a phase in which Barthes adopted the semiology of Ferdinand de Saussure (1857–1913) in order to demonstrate how meanings were communicated in literature. Before de Saussure's ideas exerted an influence (after his death), linguistics had typically been concerned with the historical evolution of language. Turning the tables, de Saussure (1959) emphasized that linguistics should concentrate upon how the elements of language interact with one another at a specific time and place. Due to this emphasis, de Saussure became concerned primarily with the fact that meaning is based upon the structural relationships of the parts of the system in contact with one another; he called this analysis semiology.[4] As the reader will readily appreciate, this method and research agenda meshes well with structural analysis.

Based upon this work, Barthes develops his critical method in *Elements of Semiology* (1968) and demonstrates that approach in *The Fashion System* (1983). This later work should be of interest to marketing/consumer researchers because it is based on the analysis of the captions under photographs in two fashion magazines. Such semiological analysis suggests that meaning is created through context; *The Fashion System* is both entertaining and a fine work of critical/cultural analysis.

So far, Barthes' work constitutes a Marxist and existentialist use of structural principles that seeks to explicate popular culture and literary texts and, in the process, reveal the structures inherent in the society. As is the case in structural analysis, during this phase of Barthes' career, he assumes it is possible for a reader to know and understand what is being communicated. In the 1970s, however, Barthes, came under the influence of Derrida and Julia Kristeva and shifted from structuralist work to poststructuralism. In his later work, such as *S/Z* (1974), Barthes points to the fact that a specific text may have different multiple meanings.[5]

In order to demonstrate the value of this approach, Barthes subjected a short novel by Balzac to an analysis about seven times longer than the work itself. Not interested in the central theme of the book or its "message," Barthes extracts different meanings from the work. He presents his case by breaking the book down into 561 separate units and beginning his analysis from there. Critics (if they approve of Barthes' method or not) tend to acknowledge that *S/Z* is a masterpiece of literary analysis and it is generally accepted that this volume of critical analysis marks the end of Barthes' structuralist era and the beginning of his poststructuralist writing. In this later period, Barthes' writing became increasingly self-reflective and his perspective lost much of its Marxist edge. As a result, this later phase may be more accessible to some marketing/consumer researchers than his earlier structuralist work.

Nonetheless, it is my opinion (in line with my social structuralist and Marxist biases) that Barthes' early structuralist work (especially *Mythologies*) is the more provocative and useful for marketing/consumer research. And, as indicated above, many of the essays he presents there focus on issues related to marketing and consumer behavior and are of particular interest for that reason.[6]

In any event, most marketing/consumer researchers will find Barthes more accessible than Derrida. First, Barthes was a literary critic, not a specialized philosopher like Derrida. Second, Barthes went through a

personal intellectual evolution that may parallel the development of mar-
keting/consumer researchers who become interested in examining literature in order to extrapolate information of value to marketing
thought. As a result, by reading Barthes, useful linkages that are not
obvious in Derrida's writings may become apparent. On a purely personal note, I find Barthes to be the most engaging and useful of the major
pioneers of poststructural thought.

Because of the diversity of Barthes' career and the fact that his thinking
evolved from structuralism to poststruturalism, it is hard to provide a
concise statement of the ways in which his thought can be employed by
marketing/consumer researchers. Barthes, however, engaged in research
that linked culture to consumption and, therefore, his methods are especially amenable to the needs of our profession. Although Barthes'
structural work looked at consumption in order to grasp an underlying
structure, the same tactics can be applied to research questions that are
centered around consumption and explore the social structure in order
to understand that process.

Barthes' fine work with semiology is equally suggestive of options that
are open to marketing/consumer researchers. After the onslaught of
poststructuralism in the 1970s, structuralism fell into disuse (if not into
actual disrepute). Semiology, however, a method of looking at relationships between parts of a system, has been able to weather this storm and
it continues to be a popular approach that is able to fulfill many of the
tasks of structural analysis. And marketing/consumer researchers have,
on occasion, made use of this research strategy (Holbrook and Grayson
1986). Those who seek to use that method may wish to consult Barthes
because he did excellent semiological analysis that concerns topics that
parallel those embraced by marketing/consumer researchers. And since
Barthes' later work focuses upon different meanings and how to interpret them, he ultimately fit himself into the poststructural camp.

Jacques Lacan

While Derrida is a philosopher and Barthes was a literary critic,
Jacques Lacan was a noted psychoanalyst. In the late 1940s and early
1950s, Lacan was the leading psychoanalytic theorist in France; at that
time he began to popularize his ideas beyond the psychoanalytic profession by presenting a series of influential public lectures that were to
inspire noted specialists from a number of fields (such as Michel Foucault, who was to emerge as a fellow leader of the poststructuralist
movement).

About that time, Lacan became involved in polemical exchanges
within the larger psychoanalytic community; eventually, the International Psychoanalytic Association stripped him of his authority, which

led Lacan to open his own psychoanalytic institute. Because his new school adopted a more liberal set of entrance requirements than other psychoanalytic training centers, it developed a cross-disciplinary flavor or ambience. The resulting environment provided Lacan with an even wider breadth.

Starting from a strong (albeit idiosyncratic) grasp of psychoanalysis, Lacan began to borrow from a number of different disciplines. Paralleling Barthes in some ways, he was influenced by Ferdinand de Saussure. Considering the work of structural anthropologist Levi-Strauss (and his mental structural approach, which emphasizes innate human response to specific situations and cultures), Lacan began to link structuralism and language with psychoanalysis. Eventually, he argued that systems may break down; this orientation transformed his work into an increasingly poststructuralist posture.

Marketing/consumer researchers are warned that Lacan is very difficult to read, and it has even been suggested that he intentionally writes in an obscure manner that is difficult to understand. Thus, marketing/consumer researchers may share my impatience with him. On the other hand, Lacan's methods have been popularized; unfortunately, according to Catherine Clement, "Lacan's thought, now fashionable, has been reduced to jargon, turned into a parody of itself" (1983: 3). Still, Lacan is widely respected within literary criticism.

In all likelihood, most marketing/consumer researchers will not make direct use of Lacan for some of the reasons outlined above. Nonetheless, he is, without doubt, an influential writer who continues to have a profound (although somewhat indirect) impact upon poststructuralism. Those interested in psychology, however, will be especially interested in his work.

Michel Foucault

Influenced by Jacques Lacan (they met through Lacan's lecture series), Michel Foucault combined a knowledge of the methods and history of philosophy with the perspectives of psychoanalysis. Early in Foucault's career, he was primarily concerned with the impact of social institutions upon culture and human behavior. Representative of this phase of his career is his acclaimed *Madness and Civilization: A History of Insanity in the Age of Reason* (1965). The key to that work centers around the various ways in which religion, philosophy, and science have viewed insanity and the impact of these disciplines upon psychiatry. Much of this description is most disturbing. While in the Middle Ages insane people tended to be treated humanely and accepted on their own terms, during the "Age of Reason" in the 18th century they became victims of profound abuse. Foucault relates this harsh treatment to the "spirit of the age" that placed supreme importance and status upon rationality; as a result, those who were not rational tended to be harshly treated.

Viewed from a structural perspective, this analysis suggests that the structure (or structured beliefs) of a society impacts the way in which phenomena is perceived and how people are viewed and, ultimately, treated. Although the resulting theories held by society may not be correct, equitable, or appropriate, Foucault affirms that they do reflect the beliefs of people and institutions. Especially useful are his observations that oppressed people are often willing accomplices who contribute to their own mistreatment. This happens when the downtrodden or stigmatized accept the logic and the rationale of their oppressors. Such an observation suggests that the oppressed should not accept the negative evaluations of those who seek to dominate them; such an orientation can easily lead to poststructuralism and the observation that one uniform vision is not appropriate for all people.

Later in his life, Foucault wrote a multivolume analysis of sexuality. Not only is this work valuable on its own terms, it is also interesting in that it is the last thoughts in regard to sexuality of a gay man dying of AIDS. The History of Sexuality (1978) is also of interest because Foucault provides a poststructural view of humanity that rejects Freud's assumption that the psyche can be viewed as relatively stable. Foucault, in contrast, replaces Freud's notions with the idea that, psychologically, the individual is really a composite of several different forces and selves. The poststructural implications of such a view are self-evident. This perspective is also of potential value to marketing/consumer researchers who seek to distinguish the different mainsprings that may influence marketplace decisions.

Although many of Fouclaut's ideas are general (such as his observation regarding the complicity of the oppressed in their own mistreatment), and although his theories can be manipulated and utilized in a number of interesting and useful ways by marketing/consumer researchers (as well as by other scholars), in recent years Foucault seems to have been most influential in the field of gay and lesbian studies. Although marketing/consumer researchers may profit from an examination of Foucault's work, many of the contemporary Foucault-influenced critical perspectives are fairly narrow and they often specialize in gender and sexuality issues; as a result, the perspectives currently inspired by this research stream may not overtly address many of the issues pursued by many marketing/consumer researchers. Resourceful thinkers, however, may be able to adapt these issues in more general ways. Although I find Barthes to be the most engaging of the poststructural pioneers, I find Foucault to be the most relevant to the needs of marketing/consumer researchers.

Julia Kristeva

Of the pioneering poststructuralists, Julia Kristeva is by far the youngest. She worked closely with Lacan, Barthes, and Foucault, and she also studied under structuralist anthropologist Levi-Strauss. Not French by birth, Kristeva was raised in Soviet-controlled Bulgaria before coming to France on an academic scholarship.

As with other poststructuralists, Kristeva was initially drawn to Ferdinand de Suassure's semiotic theory, which looked for meaning not in the words themselves but in their relationships within a larger linguistic system. Being a political activist and feminist, Kristeva expended much of her effort analyzing and/or championing specific causes. As a result, she increasingly depicted language and communication as dynamic and multifaceted. Since she feels that language and communication cannot be adequately described, she eventually embraced the essence of poststructuralism.

Due to her activism and feminism, Kristeva dealt with the fact that there are many different groups in society and that understanding and/ or communicating with them may be difficult. As a result, marketing/ consumer research that is concerned with the distinctiveness of specific groups may benefit from her work. In addition, her interest in feminist issues might make her work useful to marketing/consumer researchers who are concerned with gender issues.

In recent years, Kristeva seems to have curbed her earlier preoccupation with radical politics; this disappoints some observers, while others view this development as an indication of her growing maturity and the broader focus of her current work. In fact, this wider perspective may ultimately increase her value to marketing/consumer research. In any event, Kristeva is an able scholar, thinker, and critic in her own right, while simultaneously representing somewhat of a culmination of the poststructural tradition.

Today, marketers are often concerned with distilling the distinctiveness of specific groups and forging ways of communicating with them. This, ultimately, is the path pursued when Kristeva worked as a political activist. As a result, her career provides multiple examples of how to communicate with a distinctive group on its own terms and thereby impact its perceptions and behaviors. Most generally, this is what marketing is all about; Kristeva, therefore, has many valuable contributions to make to marketing/consumer research.

A COMPARATIVE PICTURE

Poststructuralism, therefore, emerged in France in the1960s and began to have an international impact in the 1970s. The broadness of the move-

ment is portrayed by the diversity of its five founding members. Their
variation in interests and techniques is portrayed in Figure 13.1.

Poststructuralism, therefore, is a multifaceted movement that is as divergent as the different careers and interests of its founding members.
Since poststructural thought ranges, in its origins, from formal academic
philosophy, to the psychoanalytic method, to literary criticism, to historical analysis, to cultural/social activism, the movement is diverse and
multifaceted. Yet, there is a uniformity in that members of the movement
direct attention away from the patterns within society and, therefore,
seek to transcend the methods of mental structuralism represented by
the work of Claude Levi-Strauss. They, therefore, expand existential theory and help it meet the challenge of rivalry with structural analysis

There are similarities between these five founders; all of the pioneering
founders of poststructuralism explore and scrutinize aspects of culture
and society that structuralists typically do not choose to investigate. As
has been discussed, classic structural analysis, precisely because it focuses upon the cooperation and interrelationships of various parts of the
system, is not well-designed to explore tensions, change, and ambiguity.
Poststructuralism, however, is at home dealing with such phenomena.

In addition, the diversity of the founders of poststructuralism encourages a cross-disciplinary or multidisciplinary approach. As a result, concepts (such as "the self," "male vs. female," "humanity," etc.) that seem
to be understood in one context will be ruthlessly examined from other
perspectives. As marketing/consumer research becomes increasingly
cross-disciplinary, such research agendas may become appropriate and
useful. Poststructuralism, however, can lead to intellectual excesses
which the scholar is warned to guard against.

CONCLUSION

Poststructural thought is invaluable when the researcher seeks to transcend social and/or mental structures in order to deal with influences
and tendencies that cannot be usefully depicted in structural terms. On
many occasions, marketing/consumer research is concerned with the
distinctiveness of specific groups of people and how they behave on their
own terms. This, ultimately, is the age of "target marketing" that seeks
to envision specific groups as distinctive and then establish marketing
strategies that cater to this variance. Poststructural models can be applied
usefully in such circumstances.

Although poststructuralism as a unified body of thought has some
overarching similarities that carry over from one thinker to the next,
different intellectuals deal with their own personal research agendas and

Figure 13.1
A Roster of the Pioneering Poststructuralists

	Orientation	Significance
Derrida	*Philosopher:* There is nothing outside of the text. Focuses on the actual document. Does not center upon intended meanings. "Deconstructs" in order to find true meaning or meanings.	Much consumer behavior stems from factors that lie below the level of consciousness. Much advertising deals with the subconscious. Derrida provides one (of several) ways to access such tendencies.
Barthes	*Critic:* Applied structuralism and poststructuralism to literature and to culture.	Besides being an excellent practitioner of both structuralism and poststructuralism, Barthes also delves into cultural criticism. Marketing/consumer researchers who seek to expand literary criticism into cultural analysis can profit from his examples.
Lacan	*Psychoanalyst:* Expanded classic psychoanalysis by arguing that the psyche was structured like a language and that this structure may break down.	Marketing/consumer research needs models of the human mind when conducting research. A linguistic analogy of the psyche provides a useful and easily undestood and communicated model.
Foucault	*Historian, cultural observer:* Wrote historical analyses that dealt with the mental lives of people and the impact of culture upon them.	Marketing/consumer researchers need to consider and understand the full impacts of culture and how it influences behavior. Foucault's research provides clues regarding these social impacts.
Kristeva	*Activist, feminist:* Writes on a wide variety of subjects of contemporary interest. The youngest of the poststructuralists and the only woman, she can be viewed as representing a culmination of the movement.	Represents the culmination of poststructuralism. Deals with specific groups, a strategy that has value to marketing/consumer research, especially when scholars think in terms of the distinctiveness of specific target markets.

poise their own theoretical propositions. In order to demonstrate this truth, this chapter has briefly reviewed the careers and intellectual orientations of the five key pioneers who are credited with establishing poststruturalism as a distinct and circumscribed school of thought. Even though all of these thinkers are similar in some ways, specific areas of thought where the vision of each is characteristic and idiosyncratic also exist. Today, there are many poststructural intellectuals, not just the five founders of the movement, and many of these thinkers possess their own unique vision. As a result of this variation, it is impossible to provide a brief overview of the movement.

Nonetheless, poststructuralists as a group inevitably seek to dismiss (or at least go beyond) structural relations and the models that portray them. This tendency is simultaneously the strength and the weakness of the movement.

NOTES

1. Kristeva is not French but is part of that intellectual tradition.
2. I am a student of Fiedler and he was on my dissertation committee. As a result, I am prejudice in favor of him and his approach. Nonetheless, I am providing an objective comparsion of his thought compared to Derrida's.
3. Although embraced by a school of criticism and a frequent guest professor at Yale.
4. While more eclectic and substantive critics would merely embrace various elements of the model in ad hoc ways and apply them when (and if) useful. The focus of analysis would be the substantive topic, not the method.
5. Again, intuitive cultural critics do not dispute this fact, but they do not focus upon it either.
6. It is my opinion that the embrace of critics such as Barthes and Derrida was, to a large extent, based on the desire of certain American critics to develop a more "scientific" or rigorous means of doing literary criticism. They continued to do what they always had, but used poststructuralism as an intellectual justification for their work. The fact that Northrup Frye's *Anatomy of Criticism* (1957) made a call for more scientific research while simultaneously remaining nested within criticism is another example of this tendency.

REFERENCES

Barthes, Roland. (1957). *Mythologies*. New York: Hill and Wang.
Barthes, Roland. (1968). *Elements of Semiology*. New York: Hill and Wang.
Barthes, Roland. (1974). *S/Z*. New York: Hill and Wang.
Barthes, Roland. (1983). *The Fashion System*. New York: Hill and Wang.
Clement, Catherine. (1983). *The Lives and Legend of Jacques Lacan*, trans. Arthur Goldhammer. New York: Columbia University Press.
Derrida, Jacques. (1967a). *Of Grammatology*. Baltimore: Johns Hopkins University Press.

Derrida, Jacques. (1967b). *Writing and Différence*. Chicago: University of Chicago Press.

de Saussure, Ferdinand. (1959). *Course in General Linguistics*, ed. Charley Bally and Albert Reidlinger. New York: Philosopher's Library.

Fiedler, Leslie. (1960). *Love and Death in the American Novel*. New York: Criterion.

Foucault, Michel. (1965). *Madness and Civilization: A History of Insanity in the Age of Reason*. New York: Pantheon.

Foucault, Michel. (1978). *The History of Sexuality*. New York: Pantheon.

Gasche, Rodolphe. (1986). *The Tain of the Mirror: Derrida and the Mirror of Relection*. Cambridge, MA: Harvard University Press.

Holbrook, Morris and Grayson, Mark. (1986). "The Semiology of Cinematic Consumption." *Journal of Consumer Research* 13 (December): 374–81.

Rotry, Richard. (1978–1979). "Philosophy as a Kind of Writing: An Essay on Derrida." *New Literary History* 10: 141–60.

Sapir, Edward. (1956). *Culture, Language and Personality*. Berkeley: University of California Press.

Stephens, Mitchell. (1994). "Jacques Derrida." *New York Times* (January 23): 22.

Stern, Barbara. (1994). "Authenticity and the Textual Persona." *International Journal of Research in Marketing* 11(4) (September): 381–401.

Stern, Barbara. (1996). "Deconstructive Strategy and Consumer Research: Concepts and Illustrative Exemplar." *Journal of Consumer Research* 23(2) (September): 136–48.

Whorf, Benjamin. (1956). *Language, Thought and Reality*. Cambridge, MA: Technology Press and Massachusetts Institute of Technology.

CHAPTER 14

Conflict Theory: Individualism within a Social Context

INTRODUCTION

As has been argued in earlier chapters, one of the long-held complaints against the classic structural model of the social sciences is the observation that the method is so skewed toward exploring the harmony and mutual reinforcing properties of social systems that it is often hard-pressed to meaningfully deal with conflict, strife, and individual priorities. And yet, it is self-evident that social life is filled with tensions and rivalries between different people and groups. As a result, many observers have rejected the social structural model and they actively look for (and develop) alternatives to it.

Another way of looking at this situation is (1) to recognize that individuals and circumscribed groups have their own goals, orientations, priorities, and opinions and (2) to acknowledge that those who seek to understand human behavior need to build this reality into their analysis. To reflect reality, models of society and social life must account for this complex tapestry of stress, struggle, and dissension. Although the "clockworks" structural model that employs a homeostatic metaphor (in order to deal with patterned and mutually beneficial social action) has served well in the past, many social scientists (and other cultural observers) have come to believe that they need to get beyond paradigms that are centered around harmony in order to account for discord and to deal with social tension and individual action.

Viewed in this context, one valuable contribution of the poststructural model is its ability to deal with both differences between people and with the tensions that exist between them. Indeed, the poststructural model celebrates diversity of thought and action to the point of denying that structures really exist at all. People, the poststructuralists argue, tend to be a disparate lot and they tend to view the world in their own specific ways. This premise is certainly a basic element in the philosophical underpinnings of poststructuralism (and the pronouncements of Jacques Derrida, who largely inspired it).

The resulting canon of poststructural thought, furthermore, has a valuable contribution to make to understanding social life in terms of the different visions, tensions, and priorities that are held by different people and groups. Recall, for example, Michel Foucault's emphasis upon the tensions that exist between different groups (as chronicled in his *Madness and Civilization* (1965) and his *The History of Sexuality* (1978). This kind of analysis was further amplified and broadened by the work of Julia Kristeva and her strong bent toward political/social activism. As a result of her political leanings, much of Kristeva's effort have been directed toward advancing partisan causes; she has routinely used the methods and rhetoric of poststructural theory when promoting the positions she supports.

Thus, according to poststructural theory, different people view the world in their own distinct ways. Thus, a feminist might observe that much of the available analysis regarding a certain issue has been accomplished by male authors, thinkers, or researchers. Females, the argument may continue, have their own distinct vision. As a result of this situation, it can be suggested that the dominant voice (of males) does not adequately reflect the totality of human response and, therefore, the prevailing vision is limited and in need of revision (or at least in need of being augmented by feminine visions).

The value of such observations to marketing/consumer researchers is immense. There has long been a realization that certain products tend to be bought by men while others are typically purchased by women. Our profession also acknowledges that a firm may wish to embrace women as a key target market and, therefore, seek to communicate with them on their own terms. If marketing/consumer researchers can discern specifically what women think and how women tend to respond in ways that are distinctive from men, it may be possible to extrapolate differences in women vs. men that have profound implications for consumer response and marketing communications. Thus, not only does poststructuralism point to differences between different people and groups, marketing/consumer researchers (and the practitioner world) are very interested in the strategic implications stemming from variations between distinct groups.

This chapter has no quarrel with this kind of poststructural analysis. Indeed, I applaud it. I believe, however, that the successes of poststructural analysis have been so great that they tend to overshadow useful models of conflict that stem from traditional social structural analysis and provide an alternative to the poststructural intellectual tradition. The purpose of this chapter is to discuss an array of analytic options that (1) merge structural analysis with conflict and the differences between individuals and (2) analyze tensions between various groups and segments of society in structural terms. This tradition of social research, largely stemming from structural analysis, provides a wide array of useful models that can be groomed for service by marketing/consumer researchers as well as by members of the practitioner world.

CONFLICT THEORY: ITS CONTEXT AND GROWTH

As indicated above, the classic structural/functional model of the social sciences is a clockworks model that concentrates upon internal harmony and how all members of a social group tend to interact in mutually beneficial ways that reinforce each other. Specifically, the work of Talcott Parsons (and like-minded social theorists) adapted an organic model (or metaphor) of society in which all components of society are viewed as participating within the larger community in compatible and complementary ways. According to such an approach, each element of society is viewed in terms of how it fits into the greater whole. In earlier chapters, we saw that by doing so, the organic model deemphasizes phenomena, such as stress and conflict, that do not deal with the systematic and overarching functioning of society. When the organic model does acknowledge social tensions, it tends to deal with them as sicknesses or perversions. Such a research agenda is legitimate because all models strategically seek to simplify reality in order to expand knowledge; organic social structural analysis fulfills this goal.

As is commonly the case, however, in the process of simplifying a model (in order to deal with important topics or questions), an array of significant issues and theoretical questions may simultaneously be "tabled" or ignored. Conflict theory, as a distinct sociological perspective, arose in order to deal with the fact that social life is not always harmonious and that not all groups benefit, in equal degrees, from the social arrangements that typify a society. Thus, conflict theory came to transcend the clockworks model by dealing with a larger array of issues and by acknowledging the fact that societies evolve over time in response to internal and external stress.

Besides stemming from the curiosity of various sociologists, the growth of conflict theory can be seen as reflective of the temper of the times in which it rose to prominence. In the United States, for example, the 1960s was the era of the counterculture, massive social confrontation, and the rise of conflict theory as a distinct body of social thought. The social theorists who came to intellectual maturity during that era have continued to push the boundaries of social theory in the direction of analyzing social tensions. Here, we will deal with the precedents and underlying theoretic strategies of this powerful intellectual tradition.

Indeed, many of the same social pressures that led to the vogue of poststructuralism also encouraged and gave form to what emerged as conflict theory. All people do not relate to their culture in the same way. Cultures do not always treat all people in a "fair" or "appropriate" manner. Those who examine cultures need to get beyond the notion that people think in parallel and interchangeable ways. These statements depict the stances of both poststructuralism and conflict theory.

There is a basic difference, however; conflict theory tends to work within the canon and traditions of social research and it refines social theory in ways that, expanding the organic model, acknowledge differences and tensions. Poststructuralism, in contrast, consciously seeks to replace the structural method with alternative analytic tools and pardigms.

We, as marketing/consumer researchers, can embrace either approach, but it is wise to understand the issues that are involved when choosing either course of action. Poststructuralism is a philosophical movement that has developed ways of dealing with social action; indeed, it has often become involved in the analysis of conflict as well as embracing partisan positions. In doing so, poststructuralism has gained an international following and, currently, it provides a popular and widely understood perspective and a vocabulary with which to deal with a host of important issues that are concerned with social tensions and the inequities of life. Poststructuralism, however, does not directly stem from the social sciences (although, of course, various social sciences embrace strong poststructural positions in their work).

Conflict theory, although it is at odds with the classic organic models of social structuralism, did evolve from within the mainstream of social scientific thought. Conflict theory tends to deal with many of the same issues as poststructuralism, but it does so in ways that resonate from the traditions of social theory. Thus, those who deal with conflict theory will probably find it easy to integrate a wealth of social theory into their work while poststructuralists can expect to do so with greater difficulty.

PRECEDENTS FOR CONFLICT THEORY

Although conflict theory represents a break with and an alternative to classic social structural theory, precedents for conflict theory have long existed within mainstream social research. Conflict and strife between people are obvious facts of life that no informed social scientist can totally or responsibly ignore. As we have seen, however, theorists who embraced the organic social structural model often chose to downplay stress, tensions, and differences between people and groups in order to explore other theoretic problems that are centered around the mutually beneficial aspects of society. Even during the era when the organic social structural model rose to prominence and emerged as the dominate paradigm, important social theorists continued to explore conflict and/or the distinctiveness of specific people, groups, and their unique responses. Various representative social theorists to be discussed from this perspective include Karl Marx, Max Weber, Georg Simmel, Robert K. Merton, C. Wright Mills, Lewis Coser, and Erving Goffman. By briefly reviewing the careers of these noted social theorists with reference to conflict theory, the traditions of examining tensions from within mainstream social theory are placed within a relevant perspective.

Karl Marx

As we saw in Chapter 4 and elsewhere, Karl Marx is a major social theorist who explained the nature of society in economic terms; his method is called dialectical materialism in order to draw attention to the fact that it is simultaneously based on economic concerns (the material world) on the one hand and cultural evolution (dialectics) on the other.

Without restating what was covered in Chapter 4, it is useful to remind the reader that Marxist thought possesses a primary interest in social conflict and it deals with the impact of social conflict upon the evolution and functioning of society. Although Marx was deeply concerned with social conflict, however, his theory largely ignored the individual and it focused upon examining the collective forces that transcend individual people. It is worthwhile to note, however, that Karl Marx and his collaborator, Friedrich Engels, were both well aware that they were simplifying reality in order to more effectively focus upon the impact of impersonal economic forces. Thus, in a series of letters dating from in the early 1890s (written after Marx had died in 1883), Engels complained about the hyperbolic theoretic assertions made by younger Marxist theorists and how they were flawed because they tended to ignore the individual. In essence, Engels acknowledges that Marx had overemphasized the impact of the impersonal material component of life because he was developing a new and innovative model that needed to be forcefully articulated. Unfortunately, Engels complains, later, younger theorists did not recognize this fact and they embraced the cultural material model at face value and without reservations.

Various Marxist theorists (especially those from the West) have gone on to recognize that Marxism needs a more robust theoretical underpinning, and they began to smuggle the individual back into Marxist analysis; the Frankfurt School is one prominent example of that tradition. Late in his career, Jean-Paul Sartre came to embrace a Marxist perspective and dubbed it the inevitable philosophy of the era. In so doing he linked his individualistic existentialism with Marxist theory.

Max Weber

Max Weber, in a polemical series of writings, sought to counter the economic deterministic models of Karl Marx. He did so by revising the causal chain; while Marx suggested that economic factors impacted ideology and remade it in its own image, Weber suggested that ideology and religious belief transformed the economic system. Weber's classic discussion is found in his *The Protestant Ethic and the Spirit of Capitalism* (1904–1905). There, Weber argues that religious belief helped create a milieu that justified the accumulation of wealth and encouraged its reinvestment. This orientation regarding amassing capital in turn led to the mechanism that fueled the industrial revolution. Thus, Weber, while not totally ignoring conflict, reversed the causal chain of Marx and provided a more culturally oriented view of conflict and social action.

Georg Simmel

As indicated above, Georg Simmel, a German philosopher and sociologist of the late 19th and early 20th centuries, often dealt with conflict between different groups. The pioneering work of Simmel, furthermore, has inspired marketing/consumer researchers such as Grant McCracken, who rehabilitated Simmel's trickledown theory of fashion. In essence, trickledown theory explains evolving fashions in terms of campaign by the dominant members of society that is designed to maintain their position (by flaunting fashionable clothes) while others, competing with them, seek parity via a strategy of emulation. Thus, wearing stylish and fashionable clothes are signs of power and prestige and, thereby, they provide a way for the upper classes to reinforce their dominate position. These high fashions, however, are quickly copied by those on the lower rungs of society as they seek to smuggle themselves into a higher social arena. Such attempts create a never-ending cycle in which the rich cast off current styles and adopt new ones as soon as they are trickle downed to those of lower status in an ongoing pattern of evolving styles that are designed to demonstrate status and superiority.

This kind of analysis, of course, is closely hinged upon conflict, and it is of obvious value to consumer theory. Although Simmel wrote before the vogue of the structural organic model, he is a major social theorist who has left a permanent mark on social theory by emphasizing conflict.

Robert K. Merton

While Simmel wrote before the advent of the social structural organic model, Robert K. Merton is part of that intellectual tradition and he sought to refine it by consciously dealing with the conflict that exists between various individuals and groups. In his *Social Theory and Social Structure* (1957), Merton complained that traditional social and psychological theories explain deviant behavior merely in terms of biological urges of individuals that conflict with the needs of the social system. This theory, while centering upon a type of conflict, focuses upon the inherent nature of mankind as pitted against the needs and priorities of society. Thus, it was not really a social theory in the way the term is used here.

Merton offered an alternative perspective that centered upon the differences and conflicts within the social system. According to Merton, the social system includes both socially acceptable goals and socially acceptable means of achieving them. Both of these orientations are an important part of the value system of society. In reality, however, not all people have an equal opportunity to achieve these socially defined goals in the proscribed manner. As we saw in the chapter on social structuralism, when people lack an ability to achieve socially proscribed goals in socially legitimate ways, anomie results. This anomie can result in a number of alternatives (deviant forms of response) from which individuals can choose.

Thus, modes of analysis that revolve around anomie and the patterns of behavior it triggers can be viewed as conflict theories because these models emphasize that people will choose alternatives to legitimate social action if and when they are unable to achieve their goals in any other way. Therefore, when conflicts arise, distinct social responses can (and often do) result. And, as we saw above, this theory has a significant value to marketing/consumer research.

C. Wright Mills

C. Wright Mills was an eclectic social scientist who, in the 1950s, provided a scathing analysis of the privileged minority who dominated American life. Mills' definitive work is his *White Collar* (1951), where he depicted the managerial class as the dominant force in American society. Mills' account is written from the perspective that, as an entity, this vested interest group functions to achieve its own ends and, therefore, its actions tend to be in conflict with the needs, wants, and well-being of other segments of society.

In his later work, *The Power Elite* (1956), Mills expanded his analysis to include a variety of powerful players including executives, military leaders, and politicians who, he asserted, controlled American society and transformed it for their own ends.

Mills' work demonstrates a shift in interpretation from the organic social structural theories of Talcott Parsons and Robert K. Merton. As the reader will recall, the organic social structuralists tended to deal with conflict as evidence that a system was breaking down or not functioning properly; conflict was clearly recognized, but it was dealt with as an abnormal response triggered, perhaps, by extraordinary events or rapid cultural evolution. Certainly, social structuralists recognized that this conflict can lead to a destabilization of society; nonetheless, conflict and the private priorities of individuals and circumscribed groups were dealt with as being deviant or aberrant in nature. In Mills' work, in contrast, conflict is viewed as a normal state of affairs; people, due to their situations, can be expected to be in competition with each other as they seek scarce commodities, such as material possessions or immaterial artifacts (such as social status).

Mills' emphasis that conflict is the natural state of affairs has a significant contribution to make to marketing/consumer research because it emphasizes that conflict (and behavior that is related to conflict) are key and recurring aspects of social life, not fleeting reflections of transitory imbalances in the social system. Mills also underscores the distinctiveness of individuals and circumscribed groups; he does so, however, without a reliance upon poststructural theory.

Lewis Coser

While C. Wright Mills wrote polemical diatribes that, although pointing to the role of conflict within society, criticized certain privileged groups in partisan ways, Lewis Coser's *The Functions of Social Conflict* (1956) provided a more evenhanded treatment of similar materials. Coser, for example, observes that both consensus and conflict have a significant role in maintaining the social structure. By acknowledging and responding to conflict, it becomes easier for individuals to perceive their differences and to forge ways of transcending them. This process can lead to a positive process of accommodation and the resulting reintegration of society.

Elsewhere, I have dealt with the conflict expressed in social causes (Walle 2000) and I related this phenomena to the needs of marketing/ consumer researchers. As one example, I pointed to the work of Herbert Blumer and the life cycle model of causes that he provides (Blumer 1971). The essence of my earlier analysis is to demonstrate ways in which conflict theories, which stem from the sociological tradition, have a significant role to play in marketing/consumer research. In order to deal with social conflict and the needs of circumscribed groups, it is not necessary to abandon classic social theory and embrace poststructural perspectives.

To whatever extent consumer responses are linked with (1) a demonstration of group identity and (2) the conflict that exists between groups, marketing/consumer researchers can benefit from such perspectives. Thus, during the era of the 1960s counterculture, many members of the baby boom generation felt at odds with the status quo. One way of portraying these differences was through the embrace of distinctive patterns of consumer response that were typified by males growing their hair long, wearing blue jeans, and the Rock and Roll music of the era (among others). Because of the distinctiveness of the consumer responses of a group that was in conflict with the status quo, the specific attitudes and opinions of this group became more readily apparent. And because these differences were overtly recognized and addressed, it was easier for society to ultimately be reintegrated. Of special interest to marketing/consumer research is the fact that this distinctiveness had a significant impact upon the goods consumed by this segment of the public.

Erving Goffman

In Chapter 10, which concerns the theories and methods developed by Erving Goffman, his relationship with game theoretic analysis is discussed. In essence, that discussion examines how Goffman's approach can be used to explore how people seek to manipulate social systems to their own advantage by creating a specific "impression" that is designed to impact and influence a social situation. Thus, the clothes worn, the avocations pursued, and the restaurants patronized may be strategically chosen in order to help define the situation in ways that are advantageous to the strategically minded social actor. In so doing, individuals typically attempt to "win" a zero-sum game; this process, of course, involves conflict.

According to Goffman's "dramaturgical" model, individuals consciously behave in a way that is analogous to "acting" (dramatic portrayals) so they can manipulate the social situation to their advantage. Goffman deals with the various participants in a social interaction as members of teams that are motivated by their own self-interest. This model, of course, implies conflict.

In our discussion of Goffman, we also saw how aspects of consumer response are commonly employed in order to present a particular definition of the situation. Thus, Goffman's methods combine both a strong interest in conflict and an eye toward consumer response.

As indicated throughout these discussions, classic social structural models tend to embrace an organic metaphor that does not focus upon conflict. Although classic social structural theory tends to depict conflict as abnormal, social research has a long tradition of dealing with strife and competition; in the above discussion, we have touched on some of the high points of that intellectual tradition.

Marketing/consumer research has long addressed such issues and/or tapped the insights of social theorists who focus upon aspects of consumer response that are triggered by social conflict. As a result, a rich intellectual tradition for merging traditional theories of social conflict and marketing/consumer research exists. Having made this observation, we will proceed to the mainstream of conflict theory, as it has evolved, in order to discuss what it offers to marketing/consumer research.

MODERN CONFLICT THEORY

As indicated above, although strong precedents for social conflict theory long existed within mainstream social theory, until recently, no specific school of thought had emerged. As indicated above, its current status as a freestanding subdiscipline is, in large part, a reflection of the temper of the times. The 1960s was the era of major civil rights initiatives, the birth of women's liberation movement, and it saw a major anti-war movement in the United States; conflict theory arose as a coherent means of dealing with these events.

In some ways, however, proponents for civil rights and the equitable treatment of minorities could usefully employ the traditional canon of social theory. One example of this tendency is Elliott Liebow's well-respected monograph *Tally's Corner* (1967), an analysis of the street corner existence of Black urban men. According to the author, the conduct of ghetto Blacks seems, at first glance, to be very different from the behavior and motivations of mainstream society. And yet, Liebow suggests, the behavior of this underclass clearly resonates from the goals and the status structure of the overarching American culture. Due to the opportunities available (and unavailable) to these inner-city men, however, Liebow points out that their overt behavior is much different from that of mainstream, middle-class Americans. Nonetheless, Liebow suggests, a careful analysis reveals close parallels. In essence, Liebow employs a version of Robert Merton's theory of anomie (and the typology of behavioral options that stems from it) in order to interpret the actions of a specific underclass in terms of the goals and aspirations of the larger society. And since Liebow explains this behavior with reference to mainstream American patterns of response, his work can be viewed as an example of using traditional social structural theory in order to advance the cause of minorities and/or to explain their seemingly deviant behavior in terms of the larger society.

By and large, however, the social theorists, observers, and activists who were concerned with causes such as civil rights and the anti-war movement sought alternatives to standard social structural analysis. Indeed, some of the most provocative writings on conflict theory that emerged during that era are not the work of scholars but were created by professional social activists. A classic example of this partisan and polemical tradition is Stokely Carmichael and Charles V. Hamilton's *Black Power: The Politics of Liberation in America* (1967).

Although some readers will be repelled by Carmichael's rhetoric while others will applaud his vision, most people will agree that he presents a classic example of what, in the 1960s, was emerging as conflict theory. Written during the era of the urban riots within American cities (some would argue that Carmichael fanned the flames of racial violence), *Black Power* emphasizes that profound conflicts exist within American society and that these tensions cannot be explained away in terms of social structural theories. Instead, Carmichael insists, conflict must be acknowledged for what it is and responded to accordingly. Although *Black Power* is not a theoretical work, in an academic sense it can be consulted as an example of the temper of the times. It also provides evidence regarding the degree to which social thought was transcending the organic model of society in order to better deal with tensions and conflicts that exist within the social system.

A more evenhanded and academic treatment of the same sort of situation as that analyzed by Carmichael is provided by Randall Collins in his *Conflict Sociology* (1975). Collins' work is useful in a number of ways. First, he provides an overview of the work of earlier social thinkers who dealt with conflict theory; as a result, he provides excellent background material for marketing/consumer theorists who seek a more in-depth knowledge of this area of social research. In doing so, Collins expands the underlying premises of the field and how they can be used to explore tensions created by racial, ethnic, sexual, and religious differences.

Crucial to Collins' approach is his focus upon social resources over which various people and groups actively compete. As a result of this competition, there exists a hierarchy of privilege within society, and this situation results in conflict. Although *Conflict Sociology* is over 25 years old, it is in no way a dated book and it remains both a synthesis of contributing approaches to conflict theory and a primer for those coming to the subdiscipline for the first time. As a result, *Conflict Sociology* is highly recommended for all who seek to understand what the sociological analysis of conflict has to offer marketing/consumer researchers. Collins' more recent work includes his *Theoretical Sociology* (1988), which is also recommended.

Equally valuable is the discussion of conflict to be found in Jonathan Turner's *Structure of Sociological Theory* (1982). Among other insights and observations, Turner suggests that conflict and violence go hand in hand

and that the outbreak of violence can be described as a nine step process. Many of these ideas have been revised and restated in Turner's *Societal Stratification: A Theoretical Analysis* (1984).

Of special interest to marketing/consumer researchers is the premise that those involved in conflict seek to gain prestige over each other and that, in the process of doing so, they often seek to strategically consume goods and services accordingly. This orientation has a long history going back to Thorstein Veblen's *The Theory of the Leisure Class* (1899) and the work of Georg Simmel and Grant McCracken regarding trickledown theory (which was discussed above). In dealing with strategic consumption, it is useful to recall that both material possessions and cultural pursuits tend to be used as a means of reinforcing the social prestige of the elite and, therefore, decisions regarding consumption ultimately stem from conflict between groups. A interesting work to consider in this regard is Pierre Bourdieu's *Distinction* (1984).

Any number of consumption decisions, ranging from the college chosen, to the profession pursued, to the advocations followed, to the car driven, to the brand of Scotch drunk, and so on, can be discussed in terms of conflicts over and assertions of status. This is true even if patterns of behavior become ingrained and/or even if some consumption decisions are made as ends in themselves. There, furthermore, exists a long tradition within marketing/consumer research of focusing upon the strategic nature of such behavior and how it may be encouraged and channeled by marketplace decisions. Conflict theory is a focused lens with which such trends can be analyzed and it views consumption choices from within a broad social context in ways that expand beyond poststructural analysis.

BEYOND CLOCKWORKS: CONFLICT THEORY AND MARKETING RESEARCH

Conflict theory offers a means for social structural analysis to transcend the organic model. It is one method by which the social structural model transcends viewing society according to static and uniform "clockworks" theories in order to deal with more flexible "cybernetic" models that can meaningfully deal with change, tension, and transformations over time.

Ultimately, much marketing/consumer research is concerned with change. Our discipline is profoundly interested in how patterns of consumption change over time and how present or future consumers can be groomed to adjust their behavior (or, in contrast, to maintain their brand of loyalty). Static models, although useful in many regards, do not provide the complete toolkit that marketing/consumer researchers need in order to deal with change, what causes it, and the impact of change upon behavior. In addition, marketing/consumer research is interested in the evolving behavior of individuals and specific groups, and it is not content to envision society in a generic and homogeneous manner. Conflict theory provides a way to deal with these phenomena using the traditions of social theory as they have evolved within sociology and anthropology. As a result, conflict theory has much to contribute to marketing and consumer research.

Poststructural analysis and conflict theory are equally poised to deal with distinctive groups and with tensions between groups. Currently, poststructural theory is extremely popular and it is often emphasized when dealing with conflict and the partisan goals of circumscribed groups. Conflict theory, while being nested within traditional social theory, can often be used in similar situations by marketing/consumer researchers. Researchers should feel comfortable using either method; they need, however, to consider the implications of doing so.

REFERENCES

Blumer, Herbert. (1971). "Social Problems as Collective Behavior." *Social Problems* 18(3) (Winter): 298–306.

Bourdieu, Pierre. (1984). *Distinction: A Social Critique of the Judgement of Taste*, trans. Richard Nice. Cambridge, MA: Harvard University Press.

Carmichel, Stokely, and Hamilton, Charles V. (1967). *Black Power: The Politics of Liberation in America*. New York: Vintage.

Collins, Randall. (1975). *Conflict Sociology*. New York: Academic Press.

Collins, Randall. (1988). *Theoretical Sociology*. San Diego, CA: Harcourt Brace Jovanovich.

Coser, Lewis. (1956). *The Functions of Social Conflict*. Glencoe, IL: Free Press.

Foucault, Michel. (1965). *Madness and Civilization: A History of Insanity in the Age of Reason*. New York: Pantheon.

Foucault, Michel. (1978). *The History of Sexuality*. New York: Pantheon.

Liebow, Elliott. (1967). *Tally's Corner: A Study of Streetcorner Men*. Boston: Little, Brown.

Merton, Robert K. (1957). *Social Theory and Social Structure*. Glencoe, IL: Free Press.

Mills, C. Wright. (1951). *White Collar: The American Middle Class*. New York: Oxford University Press.

Mills, C. Wright. (1956). *The Power Elite*. New York: Oxford University Press.

Turner, Jonathan. (1982). *The Structure of Sociological Theory*. Homewood, IL: Dorsey Press.

Turner, Jonathan. (1984). *Societal Stratification: A Theoretical Analysis*. New York: Columbia University Press.

Veblen, Thorstein. (1899). *The Theory of the Leisure Class*. New York: Macmillian.

Walle, Alf H. (2000). *Rethinking Marketing*. Westport, CT: Quorum Books.

Weber, Max. (1904–1905). *The Protestant Ethic and the Spirit of Capitalism*, trans. Talcott Parsons. New York: Scribner.

CHAPTER 15

Individualistic Implications and Marketing Research

INTRODUCTION

In recent years, marketing/consumer research has made significant and increased use of theories and methods that are designed to deal with the specific and distinct needs of individuals and circumscribed groups. In the process of doing so, our profession has borrowed a wide array of ideas, theories, techniques, and perspectives that derive from the humanities and the social sciences. As a result of this exciting cross-disciplinary endeavor, far-reaching transformations are currently taking place regarding the ways in which marketing/consumer researchers view people, purposeful behavior, the environment in which human conduct exists, and the consequences that derive from people's actions and choices. These are certainly exciting times for our field.

One reason for the increased importance of this kind of research stems from the fact that marketing strategies are relentlessly moving toward a greater reliance upon target marketing. Target marketing involves the process of focusing upon a distinct subsection of the population, dissecting it, analyzing its preferences, recording its behavior patterns, determining how to please this relatively small and self-contained subset of the population, and planning strategies accordingly.

Increasingly, firms are transcending the old strategy of mass marketing homogeneous products to the world at large and, as an alternative, they are adjusting both the merchandise sold and marketing arrangement employed so that strategies and policies can be effectively tailored to the precise needs, wants, and whims of circumscribed target markets that can be addressed individually and on their own terms.

As this process of tailoring products and marketing arrangements around specific groups has grown in importance, marketing/consumer researchers have become increasingly concerned with the needs of specific segments of the population and how these individuals and groups can be most effectively and efficiently analyzed. One way of dealing with circumscribed groups is with reference to poststructural analysis that evolved from and expanded out of the existential intellectual tradition. A second method of analysis consists of conflict theory that can best be viewed as a refinement of classic social theory, which nests the behavior of groups within a larger social context. Both methods are equipped, in their own ways, to address the needs of marketing/consumer researchers who seek to understand small, circumscribed market segments in order to effectively communicate with them and/or cater to their needs. It is useful to briefly discuss both of these issues on their own terms.

POSTSTRUCTURAL ANALYSIS

In many ways, poststructural analysis is tailor-made for the needs of target marketing. Thus, target marketing is little interested in the habits and preferences of large, overarching social structures and, as an alternative, it concentrates upon smaller, circumscribed groups and their more self-contained and unique attitudes and responses. The strategic needs of target marketers is closely reflected by the type of analysis that poststructural analysis is poised to provide and the issues that can, most effectively, be examined by it.

Stemming from the existential tradition and expanding beyond it in relevant ways, poststructural analysis is an international movement that provides a broad array of perspectives of profound value to those who seek to understand small segments of the market. It is also ideally suited for addressing the needs of those who wish to communicate with circumscribed market segments and who do so in distinctive and tailored ways.

In addition, many of the leaders of poststructural analysis have devised techniques for dealing with the fact that different people view the world in their own unique manner and that these people inevitably interpret and evaluate the communications they receive in a specific way that is an artifact of who they are and a reflection of their (1) past experiences and (2) the worldviews they embrace. Thus, poststructural theory assumes that a specific communication can "mean" many diverse things to various people and, therefore, it is useless to attempt to determine the universal "meaning" of the messages that are being voiced to others. These insights from poststructural analysis have a profound importance for those who are concerned with marketing communications.

The work of researchers such as Barbara Stern demonstrates that these tools can be usefully translated to the needs of our profession.

In recent years, poststructural theory has emerged as one of the mainstays of contemporary marketing/consumer research; in addition, the integration of poststructural theories and methods into the body and substance of our profession is establishing useful linkages between the work we do and the theories, methods, and priorities of other disciplines. As this process of intellectual borrowing and cross-disciplinary integration continues and deepens, we can expect (1) a growth in the prestige of our discipline, (2) a recognition of the value of our methods by others, and (3) an emergence of an intellectual environment where it is easier for us to explain our work and our theories to members of the greater intellectual community. These are positive and beneficial rewards to be reaped by the embrace of appropriate poststructural models.

CONFLICT THEORY

Not currently enjoying as high a profile within marketing/consumer research as poststructural analysis, conflict theory is largely an outgrowth and refinement of traditional social theory. Because conflict theory deals with circumscribed groups that are pitted against one another, this method is also ideally adapted for analyzing specific market segments and responding to their needs. Focused, as it is, on specific groups and the milieu in which they exist, conflict theory, like poststructural analysis, is poised to serve marketing/consumer researchers who are concerned with target marketing.

On many occasions, the members of specific market segments are consciously aware of other groups with which they may be in some sort of competition and/or from whom they want to distance themselves (by presenting or embracing some kind of alternative). Wherever this is true, conflict theory may be a suitable method that is well designed to analyze how specific market segments of society are positioned vis-à-vis other groups and/or how these relationships impact, among other things, the consumption process. In the last chapter, many of these analytic options were discussed, as well as specific examples of how they may be applied to the needs of marketing/consumer research.

Thus, like poststructural analysis, conflict theory can be applied to research questions where distinct groups/target markets stand apart, in some way, from other segments of society. While poststructural analysis evolved outside of the mainstream of classic social theory, conflict theory is clearly a product of this intellectual tradition and it can best be viewed as a refinement of and an expansion of classic social structural theory. Thus, although poststructural and conflict theories both provide ways in which to deal with the distinctiveness of specific groups, each of these

theories/methods has a different intellectual pedigree and each is poised
to accomplish an array of tasks its own distinctive way.

A STRATEGIC JUXTAPOSITION

As indicated above, a menu of options stemming both from poststructural analysis and conflict theory exist; they can be used by target
marketers who seek to understand how specific groups respond in general and react within the marketplace in particular. These alternatives
have their own intellectual history and each is ideally suited for a range
of research assignments. They can be compared and contrasted in Figure
15.1. Thus, both poststructural and conflict theory models are useful in
situations where the marketing/consumer researcher seeks to understand distinct groups of people in order to better understand how the
techniques of target marketing may be strategically deployed. Although
both methods can provide useful tools, each is very different and each
needs to be evaluated on its own terms and with reference to the particular research project being conducted.

CONCLUDING OBSERVATIONS

Currently, poststructural analysis is enjoying a high profile within
marketing/consumer research. It has emerged as a state-of-the-art
method for investigating individuals and circumscribed groups and is
useful when dealing with them as unique target markets. An alternative
to poststructural analysis is conflict theory, which emerged as a refinement of social structural analysis, which transcends the homeostatic
thrust of the classic social structural model. Although conflict theory as
a distinct subdiscipline of the social sciences has, as yet, made little direct
impact upon marketing/consumer research, its value is obvious.

By envisioning poststructural analysis and conflict theory as equally
respectable analytic options and by refusing to view them as in mortal
conflict and in inevitable competition with each other, marketing/con-
sumer researchers can develop and embrace a broad and diverse toolkit
with which to deal with issues that concern target marketing. It is hoped
that this discussion will provide a useful orientation as our field moves
in this positive direction.

Figure 15.1
Poststructuralism and Conflict Theory: A Strategic Comparison

Issue	Poststructuralism	Conflict Theory
Intellectual Tradition	Poststructuralism evolved out of and is the heir to the existential intellectual who emerged as the dominant intellectual paradigm in the 1940s and 1950s.	Conflict theory is a refinement of social structural theory, which transcends the "organic" model of society by acknowledging the stress that exists in society.
Influenced by	The repercussions of the post–World War I era, coupled with economic depression in Europe, caused people to lose faith in the ability of the collective culture to provide leadership to social groups and individuals. The horrors of World War II solidified this perspective, resulting in the mass appeal of the existential model. Later refinements led to poststructuralism.	The era of the 1960s in the United States was one of significant social conflict. Social theorists during the period needed methods that could meaningfully deal with this strife in a manner that transcended prevailing structural models, which centered upon social harmony and the mutual benefits that stem from the social structure. Conflict theory filled that theoretic void.
Representative Values	Poststructuralism, by denying that structures actually exist, gets beyond perspectives that are hinged around the assumption that phenomena can be usefully interpreted in some kind of generic manner. Instead, different people embrace their own vision.	Conflict theory provides a means of rephrasing organic social structuralism in more dynamic ways and in ways that recognize that not all groups mesh well within a social system. As such, it adds a dynamic component to structural analysis and deals with subgroups accordingly.
Representative Limits	Poststructural theory is designed to provide an alternative to structural analysis. As such it is ill equipped to embrace structural perspectives and provide leadership where structural analysis is needed.	Being derived from the social structural model (although expanding upon it), conflict theory centers upon group response, not individual thought. It, therefore, is not as well equipped as poststructural models to deal with the actual thought processes that underlie behavior.
Discussion	Both poststructural analysis and conflict theory deal with circumscribed groups and their responses. Poststructuralism, however, stems from the existential movement, which emphasizes the individual, while conflict theory derives from social theory, which is designed to explore collective behavior. Thus, while both deal with a similar universe of discourse, each method is distinct. By keeping these differences in mind, the full range of analytic options available to marketing/consumer researchers can be usefully and strategically envisioned.	

CHAPTER 16

Conclusion: A Diversity of Methods

Today, marketing/consumer research is being transformed by a wide array of methods and techniques that stem from the qualitative intellectual traditions. Those of us who champion such analytic strategies are apt to anticipate a new age in which our vision emerges as dominant and, perhaps, leads to the establishment of a new subdiscipline that overtly embraces the tactics of research and the philosophies of evidence that we espouse.

While such pleasant daydreams may come true, this state of affairs cannot be assumed to come quickly, painlessly, or inevitably. I am reminded of an observation that marketing theorist Shelby Hunt made a few years ago:

Thirty years from now, how will scholars evaluate the history of naturalistic, humanistic, and interpretative inquiry in marketing and consumer research? Will it be viewed as a significant addition to other methods? Or will it be viewed as a "blip" in the scientific enterprise, much like the motivational research of the 1950s? The . . . verdict . . . will be determined in large measure by how its practitioners and its advocates respond to challenges. (Hunt 1991: 431)

Key to Hunt's remarks is the realization that methods will not prosper simply because they are intellectually legitimate and/or because they have a valid contribution to make. Equally important is the way in which we conduct ourselves as advocates for and as champions of specific intellectual traditions. In the final analysis, our professional posture will seal the fate of the techniques we champion. In closing, it is appropriate for me to mention how I hope this book will help qualitative marketing/

consumer researchers to meet the challenge that Hunt so appropriately addresses.

Scientific and quantitative methods in marketing did not rise to prominence due to an historic accident or pure luck. These methods came to dominate because those who championed them were able to convincingly demonstrate that their research stream was superior, in certain respects, to what came before it. Portrayed in positive and constructive ways, science eventually came to dominate marketing/consumer research. Even if some of us complain that the methods of science currently stand in the way of (and/or inhibit) much-needed research, few members of our profession would discredit or underestimate the vast contributions that have been made by the application of scientific principles to an examination of the marketplace. In order to gain recognition, scientific researchers presented a point of view and demonstrated its unique value, and they have prospered accordingly. This situation is right, proper, and in line with the flow of intellectual history.

Today, qualitative (non-scientific) methods, in their turn, are struggling to establish themselves within marketing/consumer research; in order to do so, they, too, must demonstrate that they have a specific and unique role to play and that the contribution they are poised to make cannot be provided by the scientific methodologies that currently dominate. In professional boxing, a draw is a de facto victory for the reigning champion because he retains his title unless he is actually defeated; this tendency also prevails within the intellectual world. Being "just as good as" a dominant and established force does not suffice; qualitative methods must demonstrate a universe of discourse and a series of situations where they are obviously and inherently superior to the scientific method that now dominates. As in boxing, this tends to result in a victory for the established champion.

This book affirms the value of qualitative methods and presents an intellectual grounding that justifies and reinforces these methods. By doing so, the unique strength and value of qualitative methods are showcased. As qualitative methods seek parity with the dominant scientific paradigm, this kind of analysis and justification must take place. I hardly consider my musings to be a last word in this regard; I merely hope that these efforts will help to focus attention and stimulate discussion. I hope this book will be read from such a perspective.

Crucial to my argument is a juxtaposition of the legacy of the era of the Enlightenment and the heritage of the romantic era. During the era of the Enlightenment, rational thought and the scientific method completely dominated. The traditions of scientific investigation that have come down to us are a legacy from the Enlightenment. Since the use of the scientific method within marketing/consumer research is a subset of this tradition, it owes a profound debt to the Enlightenment.

While few of us would totally reject the value of the scientific method, many of us do believe that it possesses profound blind spots. Overtly or covertly, furthermore, our reservations tend to reflect the critiques of the scientific method that were advanced by members of the romantic movement. The romantic era can be viewed as a pendulum shift away from the Enlightenment's overemphasis upon rational thought and the scientific method. The romantic movement pointed to the fact that many important issues cannot be easily examined via the methods of science. It also affirmed that, due to the nature of the human mind, other legitimate means of analysis exist besides the scientific method.

Having made these observations, this book discusses a variety of theories and methods that have been developed within the humanities, liberal arts, and social sciences; I have emphasized that they, to a greater or lesser degree, are a legacy of the romantic era. These methods include (1) mental structuralism, (2) social structuralism, (3) existentialism, (4) poststructuralism, and (5) conflict theory. Each of these strong and vital intellectual traditions is discussed in terms of being an alternative to scientific analysis that grows from the stem of the romantic tradition. The value of each to qualitative marketing/consumer research is emphasized accordingly.

Coming to grips with the intellectual pedigree of such powerful and provocative paradigms is profoundly important as qualitative research in marketing/consumer research seeks to establish itself as a viable and legitimate alternative to the scientific tradition. Thus far, those who have borrowed from the qualitative traditions have tended to do so in rather eclectic ways. When following this path, the full strength and weight of the qualitative intellectual tradition (inspired as it is by recurring romantic principles) has not been emphasized. As qualitative researchers seek to affirm the distinctive nature of their paradigm, however, they need to build bridges and create linkages between their work and those of like-minded scholars. A key goal of this book is to present one framework with which this important synthesizing can take place.

As Shelby Hunt observed, we must forcefully respond to the intellectual challenges we face. Some of these struggles are external (and take the form of rival methods and "doubting Thomases"). I believe the most disabling threats, however, are internal. The humanities, liberal arts, and qualitative social sciences, while they may appear to be seductively easy to apply, are made up of complex layerings of substantive knowledge and methodological techniques. Valuable though they are, they cannot be easily mastered and they cannot be applied by rote. For qualitative methods to prosper in marketing/consumer research, this fact must be accepted. One implication of this reality is that scholars will often be required to make long-term intellectual investments in the methods they seek to master and, in some cases, postpone the realization of positive results for a significant period of time. Sadly, and shortsightedly, many tenure and promotion committees may not have adequate patience in this regard.

This situation is complicated by the way in which new ideas become part of intellectual traditions. A powerful description of this process is provided by physicist Max Planck (1936), who discussed how new paradigms and ideas become established within scholarly disciplines. Planck observed that, in general, colleagues are not "won over" to new ideas. Instead, emerging methods and paradigms become embraced by a profession "at large" only as the older generation dies off, leaving younger thinkers who accept the new proposition to fill their void.

Qualitative methods and humanistic traditions are currently gaining a beachhead in marketing/consumer research, but the scientific method, closely tied to empirical/statistical analysis, continues to dominate. Although I believe our position will ultimately prevail, it may take decades for this vision to achieve its deserved status because the old guard continues to be well entrenched. Nonetheless, I believe that our work is the wave of the future and that, ultimately, it will prevail.

Without a doubt, qualitative and humanistic methods have a profound contribution to make to marketing/consumer research. If these contributions are not made, furthermore, our profession will suffer. But need alone will not inevitably spell success; in addition, we, as advocates for a specific intellectual position, must portray ourselves in ways that will build respect, win converts, and silence detractors. I hope that, by providing an overview of how qualitative methods provide options that cannot be duplicated by scientific investigation, I have in some small way contributed to this process.

REFERENCES

Hunt, Shelby. (1991). *Modern Marketing Theory: Critical Issues in the Philosophy of Marketing Science.* Cincinnati, OH: South-Western.
Planck, Max. (1936). *The Philosophy of Physics.* New York: Norton.

Index

About the Author

ALF H. WALLE is on the faculty of the University of Alaska at Fairbanks. He specializes in qualitative methods in marketing and consumer research and translating the techniques and perspectives of the humanities in ways that serve marketing scholars and practitioners. Although he continues to work within the context of business, he publishes in other fields such as folklore, popular culture, and literary criticism. His previous works include two books published by Quorum: *Qualitative Research in Intelligence and Marketing* and *Rethinking Marketing* (both 2000).